Scots in the North American West, 1790–1917

Scots in the North American West, 1790–1917

By

Ferenc Morton Szasz

University of Oklahoma Press : Norman

Also by Ferenc Morton Szasz

The Divided Mind of Protestant America, 1880–1930 (Tuscaloosa, 1982)
(editor) *Religion in the West* (Manhattan, Kans., 1984)
The Day the Sun Rose Twice: The Story of the Trinity Site Nuclear Explosion, July 16, 1945 (Albuquerque, 1984)
The Protestant Clergy in the Great Plains and Rocky Mountains, 1865–1915 (Albuquerque, 1988)
The British Scientists and the Manhattan Project: The Los Alamos Years (New York, 1992)
(editor) *Great Mysteries of the West* (Golden, Colo., 1993)
(editor, with Richard Etulain) *Religion in Modern New Mexico* (Albuquerque, 1997)

Library of Congress Cataloging-in-Publication Data

Szasz, Ferenc Morton, 1940–
  Scots in the North American west / Ferenc Morton Szasz.
    p. cm.
  Includes bibliographical references and index.
  ISBN 978-0-8061-3253-2 (cloth)
  ISBN 978-0-8061-9125-6 (paper)
  1. Scottish Americans—West (U.S.)—History. 2. West (U.S.)—Ethnic relations. 3. West (U.S.)—History. 4. Frontier and pioneer life—West (U.S.) 5. Scots—Canada, Western—History. 6. Canada, Western—Ethnic relations. 7. Canada, Western—History. 8. Frontier and pioneer life—Canada, Western. I. Title.

F596.3.S3 S93 2000
978'.0049163—dc21

99-462090
CIP

The paper in this book meets the guidelines for permanence and durability of the Committee on Production Guidelines for Book Longevity of the Council on Library Resources, Inc. ∞

Copyright © 2000 by the University of Oklahoma Press, Norman, Publishing Division of the University. All rights reserved. Paperback published 2022. Manufactured in the U.S.A.

Dedicated to
Mary I. Szasz and the memory of Ferenc P. Szasz, as well as
Margaret
Maria
Eric
Chris
Scott
Tyler
Sean
and to Penelope P. Katson, typist extraordinaire

Contents

List of Illustrations		ix
Preface		xi
1.	Historians and the Scottish-American Connection	3
2.	Scottish Explorers and Fur Trappers: The 1790s to the 1850s	21
3.	Scotland and the American Indians	49
4.	Scotland and the Victorian West: The Reality	78
5.	Scotland and the Victorian West: The Romance	118
6.	Varieties of the Scottish-Western Experience	151
7.	The Western Canadian Alternative	185
Epilogue: Words on the Land		209
Notes		219
Select Bibliography		257
Index		265

Illustrations

PHOTOGRAPHS

Port of Stornoway, Isle of Lewis	40
Nineteenth-century crofter's house, Isle of Skye	51
St. Kilda Parliament	57
John Ross, Cherokee Chief, 1837	67
Duncan MacDonald, Missoula, Montana, 1927	75
Headquarters of the Swan Land and Cattle Company, Chugwater, Wyoming	93
End of the roundup, eastern Montana, c. 1893	95
Andy Little, the "Sheep King" of Idaho	104
Spring lambs on the Andy Little sheep ranch in Idaho, 1906	105
Statue of Robert Burns, erected in 1904, City Park, Denver, Colorado	114
Statue of Robert Burns, erected in 1927, Gilchrist Park, Cheyenne, Wyoming	115
Murthly Castle, Perthshire	127
Entrance to Murthly Castle	131

Sir Harry Lauder	144
Wild West Show program, 1886	147
Recruiting poster for Western Canada, 1903	198
Young women dancing at the Highland Games, Salt Lake City, Utah	214

MAPS

Scotland, 1790–2000	4
The North American West, 1790–2000	23

TABLES

Immigration from Scotland to the United States, 1820–1950	11
Scottish-born Population in the United States, 1850–1950	11
Scots in the Canadian West	187

Preface

"Just how did you become interested in this project?" The query, with the arched eyebrow that accompanied it, came from prize-winning poet Joseph-Charles Mackenzie of the University of New Mexico's Interlibrary Loan Division after he had processed yet another request for Scottish-American material. Had my middle name, Morton, been my surname or had I signed the requests "MacSzasz," the question might never have arisen. But it is a fair one and it deserves an answer.

While my mother maintains that our family has some Scotch-Irish ancestry from her side, as opposed to none whatsoever from my Austro-Hungarian father, I grew up without a connection to any Scots or Scots-Irish organization—excluding, perhaps, membership in the First Presbyterian Church of Bucyrus, Ohio. This study, then, springs less from a quest for historic identity than from a unique set of circumstances.

In 1991–92, my historian wife, Margaret Connell Szasz, arranged an academic exchange with Edward Ranson of the University of Aberdeen. Fortunately, I was on sabbatical leave from the University of New Mexico during the year and was able to spend many hours prowling the shelves of Aberdeen's Queen Mother Library while working on a variety of Scoto-American projects.[1] The excellent rare-book holdings of this ancient university (founded in 1495) finally convinced me that I might explore the connections between my newly adopted "nation within a nation" and my "home territory" of the Trans-Mississippi West. Here is the result.

This book is about the interaction between the Scots (I include the Ulster Scots) and the North American West from about the 1790s to about World War I. The late eighteenth century inaugurated the British exploration of the West, and the outbreak of the First World War essentially marked the start of a new era. In the intervening years, however, the Scottish-Western connection was extensive.

Scots in the North American West examines several aspects of this connection. It discusses Scots explorers, fur traders, the "Scoto-Indians," writers, sportsmen, clerics, actors, and travelers. It also considers the Scots' impact on the American range-cattle industry, the rise of western sheepherding, and the emergence of western mythology. This last item is a bit tricky. At some time during the nineteenth century, popular perceptions of both Scotland and the American West underwent a decided shift. They moved from an appreciation of authentic historical events to a celebration of dramatic pageantry. By the middle of the nineteenth century, an atmosphere of romance had engulfed both regions. Each, incidentally, delighted in the stock characters of the other. Thus, my goal in this work is less to trace the path of every Scot who ventured across the Mississippi River than to try to assess the overall impact of the Scottish presence in the Trans-Mississippi West.

I would like to begin by thanking Roy Bridges, former head of the Aberdeen History Department, and his gracious wife, Jill, for making us so welcome in a new land. Thanks, too, to Joan Pittock Wesson for offering me an appointment as a fellow in her Institute of Cultural Studies and for providing me with an office in Cromwell Tower. Lunchtime conversations with Terry Brotherstone, David Ditchburn, Till Geiger, Louise Bourdua, Rosemary Tyzack, and William Pike deepened our understanding of Scottish life, as did the fine lectures of Marjory Harper. Anne and Grant Simpson should be especially singled out for providing us with firsthand information about the links between Scotland and the American West. The expertise of archivists Colin Maclaren, Iain Beavan, and Myrtle Anderson-Smith, plus the skills of Interlibrary Loan specialist Katherine McCurdy, proved especially valuable. Both Margaret and I would like to thank Allan Macinnes, current department head, for arranging our appointments as honorary members of the Aberdeen History Department and T. M. Devine for inviting us to the 1999 conference on the Scottish diaspora. Thanks are due as well to the staffs of the Scottish Record Office, the Scottish National Library, the Edinburgh Room of the Edinburgh Public Library, the Aberdeen Public Library, and the Inverness Public Library.

I would also like to credit the often-volunteer staffs at various regional centers: The Highland Folk Museum, Kingussie; the West Highland Museum, Fort William; the Gairloch Heritage Museum; the Tomintoul Museum; the Strathnaver Museum at Bettyhill, especially Pat Rudie; the Wick Heritage Centre, especially Ian Sutherland; and the Helmsdale Heritage Centre. Special thanks are due to Chris Fraser for his critical reading of the manuscript from the Scottish perspective.

On the other side of the Atlantic, I would like to thank Carol MacGregor for alerting me to the key role played by Idaho rancher Andy Little, as well as Raphael Cristy for sharing his research on Montana mixed-blood Duncan MacDonald. Richard W. Etulain, with his photographic memory and endless set of four-by-six bibliographic cards, always kept an eye out for Scottish references. He also read the manuscript in an earlier form. David Key helped with the research, as did Bruce Erickson. Elizabeth Jameson shared her materials on Scottish labor leaders; Howard Rabinowitz offered his extensive knowledge of Scottish golfers; and Louis A. Hieb provided valuable information on Alexander MacGregor Stephen. I am indebted to them all.

Special thanks are also due to former Idaho Historical Society archivist Tomas Jaehn, now in Santa Fe, and to Eleanor Gehres, head of the Western Room of the Denver Public Library. Zimmerman Library's Kate Luger alerted me to still other Scottish-American links. My debt to Penelope P. Katson, master of the art of typecraft, can be seen in the dedication. Finally, I would like to thank Margaret and Maria for allowing me to compare my insights on the Scottish-Western experience with theirs over many a delightful dinner-table conversation.

A NOTE ON TERMINOLOGY

America, when used by Scots writers, almost always meant North America rather than simply the United States, a usage that continued until the middle of the nineteenth century.

Trans-Mississippi West in this book refers primarily to the region that stretches westward from the 98th meridian, from the Dakotas on the north to Texas on the south and over to the Pacific Ocean. On occasion it also includes parts of what is now Canada. Although the 49th-parallel boundary was finally drawn in 1846, the British and Americans shared joint occupation of the Oregon country from 1818 forward. For the Native American inhabitants of the region, of course, the national boundaries were almost devoid of meaning, as they are today. Although the Trans-Mississippi West remains my primary area of concern, during discussion of the Scoto-Indians in the late eighteenth and early nineteenth centuries in chapter 3, I occasionally draw on frontier examples from east of the Mississippi.

Scots-Irish or *Scotch-Irish* first appeared as a term around 1585. It refers to the settlers, primarily—but not exclusively—from Lowland Scotland, who settled the region of Ulster from the sixteenth century forward—a mass migration of people that ranked with the largest of its day. Irish historians tend to claim the Ulster Scots as Irish, and, indeed, Americans generally called them "Irish" until the 1830s. But the Ulsterites usually drew distinctions between themselves and the "other Irish." One Ulsterman described himself as living in "the Scottish nation in the north of Ireland." Another termed himself a "Scoto Hibernus." Yet another as a "Scot of Ireland." Fiercely Presbyterian, the Scotch-Irish detested the Roman Catholic Irish and the Anglican English with equal vigor. While *Scotch-Irish* is an admittedly awkward term, it is hard to find a substitute. *Wester Scot* and *Ulster Scot* have been suggested, but they have yet to gain widespread acceptance.

British refers to anyone from England, Scotland, Ulster, Wales, or Southern Ireland (the latter until Irish independence in 1921).

English refers solely to the people living south of the River Tweed, Scotland's "auld enemy" from well before the days of Edward I.

Scots refers solely to the people living north of the River Tweed. I reserve *Scotch* for the national drink.

Most Americans tend to confuse these last four terms, often using *English* as an umbrella phrase. But when England plays Scotland in football, the teams' supporters draw upon centuries of antagonism to cheer on their sides, suggesting that the distinctions have hardly faded even today. Cards and letters addressed to "Aberdeen, England," pain postal clerks no end. Yet these errors are not exclusively confined to foreigners. When a Scottish first-year student wrote that the Scots defeated the British at Bannockburn on June 24, 1314, it almost gave his History of Scotland instructor apoplexy.

As I focus on the Scottish experience in the American West, I will try to keep these distinctions clear.

Scots in the North American West, 1790–1917

CHAPTER ONE

Historians and the Scottish-American Connection

The links between Scotland and America stretch back over three centuries. Perhaps one can officially date them from 1650, when a group of Scots gathered in Boston to create the first Scots' Charitable Society, an organization to aid fellow immigrants who had fallen upon hard times. Scottish migration to the British North American Colonies during the seventeenth century remained sporadic, but from the early eighteenth century forward, extended bands of Highland and Lowland Scots settled all through Nova Scotia, New Jersey, Pennsylvania, and North Carolina. Simultaneously, wave after wave of Scotch-Irish migrants from Ulster landed in Philadelphia, making their way down the Appalachian valleys into Virginia and beyond.

Contemporaries were well aware of this Scots and Scotch-Irish migration to the Colonies. As James Logan, chief advisor to Pennsylvania proprietor William Penn once observed: "It looks as if Ireland [i.e., Ulster] is to send all her habitants hither; for last week not less than six ships arrived, and every day two or three are coming." These Presbyterians, the Quaker Logan

Scotland, 1790–2000

continued, were "audacious and disorderly"; they were "troublesome settlers to the government, and hard neighbors to the Indians."[1]

Since the Scots were often educated, planters in the Chesapeake region frequently hired them as tutors, although they groused at having their children acquire a Scottish accent. The *Journal* kept by Lerwick émigré John Harrower, who served a four-year indenture as a schoolmaster in Virginia, illuminates this world. At William and Mary, young Thomas Jefferson fell under the sway of Aberdonian William Small, to whom he was ever grateful.[2]

When the American Revolution broke out, at least in the Scotch-Irish version of the story, the Ulster natives leaped at the opportunity to attack the British crown. "Call this war by whatever name you may . . . ," observed one Hessian officer, "it is nothing more or less than a Scotch Irish Presbyterian rebellion."[3] King George allegedly called the conflict "a Presbyterian war," and another official stated that cousin "America has run off with the Presbyterian parson." In spite of these comments, the actual Scotch-Irish population was a bit more divided in their loyalties than legend would have it, especially in the South. Still, the Scotch-Irish generally emerged from the Revolution with an enhanced local reputation.

The same could not be said for the Scots proper. Although famed poet Robert Burns once wrote an "Ode for General Washington's Birthday," the Scots who had emigrated to Colonial America were seldom convinced by the patriots' arguments. Many had fought against the Crown only thirty years previously, but when the Revolution broke out, the majority of Scots sided with Great Britain. Of this there is little dispute. In 1776 former Paisley cleric John Witherspoon, then president of the College of New Jersey and a staunch patriot, tried to change this point of view. He gave an address (later printed as a pamphlet) to the "Natives of Scotland residing in America" that noted: "It has given me no little uneasiness to hear the word *Scotch* used as a term of reproach in the American controversy."[4] Virginian Thomas Jefferson included a condemnation of "Scotch and other foreign mercenaries" in an early draft of the Declaration of Independence, a phrase that Witherspoon discreetly helped remove. However, Jefferson continued to rail at the "Scotch Tories" for over two decades.⁵

During the era of the Revolution, Americans often denounced the Scots. In his 1776 play, *The Patriots,* Virginia author Robert Mumford named characters "M'Flint," "M'Gripe," and "M'Squeeze." Local pressure either evicted Scots from certain regions (such as the Chesapeake) or forced them to return to Scotland on their own. Flora MacDonald, Scotland's most famous heroine, left North Carolina for her native South Uist under these circumstances. Perhaps as many as five thousand Scots Tories later migrated to Canada due to their loyalty to the British crown. In the process they became the spiritual founders of Canada.⁶ In 1782 the lower house of Georgia passed a resolution declaring that the people of Scotland possessed "a decided inimicality to the Civil Liberties of America." Any Scot found in the region after three days would be "committed to Gaol."⁷

But citizens of the new Republic had short memories and this antagonism quickly passed. Paisley-born naturalist Alexander Wilson observed that he received great cooperation on his southward journey from Philadelphia to gather material for his famed *American Ornithology* (1807–18). An 1810 traveler to Charleston also noted that the ruling Tory aristocracy of South Carolina consisted of "chiefly Scotchmen."⁸ After the Peace of Paris in 1783, one finds little criticism of Scottish people.

From c. 1790 to c. 1860 the Scots and Scotch-Irish immigrants generally split their destinations between Canada and the new American republic. Figures are, unfortunately, inexact, but the majority probably sailed for Montreal and Ontario rather than Philadelphia or New York. Even so, a small but significant number found their way to the various "British colonies" established in Illinois, Iowa, Kansas, and elsewhere. When the American Civil War broke out in 1861, many a Confederate soldier bore a Scotch-Irish surname. On the other side, Chicago and New York each raised a Scottish-American regiment that fought for the Union. New York's 79th, which modeled its uniforms after the famed Black Watch, remains the most celebrated of these Scots Union military contingents. In 1893 the city of Edinburgh erected a statue of President Abraham Lincoln in the Old Calton Hill Burial Ground, the first Lincoln statue outside the United States. In an impressive ceremony the provost of Edinburgh and the American consul dedicated the ground as a burial place for five Scots soldiers who had died fighting for the Northern cause.

By the middle of the nineteenth century a number of Scots had risen to prominence in American life. By the 1840s Aberdonian George Smith had become the most famous banker of the upper Midwest. Indeed, "George Smith's money," as it was termed, often proved more sound than state or federal currency. When Smith died in 1899, he left a fortune that approached one hundred million dollars. Fellow Aberdonian Alexander Mitchell, once termed "the best known Scot in Milwaukee," also gained wealth as a banker and, later, served two terms in Congress. Clydeside émigré John Stewart Kennedy played a crucial role in financing the western railroad boom, especially the Northern Pacific line. A native of Glasgow, Allan Pinkerton rose to prominence during the Civil War as a purveyor of information (much of it wrong) to Abraham Lincoln; his name is still virtually synonymous with "detective agency." Other successes included Michael Donahoe, who established the largest foundry in Iowa, and Davis Nicholson and Dugald Crawford, who became prominent mercantile figures in St. Louis. In 1923 Robert Dollar from Falkirk inaugurated the first "round the world" passenger service. Undoubtedly, the most prominent nineteenth-century Scoto-American was Andrew Carnegie, the son of a Dunfermline weaver who ended his career as "the richest man in the world."[9]

Most Scots and Scotch-Irish immigrants, one may safely say, did not do quite that well. But nineteenth-century America had great need of miners, granite workers, cattlemen, maids, shepherds, bankers, farmers, and missionaries. Because of their history, the Scots possessed long experience with all those occupations. If the average Scots immigrant never quite equaled Carnegie's success, neither did he or she appear with regularity on the nineteenth-century welfare rolls.

American historians did not pay much attention to these Scoto-American links until the late nineteenth century. Then, faced with the arrival of thousands of immigrants from southern and eastern Europe, people of Scots or Scotch-Irish descent began vigorously to champion the role that their ancestors had played in "creating the American republic." Second- and third-generation historians wrote scores of books and articles with the contributions of the Scots or Scotch-Irish as their central theme. From the Philadelphia Centennial of 1876 forward, these filiopietistic studies appeared with regularity, bearing titles such as *Presbyterians and the Revolution* (1876); *Scotch and Irish Seeds in American Soil* (1879); *The Scotch-Irish in America* (1896); and *The Scotch-Irish in America* (1906).[10]

Turn-of-the-century popular magazines often struck the same chord. In "The Sons of Old Scotland in America" (1906) Herbert N. Casson proudly listed the most prominent Scoto-Americans of his day: California congressman James McLachlan; House speaker David Henderson; Buffalo, New York, mayor James N. Adam; New Hampshire governor John McLane; secretary of agriculture James Wilson; noted inventor Alexander Graham Bell; cleric George Gordon of Boston's Old South Church; educators William Kaller and John Kennedy; naturalist John Muir; industrialist Andrew Carnegie; and so on. "A remarkable record and a remarkable race," he concluded.[11]

The Scotch-Irish patriotic groups went even further. In 1889 they inaugurated an annual series of conferences to extol the virtues of "the race," and they faithfully did so for over a decade. Declaring their absolute neutrality on all political or religious issues, these regional and national Scotch-Irish societies declared their purpose solely "to impress upon the pages of history the heroic deeds of the sons of the Scotch-Irish race." Scottish men, incidentally, were not welcome unless they had married Scotch-Irish wives.[12] When the collected speeches of the conferences were published, they contained few surprises. Appeals to Scottish history—which the Scotch-Irish equally claimed as theirs—extolled the virtues of William Wallace, Robert the Bruce, Sir Walter Scott, and Robert Burns. One speaker in 1891 declared that the synonym for the Scotch-Irish "race" lay in the phrases "national freedom, general education, and sound scriptural faith."[13]

Such celebrations of ancestral ties formed an integral part of white middle-class fin de siècle life. It was during this era that most city libraries established genealogical divisions, and the figure of the professional genealogist became a familiar one in the nation's archives. When Scottish women formed their own ethnic organization, the Daughters of Scotia, in 1898, they reflected the same concerns that animated the national Daughters of the American Revolution (formed in 1890) and the regional United Daughters of the Confederacy (formed in 1894). By the turn of the century Caledonian societies, Burns clubs, and St. Andrew's societies had so proliferated that hardly any American or Canadian city of size lacked one. One author claimed that there were more Scottish-American organizations than their Welsh-, Irish-, or English-American counterparts.[14] All these organizations helped trumpet "Scottish contributions" to the formation of both the American nation and Canada.[15]

The articles, speeches, and books on this theme naturally varied in quality. Henry Jones Ford's *The Scotch-Irish in America* (1915) probably represented the genre at its best. A professor of politics at Princeton, a university that had long prided itself on strong Scottish-American links, Ford detailed the impact that the Scotch-Irish "race" had on America with considerable perception.[16] He acknowledged strengths and weaknesses in the interaction. But George Fraser Black's *Scotland's Mark of America* (1921) is far more representative of this variety of work. Although Black admitted at the onset that the task of "positively identifying certain individuals as of Scottish origin or descent [was] a very difficult one," he proceeded to do just that, in thirty chapters, compiling a lengthy list of Scottish men (no women) who had served in the presidency, vice presidency, senate, house of representatives, and judiciary. In addition, he listed those who had been ambassadors, state governors, military men, scientists, industrialists, bankers, journalists, and so forth.[17] Carefully distinguishing between the Irish, Scots, and Scotch-Irish, he argued for the continuous and formative influence of ancestors down to the nth generation. Black's volume ranks as the epitome of "Scot counting," the most prevalent form of late-nineteenth, early twentieth-century Scottish-American historiography.

Perhaps this is the best place to deal with the question of numbers. Historians estimate that as many as 2.33 million Scots left Britain between 1825 and 1938. The Scots were statistically more likely to emigrate than any other European people, excluding only the Irish and the Norwegians. During the mid-nineteenth century the main flow seems to have come from Scotland's rural Lowlands, due largely to the industrialization of the region. The typical Lowland emigrant moved first from farm to town and then, ultimately, overseas. In general the Lowlanders seem to have emigrated as individuals or in small family groups, while the Highlanders usually traveled later, more sporadically, and en masse, often seeking to duplicate their peasant communities in another part of the world. Most of the emigrants came to North America, although during the American Civil War (1861–65) and various depressions they tended to go to Australia and New Zealand.[18]

Historian Roland T. Berthoff has compiled the following statistics on Scottish-American Immigration:

TABLE 1.
Immigration from Scotland to the United States, 1820–1950

1820–30	3,180
1831–40	2,667
1841–50	3,712
1851–60	38,331
1861–70	38,769
1871–80	87,564
1881–90	139,869
1891–1900	44,188
1901–10	120,469
1911–20	78,357
1921–30	159,781
1931–40	6,887
1941–50	16,131
Total:	749,905

SOURCE: Roland Tappan Berthoff, *British Immigrants in Industrial America, 1790–1950* (Cambridge: Harvard, University Press, 1953), 5.

TABLE 2.
Scottish-Born Population in the United States, 1850–1950

1850	70,550
1860	108,518
1870	140,835
1880	170,136
1890	241,233
1900	233,524
1910	261,076
1920	254,570
1930	354,323
1940	279,321
1950	244,200

SOURCE: Berthoff, *British Immigrants*, 7.

As one can see from Berthoff's tables, these are not extensive figures. But numbers alone can be misleading. Although the Scots were by no stretch of the imagination a large American immigrant group, they, like the Jews, Hungarians, Greeks, Unitarians, Quakers, and Episcopalians, had an impact that often extended far beyond their numbers. Their presence proved especially significant in the more sparsely populated West, where virtually every individual counted because there were so few of them. Moreover, the impact proved long lasting. The 1990 census listing of Americans of Scottish ancestry shows that the majority still reside in the various western states.[19]

One could perhaps date the arrival of a new historical sophistication in Scottish-American historiography to Thomas Jefferson Wertenbaker's March 8, 1945, lecture to the University of Glasgow, "Early Scotch Contributions to the United States." A professor at the University of Virginia, Wertenbaker moved far beyond the mere listing of names and totting up of contributions. His analysis of Reverend James Blair, Governor Alexander Spotswood, and Governor Robert Dinwiddie highlighted Scotland's *cultural* impact on American Colonial life. In passing, Wertenbaker noted that Glasgow tobacco factors had dominated the early Chesapeake tobacco trade and that the religious revival of eighteenth-century Scotland had crossed the Atlantic to produce a number of American colleges and secondary schools. Finally, Wertenbaker argued that after c. 1700 the Scotch-Irish "more than any other group, created the first western frontier."[20]

Nine years later, the *William and Mary Quarterly* devoted its entire April 1954 issue to links between Scotland and America. All the articles were of high calibre, but John Clive and Bernard Bailyn's "England's Cultural Provinces: Scotland and America" has become a classic. Clive and Bailyn argued that Scots and Colonial Americans both felt themselves on the edge of a sophisticated, cultured world centered primarily in London.

Consequently, each nation developed a parallel sense of "cultural inferiority" regarding its native traditions. But then the stories diverge. The success of the American Revolution in 1783 allowed the United States to celebrate its distinctive cultural traditions and, eventually, to flaunt them in English faces. But the failure of the Stuart uprising in 1746 forced Scotland to consider its native traditions through a saddened, more "romantic" lens. Consequently, a shared sense of cultural inferiority, combined with sullen resentment against the English, persisted for generations in American and Scottish cultures.[21]

With T. J. Wertenbaker and the 1954 *William and Mary Quarterly*, a new era of Scottish-American historiography had begun. On the Scottish side, the foremost scholar was Professor George Shepperson of the University of Edinburgh. Over many years, Shepperson published a series of articles on Scottish-American links in the eighteenth and nineteenth centuries. He especially focused on connections between Scots and Americans during the Revolutionary era and in the abolitionist movement. Until his retirement from the University of Edinburgh, Shepperson also directed a number of Scottish-American dissertations, including two excellent ones: Robert Botsford on Scotland and the American Civil War and Helen Finnie on Scotland and Reconstruction.[22] Shepperson's friendly rival at Glasgow University, Bernard Aspinwall, concentrated on the impact of the Clyde Estuary on American life. He has also written on the transferable nature of Scottish religious identity.[23]

Thus, from the 1950s forward, scholars began to explore the links between the two cultures in a variety of areas. In 1956 Ian Graham analyzed the impact of Scottish immigration on North America up to the close of the American Revolution. He concluded that from 1768 to 1780 about twenty-five thousand Scots—mostly from the Highlands—had left the British Isles to settle in western Pennsylvania and North Carolina.[24] In 1971 Douglas Sloan's *The Scottish Enlightenment and the American College*

Ideal argued for the central role that the Scottish universities had played in forging the American educational system. The largely Presbyterian Scots, he maintained, had never feared an educated populace as had the leaders of Anglican England. Thus, Scots were far more congenial to the idea of mass education. If American education has British roots, Sloan argued, they rested in Scotland, not in England.[25]

Four years later, University of Edinburgh professor Andrew Hook's important *Scotland and America: A Study of Cultural Relations, 1750–1835* explored early literary links. Hook emphasized the impact of writers Jane Porter, Sir Walter Scott, and the essayists in *The Edinburgh Review* on early American belles lettres. He also argued that most nineteenth-century Americans viewed Scotland through a double lens: those of "the land of Rationalism" and "the land of Romance."[26] His central thesis remains unchallenged.

Specialists in eastern Colonial America have long acknowledged a prominent Scots connection in North Carolina, New Jersey, and the Chesapeake. In *The Highland Scots of North Carolina* (1961), Duane Meyer sketched part of this story.[27] Both Thomas M. Devine and Jacob M. Price have written on the crucial Scots-Chesapeake tobacco connections before the Revolution. Ian C. Graham, Wilbur Shepperson, Charlotte Erickson, and David Dobson have done the same for the theme of immigration.[28]

In 1978 sociologist William C. Lehmann expanded Scottish influence to virtually every area of Colonial life with his *Scottish and Scotch-Irish Contributions to Early American Life and Culture*. In 1980 Charles H. Haws published his monograph, *Scots in the Old Dominion, 1685–1800,* while Ned Landsman added his *Scotland and Its First American Colony, 1683–1760* five years later. The recent study by Alan L. Karras, *Sojourners in the Sun* (1992), treats the Scots in Jamaica and the Chesapeake region.[29]

During the last fifteen years, the literature has steadily expanded. While most historians have assumed that the Great

Awakening of mid-eighteenth-century America had uniquely Colonial origins, Marilyn Westerkamp and Leigh Eric Schmidt have convincingly argued that these Colonial revivals trace their origins to Scots and Ulster Scots festival communion services. Westerkamp even suggests that revivalism in general was simply part of a Scotch-Irish religiosity that found a fertile field in America.[30]

The links between the Scottish and American Enlightenments have also attracted considerable attention. Scots historian Archie Turnbull has suggested that Scotland's Declaration of Arbroath (1320) formed the "model" for Thomas Jefferson's Declaration of Independence (1776).[31] Similarly, George Shepperson has argued that the writings of William Duncan, Professor of Natural Philosophy at Marischal College, Aberdeen, and author of *Elements of Logick*, may have contributed to the phrasing of the Declaration of Independence by his use of the term *self evident*.[32] The boldest statement along these lines came from Garry Wills's *Inventing America* (1978), which suggested that Jefferson owed more to Scottish thinkers such as Thomas Reid than he did to English essayist John Locke.[33] The essays in *Scotus Americanus: A Survey of the Sources for Links between Scotland and America in the Eighteenth Century* (1982) and *Scotland and America in the Age of Enlightenment* (1980) explore in detail the numerous theological, political, economic, medical, educational, and evangelical debts that Colonial America owed to Scotland.[34] If a historian includes folkways culture, and music in the list, he or she could almost argue that the Scots and Scotch-Irish had more influence on molding early American institutions and lifeways than *any* other European group, not excluding the English, Irish, Dutch, Swiss, Germans, French, or Spanish.

The pervasive impact of Scotland upon America continues to fascinate up to the present day. In 1976, the American bicentennial year, Old Dominion University in Norfolk, Virginia, established an institute of Scottish Studies. Their scholarly journal,

Scotia, dedicated to exploring such links, first appeared in 1977. Similarly, James McLeod began a program in Scottish Studies at the College of Northern Idaho in Coeur d' Alene, an area of the state that boasted numerous Scottish settlers. Most of the renewed interest in Scottish-American scholarship, however, has concentrated on the seventeenth and eighteenth centuries. Indeed, the brunt of the American documents held by the Scottish Record Office in Edinburgh falls into that time frame.[35] But, led by C. Duncan Rice's study of Scots abolitionists, a few scholars have attempted to carry the story into the Victorian era.[36]

By far the most controversial analyses have come from southern historians Forrest McDonald, Ellen Shapiro McDonald, and Grady McWhiney. They have combined forces in a number of articles (and McWhiney has gone solo in *Cracker Culture* [1988]) to suggest that a pervasive "Celtic" (very broadly defined) influence has been *the* central feature in shaping southern life. Although Roland Berthoff denounced the descent of a "Celtic mist" over southern history, the McDonalds and McWhiney have had the best of the argument to date.[37] Even skeptics have acknowledged the persistence of Scotch-Irish cultural traits and physiognomy on the southern frontier, a theme explored in detail by Ulster folklorist E. Estyn Evans and Ulster television producer Rory Fitzpatrick.[38] The Museum of American Frontier Culture near Taunton, Virginia, also makes this a central theme of its exhibits. In 1989 historian David Hackett Fischer joined their campaign with his section in *Albion's Seed* on the links between the English/Scottish Borders region and the American frontier.[39] From farming practices to frontier folklore, from mournful Appalachian ballads to the "rebel yell," these historians argue, the Scots/Scotch-Irish/Celtic influence lay just below the surface of antebellum southern society. After all, Margaret Mitchell did name her heroine in *Gone with the Wind* "Scarlett O'Hara."

Except for these studies of the antebellum South, scholars have paid scant attention to the impact of Scots immigration on the rest of nineteenth-century America. After the Revolution, the argument goes, the Scotch-Irish and Scots largely left their communal identity behind. Thus, the Scots and Scotch-Irish who moved into the Ohio River Valley and Mississippi Delta in the early nineteenth century lost their distinctive "Scottish" connections. They moved west as "Americans." Since the infamous Highland Clearances of the nineteenth century sent immigration primarily to Australia, Canada, and New Zealand, the American aspect of the Scottish story simply stops. The Scots lost their visibility and disappeared into American life. Historian Charlotte Erickson's study, *Invisible Immigrants*, reflects this point of view in title and in argument.[40] Consequently, few historians have explored the Scottish impact on the most extensive region of the American nation: the Trans-Mississippi West.

From Ralph Waldo Emerson's time forward, the nation's western "frontier" has ever been viewed as the most American section of America. American though it may have been, the Trans-Mississippi West contained a vast array of diverse peoples. American Indians, whose cultures ranged from the buffalo hunters of the northern plains to the settled Pueblo farmers of the Rio Grande Valley to the Apache and Navajo raiders of the Mexican borderlands, claimed the region as their own. About seventy thousand Hispanic farmers in New Mexico and along the Rio Grande corridor suddenly became American citizens with the Treaty of Guadalupe Hidalgo in 1848. In the Great Basin of Utah the Latter-day Saints (Mormons) carved out a religio-cultural enclave that still dominates the region. Later, the Great Plains became home to other ethnic colonies: German Roman Catholics, Mennonites, Hutterites, Jews, Swedish Lutherans, and so on. A diversity of cultures has long characterized western life.

So, too, the diversity of the natural world. Americans east of the Mississippi proudly pointed to their natural wonders: Niagara Falls, the Natural Arch of Virginia, the Great Smokey Mountains, the White Mountains, the Valley of the Hudson River, and the Florida Everglades. Impressive though these might be, they paled beside the geography of the Far West. When travelers first enountered the undulating expanse of natural grasses of the Great Plains, they could only compare them to waves of the ocean. When they first crossed the Sierra Nevada Mountains or the Colorado Rockies, they usually likened them to the Italian or Swiss Alps. San Francisco Bay, the Columbia River Gorge, Yosemite, Yellowstone, and Mount Rainier ever challenged their descriptive skills.

The American Southwest, with canyons unmatched in any other part of the globe, seemed the most marvelous of all. Sunsets over red-rock mesas fascinated the romantic landscape artists of the era, who tried in vain to capture the moment. The discovery of abandoned Anasazi villages in Chaco Canyon, New Mexico; Canyon de Chelly, Arizona; and Mesa Verde, Colorado, further teased the Euro-American imagination. Who were these people? What had happened to them?

The Trans-Mississippi West also abounded with exotic animals and plants. Elk, deer, and antelope roamed the mountains and prairies, while chum and sockeye salmon spawned in the great rivers of the Pacific Northwest. Fur-bearing creatures, such as mink, muskrat, and, especially, beaver, lived alongside every riverbank. Uncounted (uncountable) bison ranged from the Canadian Great Plains southward into New Mexico. The gigantic strands of sequoias, pines, and firs of the Pacific Northwest stood unrivaled outside of Russia. By the time the forty-niners discovered gold in California and, later, silver in Nevada, the Trans-Mississippi West had emerged as a veritable utopia. Even regions that today are deemed of only marginal aesthetic/economic value—such as the vast, empty desert of southeast

Oregon/northern Nevada—astounded the initial settlers with their beauty and economic potential.[41] This mixture of beauty and natural abundance of the North American West, in writer Wallace Stegner's words, catered to "the common man's dream of something for nothing."[42]

The Scots and Scotch-Irish were prominent among these "common men." Although they could claim no familiarity with deserts, those from the Highland regions surely knew the solace of the mountains. Years of involvement with the English, plus the far-flung trade network that reached into the Baltic regions, had attuned Scots merchants to the art of dealing with people from different cultures. One does not have to look far in western history before coming across an émigré from Scotland or Ulster.

Still, relatively few historians have explored these connections. There have been studies of British immigration to America in general, sometimes to the West in particular, but they usually mention the Scots only in passing.[43] The two most recent books on the Scottish-American connection, by Orkney journalist Jim Hewitson and Isle of Skye historian James Hunter, do not give much attention to the links between Scotland and the West.[44]

Using a strict definition, one can find only five monographs that focus on the Scottish experience in the Trans-Mississippi West: Alexander Campbell McGregor's *Counting Sheep* (1982), the story of the McGregor agricultural enterprises of eastern Washington State; W. Turrentine Jackson's *The Enterprising Scot* (1968) and W. G. Kerr's *Scottish Capital on the American Credit Frontier* (1976), which treat Scottish investment in the American cattle industry; Bruce LeRoy's *Lairds, Bards and Mariners: The Scot in Northwest America* (1976); and James Hunter's saga of the McDonald family and Montana, *Scottish Highlanders, Indian Peoples,* published in Scotland as *Glencoe and the Indians* (1996).[45]

Similarly, only a few western Scots have been subjects of biographies. May Reed Porter and Odessa Davenport have written on nineteenth-century adventurer Sir William Drummond Stewart in *Scotsmen in Buckskin* (1963); Susan Bryant Dakin did a study of Hugo Reid, *A Scotch Paisano in Old Los Angeles* (1978); Leonard Arrington described the career of a Scottish Mormon millionaire in *David Eccles* (1974); William Norwood wrote on naturalist David Douglas in *Traveler in a Vanished Landscape* (1973); and Louise Shadduck portrayed *Andrew Little, Idaho Sheep King* (1990). The only western Scot to receive extensive biographical treatment has been naturalist John Muir.[46]

In the pages that follow I will attempt to fill in at least part of this gap. My overall thesis can be stated at the outset. For about 130 years, from c. 1790 to c. 1917, the economic and social conditions in Scotland and Ulster proved especially congruent with those of the American West. The Scots and Scotch-Irish population pressures, the economic dislocations, a heritage of wandering, a long-standing emphasis on formal education, the ancient skills of the drovers, shepherds, gardeners, ministers, miners, and granite carvers, the newly created middle-class investment corporations (which needed places to put their money), the hunting expectations of wealthy Scots lairds, and the foibles of Scots "remittance men" all meshed nicely with the American and Canadian Wests. In addition, the rich tradition of Scottish romance and myth, as seen in the traveling artists, writers, photographers, and entertainers, provided a ready infusion for what would eventually emerge as the new republic's greatest cultural export: the myth of the American West.

CHAPTER TWO

Scottish Explorers and Fur Trappers

THE 1790s TO THE 1850s

Initial interaction between Scotland and the North American West might best be grouped under two general headings: the fur trade and exploration. From the 1790s forward, Scots pioneers played crucial roles in each area. That they did so can be directly linked to the complex cultural forces that have molded the Scottish people. Since the explorers usually hailed from the Lowlands and the fur trappers from the Highlands, the Western Isles, and Orkney, perhaps it is best to begin with a bit of Scottish geography.

Situated at the northwesternmost point of Europe, Scotland is blessed with some of the most spectacular wilderness areas on the globe. Even in modern times, however, it is a harsh and demanding land. Though Scotland is a country of 520,411 square miles, only slightly over one-fourth of it is arable. Lacking an Ireland to break the Atlantic storms, it is both colder and wetter than its English neighbor to the south. In the Western Isles, for example, rain falls, on average, seven out of every nine days. The Scottish Tourist Board recently compiled a pamphlet professing to show that the climate was not really as bad as reputed, but even it noted that Paisley, near Glasgow, received only 1.3 hours of sunshine during the entire month of December 1890.[1] The cotton barons of the early nineteenth century favored Lanarkshire for their mills because the steady moisture in the air kept the cotton fibers from breaking. Eighteenth-century Highlanders used to wish their departing guests "good weather" as they saw them off.

The east-coast city of Edinburgh receives much less rainfall than the west of Scotland, but fronting the North Sea brings challenges of its own. In a famous essay on Edinburgh, Robert Louis Stevenson credited it with having one of the "vilest climates" under heaven. Said Stevenson, "The weather is raw and boisterous in winter, shifty and ungenial in summer, and a downright meteorological purgatory in the spring." Even the *Edinburgh Review* complained that their climate "would scarcely ripen an apple."[2] While other countries have climate, the old adage has it, Scotland has weather.[3]

But the Scots have been known occasionally to overstate their case. Thanks to the Gulf Stream, the west coast of Scotland provides an ideal climate for growing tropical plants, as seen today in the world-famous Inverewe Gardens. The sheltered Lowlands and the fertile northeast region also belie some of these observations. The proximity to the sea means that the northeast receives late frosts—roses may bloom until December—and the rich black soil of the land beyond the Grampian Mountains has supported cattle and sheep for millenia. Oats, barley, peas, and rye grow well, and when potatoes were introduced there and in the Western Isles in the early eighteenth century, they transformed Scottish agricultural life. Other root crops such as rutabagas and turnips, introduced at approximately the same time, flourished as animal and human food. Grass for cattle and sheep still grows abundantly in Orkney, and the sheltered Tay Valley teems with berries of all varieties. Harsh though the climate was, in short, the Scots ate well. Variety,

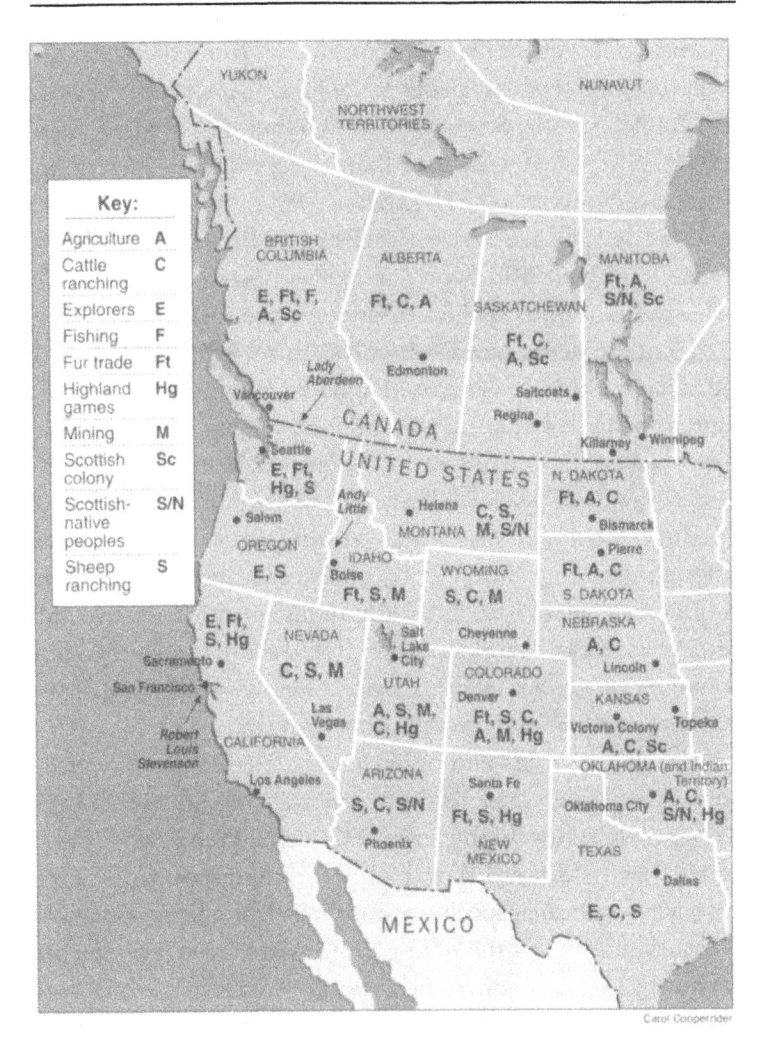

The North American West, 1790–2000

however, was another matter. Green vegetables remained rare until the early twentieth century, and Samuel Johnson's jibe that the English fed oats to the horses but in Scotland oats served as the staple for the people had a degree of truth throughout Scotland's long and complex history.[4]

Historians believe that the Scottish nation emerged from the union of several diverse peoples: the Picts, the Scots, the Britons, the Angles, and the Scandinavians. But over the centuries, these divisions were less important than a more famous dichotomy: the Lowlands versus the Highlands. Eighteenth-century travelers frequently observed the differences between the "house Scots" and the "wild Scots." The "wild Scots" spoke Gaelic, whereas the others spoke a distinct tongue related to English. Lowland Scotland had cities and culture: Edinburgh, Perth, Aberdeen, Stirling, Glasgow; Highland Scotland had scenery and romance. Perhaps, as contemporary poet Maurice Lindsay has phrased it, Scotland was really only an "attitude of mind."[5]

Lowland or Highland, however, Scotland in the eighteenth century remained very much an outpost of Europe. Even though the Scottish border lay but three hundred miles from London, as late as 1753 the Edinburgh stage made the trip only every two weeks. Travelers who ventured south frequently made out their wills as a final preparation.[6] Regular ship service from Orkney to Aberdeen did not occur until 1834.

The lack of roads and bridges in the Highlands was notorious. Since the numerous rivers generally ran parallel to each other on their way to the coast, they formed remarkable barriers to overland travel. Local guides were necessary, but even they knew only their specific regions. The Hanoverian monarchs began a series of road-building projects in the early eighteenth century in order to open the region to commerce as well as to pacify Highland supporters of the ousted Stuarts, but it was not until the railways penetrated the region in the mid-nineteenth century that Scotland became relatively easy to access. Tobias Smollett's character Mrs. Tabitha, for example, believed that one could reach Scotland only by sea.

To Scotland's geography must be added the steady pressure of population. A population explosion from c. 1750 to the late nineteenth century placed increasing pressure on a nation already short of arable lands. During the 1745–1811 period, for example, the population of the Outer Hebrides rose from 11,500 to 24,500. At least 6,000 Highlanders left for North America during the first five years of the nineteenth century. At the close of the Napoleonic wars, the Scottish growth rate approached 15.1 percent a decade. Periodic food shortages— the two most memorable being the seven ill years of William and Mary's reign and the potato famine of the late 1840s— fueled the exodus.

A central theme of Scottish history, therefore, has been emigration. Historian George Shepperson has labeled this the Scottish *Volkerwanderung*. Others have termed it the Scottish diaspora. Scotland's loss, as the National Trust Monument at Culloden currently phrases it, "has been the world's gain."[7]

To the factors of geography and population pressures one must add another: the politics of eighteenth-century Britain. The attempt by the ousted Stuart dynasty to recapture the throne culminated in the Hanoverian victory at Culloden on 16 April 1746. Afterwards, the monarchy turned to draconian measures. The crown executed a number of Stuart supporters, confiscated numerous estates, and officially banned the playing of bagpipes and the wearing of the tartan and other Highland garb. A distinct Scotophobia swept through England, and those Scots who ventured south met social hostility on a number of fronts. Since success in eighteenth-century British society depended upon the favors of highly placed patrons in government, the Scots in England found themselves at a distinct disadvantage. As a defense, they usually banded together. "No Scot ever exerted himself but for a Scot," grumbled one observer.[8]

While a Jacobite past might decidedly hinder advance in England, it proved of no significance overseas. Small wonder, then, that James Charles Stuart Strange and others whose names gave their politics away sought opportunity abroad. Indeed, as historian Linda Calley has recently noted, for many Scots "empire became a profession in itself." In certain regions, such as India and British North America, family loyalty to the lost Stuart cause might even prove an advantage. At the very least, it provoked no public outcry. Georgia Scots fur traders wore kilts in the late eighteenth century, and in 1777 a band of Scots, accompanied by pipers, marched unmolested down the streets of St. Augustine in full Highland regalia.[9]

Poverty, the pressure of population growth, and political turmoil were hardly unusual in the history of Europe. But the proximity to the sea gave the Scots an advantage that eluded the inhabitants of countries such as Switzerland, Hungary, or the Ukraine. Surrounded by the North Sea on one side and the North Atlantic on the other, no part of Scotland is more than forty-five miles from salt water. Aberdeen and Edinburgh maintained a thriving trade with Baltic Sea ports from the fourteenth century forward. Scotland also contains 787 islands, and those who lived in Orkney, Shetland, or the Western Isles met the sea on a daily basis. For example, famed nineteenth-century Arctic explorer John Rae, who grew up on Mainland Orkney, had his own boat when he was fifteen. Legend had it that a person could holler "Hey, Mac" down the engine room of any nineteenth-century steamer and receive a response. During the mid-nineteenth-century wars of empire, so the story goes, a Scottish regiment bound for India found itself stranded by a local sailors' strike. Undaunted, the soldiers—all of whom were fishermen in civilian life—simply sailed the ship themselves.

This combination of circumstances meant that, from medieval times to the present day, the Scots developed the reputation of being a "people on the move." As early as the fourteenth century, the Germans used the term *Schotte* as a synonym for trader. In Scandinavia *Schotts* carried the same meaning. During the Thirty Years War, Scottish adventurers fought all over the continent, a saga fictionalized in Sir Walter Scott's character Sir

Roderick Dhu. By the late eighteenth century, Scots merchants, fishermen, traders, and adventurers could be found stretching from Russia to the Baltic and from France to Scandinavia. Thus, when Britain began to manifest serious interest in exploring the uncharted interior of the North American continent, the Scots were well positioned to take advantage of this new situation.

One of the most significant dates in British and North American history proved to be 1667. In that year the Hudson Bay Company (HBC)—the "Great Company," as the American Indians would learn to call it—was born in Restoration London. Just emerging from a brutal and protracted Civil War, Britain was thronged with capitalist adventurers who dreamed of untold profits from the furs of North America. Five years later, poet John Dryden celebrated the company's first public sale with a bit of doggerel:

> Friend, once 'twas Fame that led thee forth
> To brave the Tropic Heat, the Frozen North,
> Late it was Gold, then beauty was the Spur;
> But now our Gallants venture, but for fur.[10]

From the mid-eighteenth century forward, the mainstays of the Hudson's Bay Company and its eventual rival, the North West Company, lay with its Scottish personnel. The HBC ships sailed from London, but they often made last calls at the Hebrides or Orkneys, where they seldom failed to find recruits. The company maintained agents in Stornoway, the Isle of Lewis, and Stromness, Orkney, for years. Orkney fur trappers in Canada complained so loudly about the unseaworthiness of American Indian birchbark canoes that they eventually brought over a modified version of their own boats to haul New World trade goods. At one time Orkneymen formed almost a majority of HBC employees. Today, Winnipeg, Manitoba, probably has the highest number of Orkney descendants of any city in the world.

Exploration and trading for fur in the eighteenth- and early nineteenth-century North American wilderness presented Europeans with some of the most formidable living conditions imaginable. The HBC trading posts established on the shores of James Bay and Hudson's Bay in Canada were surrounded by terrain known locally as "the barren grounds." Communication with supply depots at Fort York, Fort Albany, and Fort Moose was usually limited to the arrival of an annual supply ship. The winter temperature fell regularly to 40°F below zero, and travel overland was as much by lake as by land. Outside of Siberia or northern Scandinavia, Europe boasted no landscape that remotely approached this region in terms of physical challenges. One needed exceptional skills to survive in such surroundings.

Although it is true that the Scots explorers and traders lacked the religious motivation of Jesuit missionaries who traversed this wilderness, they had the next best thing. They had grown up in an environment of mountain ruggedness, lochs, and solitude that provided an ideal practical training ground for exploring the North American West. John Rae, for example, positively relished the Orkney gales. As he recalled in his reminiscences:

> I delighted in being out in the worst of weather—snowstorms in winter, rain and gales all the year round. Cared nothing for, and felt no harm from being soaking wet either with salt or fresh water all day long—for a waterproof coat was never thought of.[11]

The innumerable challenges of Highland and Island life—especially the necessity of being at the beck and call of the clan leader—produced generations of rugged men and women. The women were as hardy as the men. They often went barefoot, wearing shoes only for special occasions such as attending church. Eighteenth-century traveler Edward Burt observed barefoot Highland women stomping their washing in tubs "when their legs and feet are almost literally as red as blood with the cold."[12] During the herring season Highland women from Sutherland would walk the 130 miles to Wick in Caithness without any type of shelter. When the herring boats unloaded their catch, the women remained outside in all types of weather to gut the fish. They cleaned about thirty-five fish a minute and could keep up the pace for hours on end. Not surprisingly, these women often led Northern crofter anti-Clearance agitation. In the 1841 riot at Durness and the 1842 protest at Lochsheil, women sporting shearing hooks and with aprons filled with stones chased away the evicting officers.[13]

Such a culture thrived on stories of endurance and bravado. Legends told of Highland soldiers on maneuvers who marched overland carrying just a bag of oatmeal and a small stone on which to heat it at night. For rest, they rolled up tightly in their homespun wool plaids and stretched out on the bare ground. When the temperature dropped near freezing, they would occasionally dip their plaids into a stream to freeze them and sleep inside a coating of ice not unlike a snow cave. One clan chieftain was chaffed by his men as "soft" when he was seen making a pillow out of snow (sometimes out of a rock).

Sir John Sinclair, compiler of the first *Statistical Account of Scotland* in the 1790s, summarized this mood to perfection:

> He [the Highlander] has felt from his early youth all the privations to which he can be exposed in almost any circumstances of war. He has been accustomed to scanty fare, to rude and often wet clothing, to cold and damp houses, to sleep often in the open air or in the most uncomfortable beds, to cross dangerous rivers, to march a number of miles without stopping and with but little nourishment, and to be perpetually exposed to the attacks of a stormy atmosphere. A warrior thus trained suffers no inconvenience from what others would consider to be the greatest

possible hardships, and has an evident superiority over the native of a delicious climate, bred to every indulgence of food, dress and habitation and who is unaccustomed to marching and fatigue.[14]

Thus, unbeknownst to themselves, Scots Highlanders and Islanders grew to adulthood in the best possible "university" that could prepare them for North American exploration or the western fur trade. Not without reason was the fur-trapping territory of western Canada termed "New Caledonia."

The history of Scotland and the growth of the North American fur trade are forever intertwined. The story of trade and discovery in the American Northwest, wrote nineteenth-century journalist A. Inness Shand, "reads like a muster-roll of the clans," chiefly "the northern clans of the second order": MacTavish, MacGillivray, McKay, McLellan, McDougall, Fraser, and Stuart. Peter C. Newman, the premier historian of the HBC, has observed that virtually all the great names of the company grew up in Scotland: Simpson, Smith, Douglas, Campbell, Murray, McLean, Leith, Stuart.[15] The HBC's chief rival, the North West Company, was also run by Scots. Its early roster contained such names as Dickson, Laidlaw, Lamont, McKenzie, Kipp, Stewart, and McTavish. The Orkney surnames of Isbister, Linklater, Marwick, Sabiston, Corrigal, and Flett are common today among the Cree and Spokane Indians of Canada and the Pacific Northwest.

The Scots dominated the nineteenth-century fur trade. When John Jacob Astor founded his American Fur Company in 1800, he hired away six disgruntled employees from the North West Company; all were Scots. A later defector from the North West Company, the Paris-educated Robert Stuart, eventually became Astor's business partner. In 1812 an English traveler ventured onto the Great Plains and met a party of five fur trappers; the Scots outnumbered the French by three to two. The fur trade along the south Atlantic coast was largely controlled by two firms—Panton, Leslie and Company and John Forbes and Company—almost every member of which was born either in Aberdeenshire or in towns bordering the Moray Firth.[16]

In many of these fur-trade enterprises, kinship ties proved far more enduring than company loyalties. Historian James Hunter has described the North West Fur Company as a unique combination of business enterprise and extended family of the Highland type. There were so many Highlanders in the HBC that Lowland employees complained that the lack of a clan name led to discrimination in promotion.[17] The common language was often Gaelic. Because their chief loyalty had been to clan, Scots traders could shift from company to company or from nation to nation as circumstances warranted. For example, in the early 1790s James Mackay moved from British Canada to St. Louis, becoming a Spanish citizen, so as to better engage in the fur trade. Similarly, a generation later Ramsay Crooks from Greenock, Scotland, moved from Montreal to St. Louis, becoming an American citizen, so as to manage the American Fur Company. The St. Louis–based firm Sublette and Campbell, the only serious rival of the American Fur Company, was run with equal skill from 1836 to 1842 by Tyrone, Northern Ireland–born Robert Campbell. Angus MacDonald from the Isle of Skye entered the service of the HBC in 1838 and proved so skillful in obtaining Indian furs that in 1852 he was appointed head of the extensive Colville district, including all traditional posts north of Walla Walla, Washington, far into British Columbia. MacDonald held this position until 1871, when the HBC finally gave up its last posts in the United States, and lived the rest of his life as an American in Montana Territory.

On one occasion, John McDonald of the Canadian North West Company was discussing the fur trade with Alexander Ross, then employed by the American Fur Company. "The Americans have been very enterprising," McDonald commented.

"We are called Americans," said Ross, "but there were very few Americans among us—we were all Scotchmen like yourselves."[18]

During their heyday the Scots fur traders amassed incredible power. James Kirker was once termed "the king of New Mexico." Dr. John McLoughlin, chief factor of the HBC in Oregon, lived in regal splendor with a piper who welcomed guests. George Simpson of the HBC took a piper with him whenever he went on an inspection tour. Kenneth McKenzie, who founded Fort Union on the Upper Missouri, presided over a larger territory than many a European monarch.[19]

Since both Highland and fur-trade society were largely oral cultures, the prowess of these men soon evolved into legend. And of all the fur-trade legends, none is as remarkable as the adventures of Hugh Glass. Born in Pennsylvania of Scotch-Irish parents, Glass migrated to the western plains and in June 1823 staggered, exhausted, into Fort Atkinson in Council Bluffs, Iowa. His arrival was greeted with astonishment, because his compatriots had heard that he had been killed on the Great Plains. One version had him dispatched by Arickara Indians; another placed the blame on a white bear.

When Glass recovered enough to tell his story, the astonishment grew. The previous year, Glass had signed up to travel with Major Andrew Henry up the Missouri River. But after several weeks, he was surprised by a large white grizzly bear and badly mauled in his arms, legs, and shoulder. His mates dispatched the animal, but Glass was too severely injured to continue. As it was questionable whether he would survive, Major Henry selected two men to stay with Glass and either wait until he recovered or bury him, whichever came first. After five days the trappers chose a third alternative. They took his rifle and provisions and abandoned him. When they caught up with Henry's party, they reported that Glass had died and they had interred him as instructed.

Left for dead, the exhausted Glass dragged himself to a nearby spring where he lived for ten days on cherries and buffalo berries. Too weak to stand, he began crawling across the prairie. Fortunately for him, he stumbled onto the partial remains of a buffalo calf recently killed by wolves and thus sustained himself for several days. Fueled by revenge, he eventually made his way to Fort Kiowa, a post on the Missouri River. Shortly afterwards, a party of trappers bound for the Yellowstone River and a Mandan village at Tilton's fort stopped by the fort, and Glass joined them in pursuit of his tormentors.

When the trading party approached an Indian village, the main group went on ahead, but Glass left the boat to take a slightly different route. This proved fortunate. As he drew near the village, Glass discovered that a band of Arickara Indians had attacked and killed all the traders. Glass immediately fled into the high grasses and escaped capture. He spent the next thirty-eight days alone before he arrived at Major Henry's establishment on the Big Horn River, where he spent the winter recovering.

Discovering that his main betrayer had moved on to Fort Atkinson in Iowa, Glass volunteered to carry letters to this post. With four companions, he left Henry's camp on February 29, 1824, for the Powder River, the Platte, and finally the lower end of the Black Hills. There the party was again attacked by a band of Arickara, this time led by Elk's Tongue, and again Glass barely escaped into the wilderness. As Glass phrased it,

> Although I have lost my rifle and all my plunder, I felt quite rich, when I found my knife, flint, and steel in my shot pouch. These little fixers make a man feel right *peart,* when he is three or four hundred miles *from any body* or *any place*—all alone among the *painters* and wild *varmints.*[20]

Fifteen days' journey brought him to Fort Kiowa, then finally on to Fort Atkinson at Council Bluffs. There he confronted his old antagonist. But his opponent had since enlisted in the army, and Glass found he could not bring charges against him. The officer in command resolved the quarrel by providing Glass with a new rifle and other necessary provisions. Then Hugh Glass went back to life in the fur trade.

This saga remains today as the premier frontier adventure story. Other than Glass himself, however, there is no proof for the tale. Consequently, it probably reflects the Scottish folk legends of endurance and triumph over treachery as much as it does life in the American fur trade. The oral culture of the immigrants proved remarkably flexible.[21]

Although not, perhaps, quite so dramatic, the lives of several other Scots or Scotch-Irish trappers achieved similar regional fame. James Kirker, "Don Santiago Kirker, the king of New Mexico," proved the most notorious of the lot. Born in Kilross, near Belfast, in 1743, Kirker arrived in New York in 1810, where he served on an American privateer during the War of 1812. In 1821 he made his way to St. Louis, where he dabbled in the fur trade and three years later began trapping in earnest in the Mexican Southwest, chiefly in the Rio Gila region of western New Mexico. In 1835 he was licensed to trade with the Apaches of the region and learned their ways well. On occasion he seems to have served as a fence for their stolen goods. Political and commercial difficulties sent him farther south, and the governor of Chihuahua eventually contracted with him to raise a private army to raid the Apaches. Kirker's army, composed of Shawnee Indians plus assorted renegades, then began a systematic compaign of murder. The Mexican government allegedly promised him two hundred dollars for each Apache scalp. By his own account, Kirker killed 487 people. After this, he accepted Mexican citizenship and a colonel's commission in the Mexican army. (By this time he had a Mexican wife and family, in addition to a neglected New York wife and family.) When the Mexican-American War broke out in 1846, Kirker again switched sides, becoming both a spy and an advisor for the Missouri Volunteers. In turn, the Mexican government placed a ten-thousand-dollar bounty on his head, which forever prohibited his return to Mexico.

The sole surviving daguerreotype of Kirker reveals a dark-skinned man with a fierce countenance. A profile in an 1847 St. Louis newspaper commented favorably on Kirker's intelligence, demeanor, and accent, the latter so unique "that few would suspect him of being a son of the Emerald Isle." After serving as guide and scout, James Kirker died in California in 1853, an acknowledged "bad man."[22]

A Scots trader named Craigie earned a much more admirable reputation during his sojourn in the northern Rockies. In the late 1840s through the 1850s he served as the fort master at Fort Walla Walla on the Oregon Trail. Craigie arrived in America as a common laborer with the HBC and rose steadily in the ranks. His home by the Boise River brought him the occasional salmon, but he and his Panack (Bannock) wife existed marginally on hunting and a few vegetables. He had almost no contact with whites save those who came through on the trail.

Craigie's reputation derived from his understanding of Christian stewardship. Over the years he housed and cared for a number of exhausted travelers who surely would have perished without him. When English visitor Henry J. Coke rode to Oregon in 1850, he found Craigie caring for a Swiss who had been severely injured when his rifle exploded. "Many are the instances of his charitable deeds," Coke wrote, "and many are the travellers on these plains who survive to pray for blessings on this disinterested and generous being, to whom they owe their preservation."[23]

The French trappers were prominent on the northern fur-trade frontier. Their Spanish counterparts played the same role on the southwestern frontier. But Scots and Scotch-Irish fur trappers were ubiquitous. No area of the Trans-Mississippi West was without them.

EXPLORERS

If the Highland and Island Scots dominated the North American fur trade, Lowland Scots often, though not always, led the way as explorers of the West. The motivation of the explorers, however, derived less from the geography of their homeland than from the geography of the mind. And here we must turn to the Scottish Reformation and the Scottish Enlightenment.

The Reformation of 1560 created a sense of Scottish destiny that manifested itself in a myriad of ways. The leaders of the Reformation began to create a distinctive semireligious mythology: like ancient Israel, Scotland was a poor and seemingly insignificant nation. But like Israel, God had chosen it to play a leading role in His plans for the establishment of true religion and the betterment of humankind.[24]

A key means to this end emerged in the scheme devised by reformer John Knox to educate Scottish youth. Knox's plan was to place a school in every parish to teach reading, writing, and catechism. The goal was to allow people to read Scripture for themselves, for no priest could assist a person in achieving salvation. The second level of schooling consisted of a grammar school in every town to teach grammar and Latin; next came a high school or college in the most important towns to further classical studies. The culmination came with a university system that boasted a three-year arts course plus medicine, law, and divinity. The ancient Scottish unversities—St. Andrews (founded 1410), Glasgow (1451), Edinburgh (1583), King's College, Old Aberdeen (1495), and Marischal (1593)—provided the capstone to a system that far outclassed the educational structures of England or the Continent.

The system was not exactly free, since parents usually paid tuition fees (sometimes in kind, such as peat for the stoves). But the teachers' salaries were paid in part by a tax on heritors and tenants or from burgh municipal funds. The educational conditions in the Highlands and Islands proved so challenging that the Society in Scotland for Propagating Christian Knowledge (SSPCK) also established a parallel system of schools. The various Scottish statistical accounts show the enormous influence that Scottish education had in the eighteenth- and early nineteenth-century rural Lowlands, the only area that approximated Knox's ideal.

Scotland's goal of a basic education for all males proved a far cry from contemporary English distrust of the educated masses. Philosopher George Davie has argued that because of its educational system, Scotland produced a "democratic intellect" with a mythology to match. Indeed, Scots have always valued a man who could "better himself." The popular image of the poor lad (the "lad-o-pairts") carrying oatmeal and herring en route to a university proved a common one. Myth though it was, it reflected a degree of truth. All through the nineteenth century, Scots scored well in any survey of literacy. In the parlance of the day, only the Jews rivaled the Scots in their respect for scholarship.

Knox's concern for education culminated in the famous Scottish Enlightenment of c. 1750–1810. The names of philosopher David Hume, economist Adam Smith, historian William Robinson, educator William Small, architect Robert Adam, and philosopher Lord Kames reflected the high calibre of Scottish thought. In a manner far different from that of the French Enlightenment, Presbyterian clerics often stood at the very center of the Scottish Age of Reason. Lawyers, economists, and geographers were equally common. In eighteenth-century Edinburgh, it was said, a person could stand at the Market Square and shake hands with fifty men of genius in an hour. Just one statistic will illustrate this point: from 1750 to 1850, the Scottish universities educated ten thousand medical doctors; Oxford and Cambridge in the same period educated five hundred.[25] Historians are still trying to comprehend the period when

Scotland led the Western world in the realms of medicine, economics, history, and jurisprudence.[26]

This emphasis on schooling and scientific advances helped produce some of the first explorers of the North American West. The range of firsthand Scottish western adventurers is remarkable. One should probably begin with the story of James Cook. Son of a Scots farm worker who had moved to the Yorkshire town of Marton, Cook rose rapidly in the service of the British navy. Later he entered historical legend as the "Pacific Columbus," for just as Columbus "discovered" America en route to India, Cook "discovered" Hawaii while searching for the elusive Northwest Passage.

On March 29, 1778, Cook's flagship the *Revolution,* with a companion vessel, *Discovery,* sailed into what is now Nootka Sound on Vancouver Island. They remained there almost a month, recording detailed scientific, geographical, and meteorological data of the region. Although Cook was a naval officer, not a businessman, he anticipated that great profits could be made by trading British goods for fur from the Natives. Unfortunately, the most famous Scottish sea captain of his generation died the next year in Hawaii; his crew returned to Britain in 1780.[27]

Six years later, a ship named in his honor, *Captain Cook,* deposited another Scot in the region, surgeon John Mackay. Mackay had volunteered to spend a year living with the Nootka natives. Supplied with paper, pens, and ink, plus a Native wife, Mackay gradually learned the language and customs of his hosts. Although Mackay's records eventually proved disappointing, his venture still ranks as the first attempt at serious New World ethnography. A contemporary Scottish merchant from St. Louis showed a similar scientific orientation. When he helped outfit Welshman John Evans for an exploratory trip up the Missouri River, he urged Evans to keep an eye out for "an animal which has only one horn on its forehead."[28]

Three further stories illustrate the theme of Scots exploration of the Trans-Mississippi West in more detail.

ALEXANDER MACKENZIE

Mackenzie was born c. 1767 in Stornoway, Western Isles. His *Voyages from Montreal, on the River St. Laurence, through the Continent of North America, to the Frozen and Pacific Oceans,* published in December 1801, became one of the most influential books of its day.[29] Based on two lengthy overland trips that Mackenzie took in 1789 and 1793, the book related the saga of the fur trade as well as his own adventures. These two overland journeys proved landmarks in the exploration of the North American continent. On the first, a journey of 102 days, Mackenzie traversed the region from Fort Chippewayen at the head of Lake Athabasca to the Arctic Sea down a mighty river that currently bears his name. On the second he became the first white man to cross the Rocky Mountains and reach the Pacific Ocean.

Mackenzie's ultimate goal in each case had been to solve the three-hundred-year question that had animated Captain Cook: was there a Northwest Passage? Publication of his *Voyages* proved conclusively that there was no practical sea route across the continent. The only way lay by overland travel, and this involved crossing 50 large lakes, 200 rapids, and 130 carrying places, which ranged from 25 paces to over 13 miles.[30]

Mackenzie's *Voyages* also revealed the scientific bent of the Scots Enlightenment. Armed with the latest instruments, he carefully recorded latitude and longitude readings at every step, often while his crew anxiously looked over their shoulders in fear of possible Native attack. On occasion Mackenzie would borrow vermilion, mix it with melted grease, and write his name and the date on nearby rocks. On a rock in Dean Channel near

The port of Stornoway, Isle of Lewis, was the birthplace of famed explorer Alexander Mackenzie and the departure point for thousands of other Scottish immigrants to North America. (The George Washington Wilson Collection, Aberdeen University Library. Print F0309.)

Vancouver on the Pacific Coast, he wrote his most famous grease-and-vermilion inscription: "Alexander Mackenzie, from Canada, by land, the twenty-second of July, one thousand seven hundred and ninety-three." This rock has been positively identified, and a permanent plaque now marks the spot.

A shrewd observer, Mackenzie made a number of trenchant comments about the terrain and Native peoples of North America. He noted that the climate on the Pacific Coast was far more similar to European climates of the same latitude than was the climate of the interior, although he believed the weather of the interior was improving. He also discovered that the interior tribes, who had had much less contact with white traders, were much easier to bargain with than the coastal bands, who had dealt with traders for generations. Not unnaturally, some tribes viewed his queries about the nature of the land with considerable suspicion.[31] One coastal group, the Bella Coolas, whose leader had once been shot at by whites, treated Mackenzie with great contempt. So eager were they to have him leave, he noted, they provided him with poles and food to speed him along. Mackenzie devoted much space to American Indian matters and the attractiveness of their way of living. So enticing was their life, he observed, that it took less time for Europeans to adopt their ways than for the Natives "to rise to civilization."[32]

Mackenzie dedicated his book to George III, and in February 1802 received a knighthood. Although the rest of his career proved somewhat anticlimactic, the reputation of his *Voyages* has never faded. It probably influenced Lord Selkirk to try his Highland resettlement scheme in Red River, Manitoba, and it certainly alerted Thomas Jefferson to the potential of British rivalry for the rich lands of the Pacific Northwest. Spurred on by reading Mackenzie's *Voyages*, Jefferson outfitted the famed expedition of Lewis and Clark in 1803. Thus, Mackenzie's account of his trips across the continent proved one of the most pivotal books in the entire history of the North American West.[33]

The Travelling Botanists

Scottish culture has long admired those men and women who could master the intricacies of the natural world. The gentleman or lady farmer remains a highly respected person today. As historian Susan Delano McKelvey has shown in her study of nineteenth-century botanist-explorers, Scots naturalists led the way in the botanizing of the North American West.[34]

Archibald Menzies was the first Scots botanist to explore the Pacific Coast. Born in Weem, Menzies studied flora at his ancestral home, Castle Menzies, but eventually trained as a surgeon at the University of Edinburgh. Appointed assistant surgeon in the British Navy, Menzies sailed to the Pacific Northwest with Captain George Vancouver in 1792, 1793, and 1794. Whilst there he catalogued over one hundred varieties of flowering plants. Menzies' extensive journal (1792–94; first published, in part, in 1923) is very revealing. It shows Menzies' awareness that he had stumbled onto a genuinely new natural world. About sixteen species are dedicated to him, and he introduced Britons to a wide variety of trees and plants, including the California poppy, the tree lupin, and the Sitka spruce.[35]

Menzies' forays remained confined to the Pacific Coast. Thus, John Bradbury has been acknowledged as the first trained botanist to explore the interior of the great West systematically. Historians dispute whether Bradbury was born in England or Scotland, but they agree that his 1809 botanizing journey west from St. Louis was the first of its kind. Working under the auspices of the Botanical Society of Liverpool, Bradbury catalogued almost one hundred of "the more rare or valuable plants discovered in the neighborhood of St. Louis and on the Missouri." The 1817 publication of his *Travels in the Interior of America* was eagerly read on both sides of the Atlantic, as it provided the first description of the great valley of the Mississippi River.[36]

Menzies and Bradbury had a number of successors. Thomas Drummond of Perthshire botanized through Texas from 1833 to 1835 before dying in Havana while on his way home. William Frazer Tolmie from Inverness, officially employed as an HBC physician and surgeon, was the first to collect plants from the lower slopes of Mount Rainier in 1833. Historians have finally identified the "friend of Mr. Tolmie," who supplied him with scores of additional regional specimens, as HBC fur trader John MacLeod. Tolmie's colleague, Meredith Gardiner, also did sporadic botanizing in the region before ill health drove him to Hawaii.[37]

The Americans lagged somewhat in this department. Jefferson instructed Lewis and Clark to gather plants on their way west in 1804–1806, but Washington did not formally explore the natural world of the Pacific Northwest until the famed Wilkes Expedition of 1841. The chief botanist for this venture was William Dunlop Brackenridge of Ayrshire, now acknowledged as the first person to assess the natural resources of Washington Territory systematically.[38]

The most famous of all the Scots explorer-botanists was David Douglas. Born at Scone in Perthshire in 1798, Douglas was early apprenticed to William Beattie, head gardener at Scone Palace, who was in charge of the Earl of Mansfield's estate. Ever curious, Douglas enrolled in classes in science and mathematics; by 1817 he had risen to the position of undergardener to Sir Robert Preston at Valleyfield. While there, he read through Sir Robert's extensive library of botanical works. Shortly afterwards, he moved to Glasgow's famed Botanical Garden, where Professor William J. Hooker noticed him and took him along on a botanical trip to the Highlands to gather strange and exotic plants.

In 1824 the HBC and the Royal Horticultural Society sent Douglas, then twenty-five, to the United States on a similar mission. The next year he took a longer voyage around Cape Horn, landing at Fort Vancouver in April 1825. During this lengthy journey he discovered and catalogued a vast range of new animals, including the California vulture and the California sheep. He found several species of pines, but his name will always be associated with the majestic conifer, the Douglas fir, whose Latin name, *Pseudetsiga menziessi,* also commemorates the botanical efforts of Archibald Menzies.

Douglas delighted in the exploration of the American West. "Not a day passed but brought something new or interesting either in botany or zoology," he noted in his diary on March 20, 1827.[39] Virtually all his writings reveal his sense of wonder regarding the world of nature, in which he saw evidence of "an infinite intelligence and power in the Almighty hand." This combination of scientific accuracy and romantic theism reflected two of the central themes of the Scottish Enlightenment.

Both the Natives and the trappers of the Columbia River basin looked with amusement on the shy, intense explorer tracking "the vegetable treasures" of the region. The Natives termed him "King George's Chief" and marveled at how he could light his pipe with the sun by way of a lens. They also nicknamed him *Olla-Diska,* Chinook jargon for *fire.*[40] As his journal shows, Douglas interacted well with the Chinook. Indeed, he often relied on Natives or trappers to bring him specimens. Later, he also enjoyed the friendship of the Franciscan friars of California. By no means a modern ecologist (he amused himself by shooting seals and killing birds), Douglas nevertheless collected avidly wherever he went.

Over the years, Douglas made several trips to the Pacific Coast. He voyaged to America in 1823 and again in 1824–25. In 1827 Douglas crossed the Rocky Mountains eastward on his way to Hudson's Bay, and from there he returned to England. Brewster's *Edinburgh Journal* published extracts from his letters, and his journals were later serialized in W. J. Hooker's *Companion to the Botanical Magazine.* Although he received several offers to publish his travels, he never finished the manuscript. His *Journal Kept by David Douglas During His Travels in North*

America, 1823–1827 did not appear in print until 1914. In the fall of 1829 he sailed again for the West and spent 1829–32 in California; during the next two years he lived largely on the Fraser River in Canada. From 1829 forward, he was lionized in Great Britain, consulted on matters of botany as well as foreign policy. (He stoutly insisted that the Columbia River was the most logical boundary between the United States and Canada.)

Douglas's years in the public limelight did not prove happy ones. Uncomfortable with all the attention, he became sour and difficult to work with. Even his friends tired of his extreme irritability. His mentor, W. J. Hooker, noted that they "could not wish, as he himself did, that he were again occupied in the honorable task of exploring North West America."[41]

In the summer of 1834 Douglas sailed to Honolulu, where he mysteriously disappeared. Later, his body was found in a cattle trap. The cause of his death has remained an item of speculation. Notoriously shortsighted, he had a habit of wandering into difficult situations. (While in Oregon country, trappers once had to rescue him from a ravine into which he had fallen and had lain injured for several hours.) Others, however, have suggested either murder or suicide.[42]

Still, his fame rests less with his words than with the approximately seven thousand species he sent back to Britain, largely to the Kew Gardens and the Linneaus Society, which made up approximately 13 percent of the then-known species of plants in the world. He singlehandedly introduced twenty-four plants to Britain. David Douglas was also the first travelling botanist to become a national hero, and even those who have forogtten his actual deeds recall his name through the Douglas fir.[43]

ALEXANDER FORBES

Although Mackenzie and Douglas achieved the greatest reputations, other Scots explorer-writers earned lesser fame as well. One was merchant and adventurer Alexander Forbes. In *California: A History of Upper and Lower California* (1839), Forbes penned what is probably the first full account in English of the Pacific Coast. A friend of the Franciscan padres, who had established missions in the area, Forbes drew upon their knowledge and experience for his study. He especially relied upon Fr. Francisco Palou's *A Life of the Chief Missionary Father Junipero Serra*, published in Mexico in 1787; an unpublished manuscript of a 1715 journey from Sonora to Upper California; and the 1776 journal of the travels of Padres Dominguez and Escalante across the Southwest. Staunch Protestant though he was, Forbes found much to praise in the Franciscan priests.[44]

Although he admired the Franciscans as individuals—especially Father Antonio Peyri, the head of Mission San Luis Rey for thirty-four years—Forbes had little good to say about the Spanish mission system in general. He compared the California mission system to the enslavement of the Blacks in the West Indies and observed that although the Spanish termed themselves "rational creatures" (*gente de razon*), they called the Natives "beasts" (*bestias*).[45]

His descriptions of Spanish agricultural innovations were extensive. He praised California cattle, potatoes, flax, grapes, and olives, but he termed their farming methods "most rude and backward." Still, even Forbes's cautious praise of Spanish enterprise marked him out as unique, since the Black Legend fueled most British commentaries on early California. For example, English traveler George Ruxton could not find a single redeeming Mexican trait when he visited California in 1847.[46]

Though Forbes dismissed the mission system and Spanish agriculture on the whole, he was fascinated by the California landscape. Since he viewed California as a unique region having nothing in common with Mexico save Spanish culture, he predicted that it would eventually become a major power in its own right. Because Mexico owed Britain monies due on a recent loan, Forbes suggested the Mexican government might cede California to Britain as full payment. The British Isles teemed with a surplus population of "human beings with superior intellects," he noted. If they could only be settled in California, they would turn the region into a breadbasket. If California were placed under good management and with a British population, the region would most certainly realize all that had been predicted for it.[47]

The idea that Britain might colonize California received serious consideration in London. But the vast lands of Australia, Canada, and New Zealand provided sufficient alternative outlets for surplus population, so no serious attempts were launched. By the time of the 1849 Gold Rush, all such ideas had been abandoned.[48]

But others read Forbes's writings, too. By the late 1830s, native Californians worried aloud about the impending invasion by the Americans. Even though the Russians were firmly established in Fort Ross at Bodega Bay, they were not half as feared as the dreaded "Yankees." If Santa Anna had won in Texas in 1836 (where, incidentally, five Scots, including a piper, died at the Alamo), rumor had it that the Americans would have overrun California within a year.[49] Forbes's predictions that California would come under civic rather than ecclesiastical control and that an English-speaking population utilizing western management techniques would turn it into a cornucopia were eventually realized, but by a far different group of people than he had envisioned.

Forbes was not the only Scot who tried to make his fortune in pre–Gold Rush California. At least fifty identifiable Scots plied their trade in this region well before the Americans arrived. Their number included Mary Anderson, wife of a Monterey shipbuilder, who is usually cited as the first English-speaking woman on the West Coast and the mother of the first child of foreign parents, and Alfred Robinson, the first traveler to sketch the San Luis Rey Mission in 1829.[50] Other Scots included Hugo Reid of Cardross, who had studied at Cambridge. His twenty-two essays, published as *Letters on the Los Angeles County Indians* (the tribe of his wife), became a valuable source for anthropologists and historians. William Money's *The Reform of the New Testament Church,* set in parallel columns of Spanish and English type, has been hailed as the first book published in Los Angeles. Money has also earned the dubious distinction of being the "first outstanding eccentric of Los Angeles," thus inaugurating a lengthy tradition.[51]

The books penned by these Scottish explorers of the American West not only reflected the influence of the Enlightenment, they also achieved the status of classics in western writing. The *Journal of Captain Cook's Last Voyage to the Pacific Ocean* (1781), Menzies' *Journals* (1792–94), Mackenzie's *Voyages* (1801), Bradbury's *Travels* (1877), Douglas's *Journal* (1828–29), Forbes's *California* (1839), and Reid's *Letters* (1852) have become vital firsthand accounts for understanding this period. One might also include Canadian Alexander Ross's studies: *Manitoba, Adventures of the First Settlers on the Oregon or Columbia River* (1849), his two-volume *The Fur Hunters of the Far West* (1852) and *The Red River Settlement* (1853). In fact, no other books of the era began to approach these Scottish accounts, either for accuracy or for historical significance. The legacy of the Scottish Enlightenment traveled well beyond the north of Britain. It had a major impact on the American West as well.

CHAPTER THREE

Scotland and the American Indians

In 1964 the principal chief of the Creek Nation of Oklahoma, who boasted the surname McIntosh, attended the annual gathering of his clan in the Highlands. To everyone's surprise, he appeared in full Native regalia. The Plains Indian headdress, beaded shirt, and moccasins contrasted sharply with the kilts, sporrans, and dirks. To a bagpipe audience, he explained his pride in his dual Creek-Scottish ancestry.[1]

The story of these Scoto-Indians is a fascinating one. Like their French and Spanish counterparts, the Scots fur traders arrived in the West largely as single men. Like the other Europeans, they soon aligned with Native women, usually "in the fashion of the country." As historian Sylvia Van Kirk has noted, this form of "country marriage" facilitated trade because the Native wives usually taught their husbands the tribal language. The Montreal-based North West Company actively encouraged this policy, whereas the HBC discouraged it, because of expense, until the 1820s. Eventually, however, all the fur-trade enterprises acknowledged the key role that Native wives played in their operations.[2]

In Indian country these unions were considered as binding as Christian church ceremonies. Later, however, if a trader returned to Britain, he often "turned off" his country wife to her family, although he usually maintained a minimum of economic responsibility for her and the children. For example, Sir George Simpson, head of the Athabasca District of the HBC and one of Canada's most powerful figures, left his country wife to marry his cousin in London in 1830. J. G. Mactavish, head of York factory for most of the 1820s, William Conolly, chief factor in charge of New Caledonia, and countless other Scots followed along similar paths. The same situation occurred in the South Atlantic region. One scholar has estimated that in late eighteenth- to early nineteenth-century Georgia, Indian women raised about four hundred mixed-blood offspring by themselves.[3]

But not all Scots fur traders left their Native consorts. Alexander Ross remained devoted to his Indian wife, as did Angus McDonald, Donald A. Smith, John McLoughlin, and a number of others who stayed with their Native or mixed-blood women for life. Whichever arrangement prevailed, however, the end result was to produce a number of Scoto-Indians.

The emergence of these Scoto-Indians should not be all that surprising. Historically there were a number of parallels between the American Indians and the Highland and Island world from which the traders usually came. In each case the physical conditions of life, governed by the change of seasons and often perched on the edge of hunger, proved similar. There could not have been much difference between an Isle of Lewis beehive shieling and a Great Plains tipi or a Mandan earthen lodge.

The two groups shared cultural similarities as well. Each was an indigenous people. Each had fought lengthy battles, stretching over centuries, both against one another and against English-speaking invaders. Each had achieved partial, but by no means complete, success in fending off the invasions.

This nineteenth-century crofter's house on the Isle of Skye must have resembled many Native American lodgings in the western territories. (The George Washington Wilson Collection, Aberdeen University Library. Print C0732.)

As indigenous peoples, their social structures reflected numerous similarities. Each viewed land as essentially a communal resource, not a commodity to be bought and sold for profit. Each identified itself by bands or clans, and since chiefdom descended through lineage, each devised a system flexible enough to allow selection of the best person for the job. (The British monarchy found itself much more restricted in this regard.) Some anthropologists have found parallels between the fall Indian Green Corn dances and the Highland Beltane fires and harvest ceremonies. Since the cultures were primarily oral, each group accorded the bard or orator a position of great significance. The ballads, songs, folklore, and stories passed on to the children contained the distilled wisdom of their people.[4]

One even finds a similarity between Native and Scottish naming practices. Historian George MacDonald Fraser has argued that many a Scots Borders name, such as Hob the King, Dand the Man, Red Cloak, and Wynking Will, carried special meaning. The similarity to American Indian names such as Black Elk, Crazy Horse, Red Shirt, and Rain-in-the-Face is intriguing. In each case these names must have carried connotations of social significance, "elegant recklessness," and prowess that modern researchers can only estimate.[5] That members of both groups were driven from their homelands, one by the infamous Highland Clearances, the other by white encroachment and Indian removal, deepens the parallel. Finally, the deep wisdom and strength of character that each group has displayed over the centuries has allowed them to endure these calamities with dignity.

Viewed historically, the Highland Scots and the American Indians were tribal peoples. Modern Scottish clan maps show how each chieftain drew the lines of his territory. For the laird, having a group of men at his call alone meant security. The symbol for gathering—a fiery cross sent around from village to village—later took on far more sinister connotations in the United States.

Anyone who looks at Scottish history is astounded by the constant round of violence and murder. No element of society was spared. Of the six Stuart sovereigns from James I to Mary Queen of Scots, for example, only one died a natural death. The ultimate symbolic event of the internecine warfare occurred in the valley of Glencoe, where, on February 13, 1692, the Campbells massacred the MacDonalds after enjoying their hospitality for several weeks.

It has been said that Glencoe symbolizes the end of the old Highland social order, as the traditional hospitality fell victim to political considerations. As historian Allan I. Macinnes has shown, the shift from a traditional to a commercialized society began as early as the seventeenth century. From that time forward the various clan leaders themselves, not just outside forces, helped accelerate the demise of traditional Highland society.[6] The power of the clans was not finally broken until the battle of Culloden in 1746, after which the traditional rivalry was siphoned off into wars of empire and, later, the sporting contests of the famed Highland games. The Scottish tradition of using clan names for fore- and surnames (Gordon Ross; Ross Gordon) shows the desire to keep these clan distinctions alive.

The lack of written records makes the re-creation of Native history before contact a bit more problematic, but anthropologists agree that the band or town served as the chief social unit here, too. As among the Scottish clans, trading and raiding against one another proved commonplace among the American Indians. The Peace River in northern Canada drew its name from a reconciliation between two warring tribes, the Cree and the Beaver. Navajos and Apaches regularly attacked the Pueblos of the Southwest. The Huron despised the Iroquois, the Crow distrusted the Blackfeet, and the Sioux were disliked by all their neighbors. Indeed, one reason why the British, Spanish, and French could gain their initial footholds on the continent was that Native bands were willing to use the

Europeans in their long-standing conflicts with their neighbors. The Pan-Indian movement did not really gain ground until the late nineteenth century.

A number of nineteenth-century travelers remarked on these Celtic-Native similarities. In 1838 Hugh Murray admired the bonds within the tribal union. "The honour and welfare of the clan supply the ruling principle," noted Murray, "and are cherished with an ardour not surpassed in the most brilliant eras of Greek and Roman patriotism." He commented that, like the Highland clans, so long as any tribal member had sufficient food, no one was in the least danger of starvation.[7] Another traveler, D. B. Warden, observed how tribes recognized basic boundaries between groups as they wandered over the Great Plains. Impressed by the hospitality and kindness of certain tribes to their friends, he saw an obvious Celtic-Indian link. "So unbounded is the hospitality of the Osages," he wrote, "that cooks are sent about to cry as in some parts of Ireland, come, come, and partake of the feast of the chief man of the village; and to refuse this invitation is a proof of bad manners."[8] In *The Heart of Midlothian* (1818) Sir Walter Scott told of a Highland outlaw who escaped to America to become an Indian chief. Almost fifty years later Lady Aberdeen found among the Blackfeet "many faces reminding us of Scottish characteristics."[9]

From the early nineteenth century forward, many observers believed that both Highland and American Indian cultures were on the inevitable road to extinction. Given the evolutionary anthropology of the time, this made perfect sense. All societies were seen as climbing the "ladder of culture" and the more "primitive" ones would soon disappear. In 1840 Highland traveler James Browne concluded his massive three-volume study, *A History of the Highlands and of the Island Clans*, with the prediction that the old feelings, habits, customs, traditions, and superstitions would vanish within a few years.[10] Across the Atlantic, many held similar views regarding the Indians. Writing in America's centennial years, British observer W. Bond Dawkins urged people to record the "red man's history" immediately or it would be lost forever. A few years later, photographer Edward Curtis began his massive documentary program with just this theme in mind. Curtis's famed image, "The Vanishing Race," reflects this perspective.[11]

Such facile assumptions took more than a century to pass from view. In the 1990s the American Indian birthrate considerably exceeds the national average. So, too, are the Western Isles of Scotland gaining in population. Not only that, the Highland Gaels and the American Indians have assumed almost mythic proportions for their respective nations. Bagpipes, kilts, and misty glens entice tourists north of the Tweed just as Indian festivals, powwows, and reservations lure them to the western American states. As Tom Sawyer might have remarked, the story of their demise has been greatly exaggerated.

Since both Highland and Native societies revolved around a fluid oral culture, no figure was as central to their life as the bard. A warrior might perform valiant deeds, but his fame would soon vanish if he had no bard to record them for posterity. The bardic tradition had especially deep roots in Scottish life. In the early fourteenth century poet Blind Harry composed his *Wallace*, which was followed in 1375 by John Barbour's *The Brus*. The quasi-fictional work by eighteenth-century poet James MacPherson, attributed to an ancient Celtic bard, Ossian, drew from this oral tradition. About the same time, the vernacular bards merged their songs with a set of Jacobite lyrics. Since political Jacobitism was no longer a serious threat by the late eighteenth century, the Jacobite popular song gradually emerged as the focal point of Scottish culture.[12] Robert Burns, Scotland's most famous bard, drew heavily upon these songs for his poetry, as did Sir Walter Scott. When one thinks of Scotland, the ballads, poetry, and music always emerge as prominent cultural elements.

The American Indians had a similar oral culture. At the time of contact the bands of North America spoke more than five hundred mutually unintelligible languages, representing perhaps the greatest linguistic diversity in the history of the world. Early negotiators of treaties recognized how important the orator was for this world. Gilbert Imlay's 1792 description of the western territory of North America remarked on the Indians' "talents of natural eloquence."[13] A generation later, Hugh Murray observed how the Indians of New York State had mastered all the tricks of European diplomacy. He marveled even more at the oratorical skills of the Iroquois leader. When the chief of the Iroquois spoke to the French governor, he informed him in no uncertain terms that he spoke for all the five nations. "The function of oratory among the five nations," Murray noted, "had become a separate profession, held in equal or higher honour than that of the warrior."[14]

A native folk wisdom permeated these oral traditions at every juncture. The Celtic lands of Eire, Northern Ireland, and western Scotland are replete with folk legends. In fact, this region may well have produced the richest folk tradition on the face of the globe. Highland folklore abounded with tales of the invisible "little people" (faeries) who moved easily between seen and unseen worlds. Legends of mermaids, banshees, sea monsters, black dogs, kelpies, charms, potions, and enchanted wells have long infused Highland life. Most of these creatures proved troublesome, and few humans meddled in their affairs without sorrow.[15] For example, modern *New Yorker* writer John McPhee spoke of a man who was wandering along the coast of the island of Colonsay when a city woman popped up from behind the bushes to warn him not to kiss any faeries he might encounter (which is certainly good advice).[16]

A number of these tales crossed to America with the Scots settlers. Both the southern Appalachian frontier and the Ozarks abound with such stories. If a cock crows at midnight, a death

As this image of the St. Kilda parliament shows, life in the nineteenth-century Highlands and Islands often proved very rugged. (The George Washington Wilson Collection, Aberdeen University Library. Print C7107.)

will follow; to break a mirror brings seven years' bad luck; black cats mean trouble; wearing a garment wrong side out brings luck to those involved in water witching; "charming" a rifle makes it more accurate—it can even remove an enemy spell, if one has been cast upon it. The list could be extended.

Yet the brunt of Celtic folklore remained firmly anchored on the British side of the Atlantic. Castles, dungeons, ruined manses, haunted wells, and spirit stones proved essential habitats for the elves, faeries, and brownies. Similarly, American sheep raising did not provide a suitable setting for shepherds' pipes or for beautiful shepherdesses dancing on the green. The absence of enchanted forests, deserted valleys, and "castles mouldering into ruin" meant that the New World would produce a different type of folk tradition. No invisible spirits could live in a log cabin, remarked traveler Judge James Hall. The Indians produced no accounts of aboriginal ghosts or "copper coloured brownies."[17]

Judge Hall, however, missed the point. If the Native folklore tradition did not produce any "little people," it did produce a number of "little animals." The Native stories frequently touched on a time long, long ago, when humans and animals could speak with one another. Spider Woman taught the Navajos of the Southwest to weave, and Beaver taught the Eastern Woodland peoples how to work with wood. From the birds, the Natives learned which berries to harvest and which to avoid. Tales of the half-human Sasquatch of the Pacific Northwest kept children near the campfires at night. The legend of Buffalo Calf Woman is still central to the Northern Plains people, and the story of the White Buffalo calf is an essential item of faith.

No character achieved more fame in Native folklore than Coyote. The universal trickster of virtually all western bands, Coyote always caused trouble for the other animals, and he dearly paid for it in the end. Native children loved Coyote stories, for the moral was obvious. Indian parents have used them for centuries to teach their children. (I will discuss Coyote in more detail later in the chapter.) Whether spoken around Native campfires during the winter storytelling season or woven into hundreds of songs and poems in Gaelic communities across the world, folk narratives such as these have embodied a social wisdom that has endured for generations.

Such wisdom proved especially necessary in times of trouble, and both groups have experienced more than their share of it. As the Highland crofters lived through the infamous Clearances of the eighteenth and nineteenth centuries, so, too, did the Natives of North America suffer through a series of removals that began in the seventeenth century and culminated in the 1830s. Overlooked for years by the dominant culture, the stories of the Cherokee Trail of Tears and the Navajo Long Walk are slowly becoming better known. The books by historian Angie Debo, a number of recent films, and the decision by the National Park Service to officially demark the main spots on the Trail of Tears have led to a renewed consciousness of this tragic aspect of America's past.[18]

Although the saga of the Scottish Clearances is well known in Canada, it is much less widely recognized in the United States. Yet this forced and semiforced exodus continued for over a century. Historian Michael Lynch has noted that because of the varied nature of crofter society, the Clearances emerged as hundreds of "local tragedies."[19]

Emigration from the Highlands and Islands varied considerably over the years. During the late eighteenth century, many emigrants left voluntarily, often in opposition to the wishes of their landlords. Historian J. M. Bumsted has termed this wave of departures the "people's" Clearance. It was this group that James Boswell observed, on his famous 1773 trip to the Western Isles, poignantly performing a "dance called America." From the early nineteenth century onward, however, most Clearances contained an element of explicit or implicit force. Almost fifteen thousand left the Sutherland estates alone during the first part of the century; perhaps sixteen thousand emigrated from the Highlands and Islands in the aftermath of the potato famine of the 1840s. Although the worst Clearances came at the hands of mid-nineteenth-century absentee landlords, Highland folk memory has seized on the expulsions from the northern county of Sutherland—c. 1806 to c. 1820, led by the infamous factor Patrick Sellar—as the most heartless. Even today, locals term the Sutherland Clearances "the evictions."

The population losses proved both severe and permanent. In Sutherland, for example, a region that had once supported two thousand people soon contained a work force of about thirty shepherds herding countless sheep. In other areas, such as Upper Deeside, the straths have never again been brought under cultivation.

Given the population pressure and scarcity of land, many nineteenth-century reformers touted emigration as the best answer to Highland and Island social problems, although one observer compared the task to that of Sisyphus.[20] The emigration from the Outer Hebrides continued well into the twentieth century. A 1923 account describing the departure of the *Metagama*, with three hundred from the Isle of Lewis on board, would easily have been recognized in Boswell's time:

> Since the lights of the *Metagama* dipped below the horizon, we have all been conscious of a lack in our lives and have engaged in our daily occupations with a heaviness of spirit mingled at times with a sense of buoyancy born of our hopes for the future—probably prophetic of the days when our young men and women will return to us richer in material benefits, and with the moral qualities characteristic of our Celtic nature, refined and matured by contact with the sterner fires of nature which are to be met with in the land of their adoption.[21]

Through countless retellings over the years, the emigration from the Highlands and Islands and the removal of the American Indians from the east to Oklahoma have assumed mythological proportions.[22] These narratives operate on many levels, of course, but their chief function is to anchor the present firmly in the past. Thus, for those who think primarily in images, as most oral cultures do, the present retains a distinct historical echo. For oral cultures, place looms as far more significant than time. Whenever one passes by the location of a major event, whenever it may have occurred, one recalls the story in all its splendor.

Thus, for both Native and Celtic cultures, the past is never very far away. "The Highlander loves his past and his native land with a passionate attachment and the story of the Clearances is still deeply embedded in his mind," wrote Ian MacPherson.[23] "A storekeeper in Edinburgh's High Street or a fishmonger in Perth can no more get away from the past than can an inhabitant of Hawaii get away from the Pacific Ocean," observed historian Geddes MacGregor.[24] In many areas of the Highlands local folk memory still blames the Clearances for the collapse of traditional forms of life. A telling incident to this effect occurred during the early 1970s, when a radical Scottish theatre group performed a traveling drama that reenacted the infamous Sutherland Clearances onstage. One weekend they performed for some isolated Highland villagers, and during the play a woman stood up to denounce the character playing the chief villain of the piece, Patrick Sellar. Why, she asked him, had he done such terrible things to her people?[25]

One finds a similar "presence of the past" in American Indian cultures. Pueblo Indians of the Southwest annually observe the anniversary of the 1680 revolt that drove the Spanish invaders to El Paso for a decade. A number of Pueblos are still critical of Isleta Pueblo, which generally sided with the Spanish in this conflict. Whether contemporary New Englanders would harbor the same intensity of feeling about the Salem witchcraft trials of 1692 is an open question. In the late 1930s some Bureau of Indian Affairs reformers were explaining the then-little-known Battle of Wounded Knee to a group of congressmen. "When did all this occur?" one asked. Eighteen ninety was the reply. "Why, that's ancient history, isn't it?" he snapped. For the congressman, yes—but not for the Sioux.[26] Perhaps it is no accident that some contemporary Scots term the English who move to their land "white settlers."

The cultural similarity between these two tribal societies meant that the Scotch-Native interaction could assume many forms. Take, for example, the cross-cultural borrowing of clothing styles. In the Rocky Mountain region local tribes adopted the Scottish brimmed cap, often embellishing it with designs of their own. Similarly, the New York Iroquois added elaborate beadwork to produce a modified Highland Glengarry bonnet. The most documented Scottish influence on Native clothing, however, occurred among the Cherokee, Creek, and Seminole of the Southeast.[27]

As early as the 1730s, British philanthropist James Oglethorpe enticed a band of Highlanders, mostly from the Inverness region, to settle in Georgia with the hope that this Presbyterian group would serve as a buffer against the Catholic Spanish in Florida. The settlers thrived, and by midcentury members of Clan Chattan virtually controlled all the Indian trade within the Creek nation. One trade item that proved popular was cloth for a kilt, for by coincidence the outlawed Scottish kilt resembled the traditional male Creek breechcloth. Both of these skirtlike outfits proved especially suitable for Georgia's wet, marshy terrain, and traveler William Bartram once likened Creek dress to the Highland kilt.[28] The Scots traders influenced Creek headgear as well, selling a number of turbanlike coverings, to which the Natives usually added feathers. With each passing decade, noted historian J. Leitch Wright, Jr., "the dress of Muscogulge warriors seemed more like that of Highland lairds."[29]

The cultural borrowing between Scots and southeastern Natives did not stop with the modification of material objects. Ideas, stories, and legends must have been exchanged as well. Although these are hard to trace with any precision, they are potentially far more powerful. In the legends surrounding the Battle of Culloden, one meets, perhaps, the most extensive Scots-Native borrowing of all.

The battle of Culloden in 1746 did far more than simply send Jacobite sympathizers to North America. This last dramatic rallying of the Scots clans may also have had an impact on the evolution of American Indian resistance strategy against the Euro-American settlers. Although this is admittedly a speculative argument—no documentary evidence exists one way or the other—it has the benefit of historical logic. The case revolves largely around the activities of the McGillivray clan.

Clan McGillivray proved one of the most staunch supporters of the Stuart cause. McGillivray of Dunnaglas led Clan Chattan at Culloden. A number of Jacobite ballads celebrate the name McGillivray. An early list of members of the Charleston St. Andrew's Society (founded in 1729) contains the names of several people banished to the Colonies after the 1715 Jacobite uprising, including John and Lachlan McGillivray.[30] This Lachlan McGillivray is almost certainly the fur trader who in the 1750s married a mixed-blood Creek-French woman from the prestigious Creek Wind clan. In c. 1759, she had a son, Alexander McGillivray, who would become the most powerful Native leader of his generation.

In the early 1770s Lachlan sent young Alexander to Charleston, South Carolina, to study with his cousin, Presbyterian minister Farquahar McGillivray. There Alexander was tutored in Greek, Latin, British history, and literature. He also briefly worked in a mercantile firm. During these years, Alexander certainly must have listened to tales of Culloden and the massing of the clans, especially Clan McGillivray.

These stories of Culloden would almost assuredly have assumed the form of "might have beens." "If only" the prince's army had not been so weary; they had not been forced to fight on a badly chosen field; all the clans had rallied and they had not been so outnumbered; the powerful Clan MacPherson had been available; Clan McDonald, which had fought on the right with Robert Bruce at Bannockburn, had not been shifted to the left at Culloden (confirming the old prophecy in the Western Isles that when Scotland's right hand in battle was withdrawn from the McDonalds, bad luck would follow); and so on. As the initial romantic lost cause, the Jacobite defeat of 1746 emerged in legend, story, and song as the first "revisionist" history. As such, it assumed protean forms.

When the American Revolution broke out, the senior McGillivray supported the British and eventually retired to an estate in the Highlands. Alexander, however, returned to his Creek homeland. There he lived in a style reminiscent of a country squire, owning a large estate and several slaves.

From this time forward, Alexander McGillivray tried to steer his divided Creek peple through the intense political realities of the day. Termed "the American Tallyrand," he negotiated with the British, Spanish, and Americans regarding the Creek homeland. Since he boasted that he could call out ten thousand Creek warriors at a moment's notice (a Scottish clan pattern as well), the Euro-Americans treated him with respect. The Spanish put him on their payroll; the Florida-based British trade firm of Panton, Leslie and Company employed him; and George Washington gave him annual payments. When McGillivray visited New York City at Washington's invitation, the new government entertained him like visiting royalty, which, in a sense, he was.[31]

A shrewd negotiator and prolific letter writer, McGillivray presented the Creek case with skill. In 1784 he denounced the

Treaty of Paris that ended the Revolution, declaring that the Creeks had always been a free people and that the British king had no right to give away their ancestral lands to the Americans. He even spoke with a U.S. congressman's representative about the possibility of the Creek Nation's entering the American Union as a distinct "ethnic state." Since Canada and Florida remained in British hands, the eastern seaboard with the Americans, and Louisiana and St. Louis in Spanish control, the diplomacy proved intricate. McGillivray once predicted that "Three Kings" (British, Spanish, and American) would soon divide the continent.[32]

Yet the heart of McGillivray's plan was to unite the often quarrelsome Creek factions, plus the other usually antagonistic southeastern tribes, into a pan-Indian movement to halt the inexorable American advance into Georgia, Kentucky, and Tennessee. He even negotiated—unsuccessfully—with northern tribes on this matter. His fragile southeastern alliance held, more or less, until his death in 1793. Afterwards, Native factionalism in the Southeast brought further pan-Indian efforts to an end.[33]

A generation later, the Shawnee leader Tecumseh and his brother, the Prophet, created a similar, even more successful pan-Indian confederation to resist the encroachment of the Americans. Tecumseh's mother, Metheataske (Turtle Laying Its Eggs), it should be noted, was an Alabama Creek of McGillivray's generation.[34] She must have been aware of McGillivray's earlier efforts to unite the Creeks against the European invaders.

Even if Culloden had not occurred, there is little doubt that the American Indians would have adopted a similar pan-Indian defensive tactic. The Ottawa chief Pontiac attempted this in his 1763 uprising, drawing Shawnees, Delawares, Hurons, Senecas, Miamis, Potawatomis, and Chippewas into his movement. But since the saga of the massing of the clans had surely been part of McGillivray's household, it is *possible*—the evidence will support no stronger statement—that the famed Creek leader also drew on the historic legend of Culloden to bolster his own case. In truth, it would be astonishing if he did not.

Although Alexander McGillivray was the most prominent southeastern Scoto-Indian, he was not alone. The surnames McPherson and McIntosh (originally from the Inverness region) remain prominent in Creek history, especially in the Removal Era. The Colbert family played a role in Chickasaw life all through the nineteenth century, as did the McCoys and McKennans for the Choctaws.

The most famous Scoto-Indian of the early nineteenth century, the leader who oversaw Cherokee removal to Oklahoma, was John Ross. By blood Ross was seven-eighths Scots and one-eighth Cherokee. Educated by clergymen, he always spoke English better than Cherokee, although he understood it fluently. A visitor to Ross's boyhood home once likened it to a Scottish manor house.[35]

John Ross never forgot his Scottish links. During the spring of 1847 he read of the efforts of a Philadelphia organization to aid the Highland poor—estimated to number three hundred thousand—who were suffering from the potato famine. "Have the Scotch no claim on the Cherokees?" Ross asked. "Have they not a very especial claim? They have." Thus, he wrote to the *Cherokee Advocate* to request that the tribe meet in Tahlequah to raise money for the cause. The Cherokees met, appointed a relief committee, and in May 1847, sent $190 to a New York bank "for the relief of those who are suffering by the famine in Scotland."[36] Many an Oklahoma Indian surname today harkens back to a distant Scottish ancestor.

The Southeast was not alone in this regard, for many other regions boasted Scoto-Indians as well. In Hispanic California, for example, Hugo Reid, originally from Cardross, married a wealthy Gabrieleno woman, Doña Victoria. By this union he inherited two ranchos and two adopted sons, Felipe and José,

John Ross, Cherokee chief, 1837. Seven-eighths Scottish and one-eighth Cherokee, John Ross was perhaps the most famous Scoto-Indian of the nineteenth century. (Archives and Manuscripts Division of the Oklahoma Historical Society. Photo 20516.3.23.)

who soon sported imported kilts and went by the surname Reid. Unfortunately, neither lived long enough to continue the line.[37] In the 1840s Rev. David Macrae found a common bond with an Iroquois leader whose mother was a "Mac" and who proudly claimed Scottish blood.[38] In 1850 William Ferguson encountered a Scoto-Indian woman near Galena, Illinois, who lived in a wigwam near the town.[39] Scoto-Indians became especially prominent in the Pacific Northwest. James Findlay, pioneer explorer of Saskatchewan, sired a son, Jacco Findlay, who was a leading figure in Spokane until his death in 1828. J. G. MacTavish, who forced the surrender of John Jacob Astor's Fort Astoria in 1813, fathered many children by Native women, as did Aberdonian trapper of the Columbia, Finian MacDonald. The list could be extended.[40]

On several occasions these fathers renewed their connections to Scotland by returning there with their families or by sending the children overseas for a European education. The most outstanding early twentieth-century athlete on the Isle of Lewis, for example, had an Indian mother.[41] So many Orkney men returned with their American families that the islanders erected a small college in St. Margaret's Hope on South Ronaldsay to educate the mixed-blood children.[42] One of these returnees, a lad named "Huskie" Sanders, arrived in Stromness in 1886. Product of an Orkney father and a Cree mother, Sanders was sent to Orkney to be educated by his grandparents. For three years young Sanders participated in the life of a Scottish schoolboy, but he longed to return to Canada and finally his family agreed. When he boarded the ship in 1889, his schoolmates cheered his departure until the ship rounded Hoy and disappeared from view.[43]

Probably the most articulate of these Scoto-Indian returnees was Alexander Kennedy Isbister. Son of a Scots HBC clerk and a Cree mother, Isbister lived in Red River, Canada, until his father sent him to enroll at King's College, Aberdeen, from which he graduated in 1842. He later became a dean of a British teachers' college. From this post he lobbied both Westminster and the Colonial Office on behalf of the Red River Métis. Eventually, he denounced the HBC's treatment of Indians and mixed-bloods in a pamphlet, *A Few Words on the Hudson's Bay Company, with a Statement of Grievances of the Native and Half Cast Indians, Addressed to the British Government Through Their Delegates Now in London* (1847). In one eloquent passage he compared their lives to those of the slaves in the American South.[44]

Historians have just begun to pay attention to the Scoto-Indians. Both Sylvia Van Kirk and Jennifer S. H. Brown have recently provided major contributions to our understanding of these peoples, but a great deal needs to be done. One generalization can be tentatively set forward. During the nineteenth century, French Métis often adopted different life-styles from those of the Scottish mixed-bloods. Captain John Palliser, who explored western Canada during the 1850s, observed that the Métis preferred Native life, whereas the "Scotch half-breeds" were anxious "to profit by the advance of civilization in the old country as well as [they] can."[45]

Perhaps Palliser's off-the-cuff observation contains a grain of truth. If so, the most likely reason for this would rest with the father's influence. From the mother, a young mixed-blood person would learn North American survival skills; from the father he or she would hear stories about another version of education. The French and Scottish fur traders came largely from the same social class. But the Scots retained a respect for "democratic learning" that the French trappers often lacked. And the heart of this attitude involved literacy. Rev. John West, HBC Episcopal chaplain to Red River in the 1820s, was astounded to discover on his trip over that the Scots sailors were both well and scripturally informed. Every one of them could read the New Testament.[46]

Consequently, many Scoto-Indians were exposed to at least a smattering of Western-style education. This, in turn, allowed them to assume yet another social role: that of cultural broker. One can find a number of nineteenth-century Scoto-Indians who served as cultural brokers or intermediaries between the Native and white worlds.[47]

One does not have to look far for examples. James Ross, son of Alexander Ross and an Okanogan mother, received a formal education and served for years as night editor for the *Toronto Globe*.[48] Jerry Potts, a mixed-blood son of a Scots trader and a Piegan woman, played a similarly important role in Northern Plains history. Potts participated in the Blood and Piegan victory over the Cree and Assiniboins in the fall of 1870 and for years was highly valued by the Canadian government for the skill with which he explained the ways of the Canadian Mounted Police to his people. He was also a leader in the destruction of the illegal whiskey trade to the Piegans. The Canadian Mounties thought highly of him.[49]

James R. Murie, who was born in Nebraska in 1862, had a Scottish father and a Skiri Pawnee mother. He enrolled in Hampton Institute in Virginia in 1879 and graduated in 1884 with skills in printing and teaching; he was also confirmed in the Protestant Episcopal Church. After rejoining his mother's group—then removed to Oklahoma—in the 1890s, Murie faced great difficulty in readjusting to Native life until he began work as an ethnographer.

At some time during the 1890s a Pawnee priest, Kurabus, taught Murie an elaborate Pawnee ceremony, which Murie recorded on the old Edison wax cylinders. For over fifteen years he continued to collect, annotate, and record a large body of Pawnee songs, stories, and dances on the cylinders. Pioneer anthropologist Alice Fletcher Cunningham relied heavily on his aid for her studies, as did Smithsonian curator George A. Dorsey. In 1914 James R. Murie published *Pawnee Indian Societies*, one of the most important works on Pawnee cultural traditions. Thus, Murie served as an effective "broker" between Pawnee and white worlds.[50]

Army scout Archie McIntosh served as a cultural broker in quite another manner, both in the Pacific Northwest and in the desert Southwest. Born at Fort William, Michigan, of Scots/

Chippewa ancestry, Archie's father moved to the Fraser River with the HBC. During their stay there, the senior McIntosh taught Archie to spell and do elementary mathematics while the two of them canoed the lakes to check their traps. After his father's murder by an unknown assailant (at the time believed to be a Native jealous of white trappers), Archie was sent to Vancouver for two years of school. At age twelve he was put on a ship to Edinburgh to live with relatives, and he received two more years of Scottish education. Upon his return to Vancouver he worked as a clerk with the HBC for about a year.

In 1855 Archie McIntosh entered the service of the U.S. Army as a scout. Working with another Scoto-Indian, Donald McKay, he saved a band of U.S. soldiers from a number of Columbia River Native attacks. As one contemporary reporter observed, "The whole body of troopers would have been massacred had it not been for the strategy of those two cunning half breeds."[51]

McIntosh's reputation grew steadily, and he soon became General George Crook's favorite scout. Crook trusted him implicitly, and McIntosh played a major role in the campaign against the Pitt River Indians and the Piutes of Northern California. The common soldiers also respected his skills. This respect grew to semimythical proportions in January 1867, when Archie McIntosh led General Crook and his men through a blinding blizzard to safety at Camp Warner in Oregon. In 1896 McIntosh confessed to a reporter how he did it:

> I knew there was going to be a blizzard and watched the course of the wind. When it [the blizzard] was upon us, General Crook asked if we had not better go into camp until it passed over, but I said "follow me and I will put you into Camp Warner by 4 o'clock p.m." So the General said no more but kept close behind me, and you bet I kept the wind on my right cheek for nine long hours, but had it

changed its direction ten degrees my goose would have been cooked.[52]

McIntosh battled a drinking problem all through his military career, but his skills were so admired that his commanders usually overlooked it. In 1871 he was again assigned to General Crook, who had recently been sent to Arizona Territory to battle the San Carlos and Tonto Apaches. There he fought in the 1874 clashes near Florence and Globe and participated in Crook's last campaign against Geronimo. McIntosh was present in Geronimo's camp in the Sierra Madre mountains of Mexico when Crook had his famous interview with the Apache chief. The situation was so tense, McIntosh recalled later, that if a gun had accidentally discharged, all the whites would have been killed.[53]

After the close of the Apache campaign McIntosh married a San Carlos woman (he seems to have had an earlier Pacific Northwest family as well) and settled on the San Carlos reservation in Arizona. There he gained a reputation as a great teller of stories. He later sent his son to Carlisle Indian School in Pennsylvania, and McIntosh descendants held important roles in San Carlos affairs well into the twentieth century.[54] Praised at the time for his "gallant and invaluable service" as a scout, Archie McIntosh played an important broker's role in both Oregon and Arizona.[55]

Perhaps the most famous Scoto-Indian cultural broker of his generation was Montana's Duncan McDonald. McDonald was born in 1849 at Fort Connen, the last HBC post established within the present boundaries of the United States. His father, Angus McDonald, was born in Ross Shire in 1816, joined the HBC in 1838, and was posted to Fort Colville in Oregon Territory. Fluent in Gaelic, French, and several Native languages, Angus soon became well respected in both Indian and white circles. Territorial governor Isaac I. Stevens thought very highly of him. Duncan's mother was full-blood, Salish-speaking Flathead.

Thus, Duncan McDonald grew to maturity with one foot in both the Indian and white worlds.

After retiring from the HBC McDonald senior ran large herds of cattle on the plains of Montana. He died in 1889, the year Montana became a state. McDonald had hired tutors to teach Duncan to read and write, talents that allowed his son to become the most prominent mixed-blood spokesman in Montana's history.

Duncan gained his initial audience shortly after the Nez Perce war of 1877. Both McDonalds believed that the Native version of the conflict deserved publicity. They contacted a local newspaper, the Deer Lodge *New North-West,* and the paper paid Duncan's expenses to travel to Canada to interview White Bird, to whom he was related, plus a number of other Nez Perce leaders. Together with his father, Duncan reworked his extensive notes into a series of essays that the *New North-West* published in several installments from January 1879 forward. The editors boasted that the data in the articles "can be relied upon as authentic from the Nez Perce standpoint."

The lengthy articles on the war and the Native retreat were both well written and crammed with detail. There was no question of McDonald's perspective. "The gallant Seventh Infantry!" he said. "It should be called the cursed Seventh. They were not satisfied in killing Indians whom they found asleep. They must kill women and children, too." The articles also provoked several white responses: one merely asked for more details, but another accused McDonald of down playing Native atrocities against white families. These newspaper essays by Duncan McDonald were probably the first authentic historical accounts written from the Indian perspective.[56]

Although McDonald once replied to a question about his schooling, "Education—I never had any education," his later career belies that comment. Although almost completely self-taught, over the years he became highly skilled with words.

An astute observer, he moved easily in the Salish world and that of Montana white society. Toward the end of his long life (he lived until 1937), newspaper reporters turned to him regularly on a variety of Native issues. One reporter, M. O. Hammond of Toronto, called him "well read and bright." Another, Ellen Nye, termed him "almost a savant among his red brethren." Reporter H. T. Balley called him "the sage of the Flathead."[57] In 1922 McDonald led a group of newspeople to the remains of the Kullyspell house, the first trading post in the Northwest, which was established by Welsh explorer David Thompson in 1809. On another trip he led Montana reporters to the site of the first Flathead Indian agency. On many an occasion McDonald spoke of his boyhood growing up on the old HBC trading post.[58]

Duncan McDonald assumed many roles in Montana society. Not only did he write the first Indian-perspective history, he was also the first American Indian to compile a list of Coyote tales and systematically present them to white audiences.[59] Like his father, an inveterate storyteller, McDonald first told his versions of Coyote tales over several sittings to University of Montana journalism dean A. L. Stone, who later printed them in a series of articles in 1912.[60]

Coyote tales played an important role in almost all American Indian societies. Trickster, sexual athlete, and general all-around nuisance, Coyote served as a perfect source to explain the origin of things as well as to convey moral lessons about behavior. Psychiatrist Carl Jung later became fascinated with Coyote. Modern Indian educators still draw on Coyote tales, and today they are formally taught in elementary schools across the Navajo Nation. Working with Stone, McDonald was probably the first person to make them available to white audieces. One Coyote tale will suffice here:

> One day long ago, the Holy People began to hang the stars in the heavens. The stars lay in a heap in a large

Duncan McDonald, Missoula, Montana, 1927. Son of a Scots father and a Flathead mother, Duncan McDonald served as an important cultural broker for the Pacific Northwest, interpreting the Native world to whites and vice versa. (Dorian Studio portrait, Montana Historical Society, Helena. Photo 943-626.)

wicker basket, and one by one, the Holy People picked them up to hang in their proper places.

Coyote wanted to help. "Let me hang stars, too," he said. "I would be very good at this."

The Holy People said no. You're too untidy, they told him. This task has to be done with great precision. We can't have sloppy, careless people like you hanging the stars.

Coyote sulked and went away. For days he hid behind the bushes watching. It seemed to him that the Holy People took forever just to hang a single star. They would never be able to finish at this rate.

Finally, Coyote could stand it no longer. One day when everyone was away, Coyote raced over to the basket full of stars. He grabbed it and ran to the edge of the mesa. With a great heave he scattered the stars all across the heavens.

And that's why the stars look the way they do today.[61]

Duncan McDonald became a fixture of early twentieth-century Montana society. Tourists who frequented the region often sought him out, and in 1909 he enthralled a group at the Roman Buffalo Round-up with Coyote tales and stories of early Montana. A Toronto *Globe* reporter listened to McDonald's yarns for more than two hours, later remarking: "It was most interesting, and we had quite a discussion over the morality of the white and red men."[62]

Famed Montana artist Charles M. Russell knew and respected Duncan McDonald. Once they even worked together to help move a buffalo herd to Canada. In turn, McDonald praised Russell as a skilled student of Indian life and sign language. In a collection of short stories, *Trails Plowed Under* (1927), Russell immortalized him in a short story, "Dunc McDonald," which told of his harrowing escape from a wounded cow buffalo.[63] Duncan McDonald thus emerges as the most famed Scoto-Indian cultural broker of the modern American West.

In 1984 historian L. G. Moses was doing research in the Indian Archives Division of the Oklahoma Historical Society in Oklahoma City. He observed many "Anglo"-looking people approaching the archivists for help in tracing down a lost grandmother, usually described as a Cherokee "princess." (The Cherokees have no princesses.) Often the archivists rolled their eyes as they assisted the researchers. Shortly afterwards, Moses was examining Native American materials at the South Dakota Historical Society in Pierre. There he observed a Brule Sioux from the nearby Rosebud Reservation seeking out the archivists. The man wanted to look through the records, he said, because he had just learned that he was descended from a Scottish nobleman.[64] The saga of the Scoto-Indians, it seems, appeals to both sides.

CHAPTER FOUR

Scotland and the Victorian West

THE REALITY

Just before the American Revolution, Philip Fithian, tutor to Robert Carter III's tidewater household, observed that being called a "Scotsman" ranked with being called a "buckskin," "lubber," or "thick-skull" and was legitimate grounds for a fight.[1] But this antagonism faded quickly during the early years of the American republic. Over the course of the century, Scots entered without difficulty into virtually every aspect of American life. They became farmers, miners, cattle ranchers, housewives, missionaries, hermits, prostitutes, vigilantes, artists, writers, labor organizers, teachers, professional golfers, and Rough Riders, just to name a few occupations. It would be no exaggeration to say that by c. 1920 the Scots had become America's favorite immigrant group.[2]

By happenstance American prejudices and social ideals fit nicely with their Scottish counterparts. Both cultures denounced the English system of social hierarchy. For example, when John Howison visited upper Canada in 1822, he discovered that the ultimate English term for social impudence was "Scotch Yankey."[3] All through the nineteenth century, Americans utilized the Fourth of July as a chance to twist the English lion's tail. Scots who celebrated a romantic homeland (but not a nation) could sometimes be coaxed to join in. Americans' fears of Roman Catholicism generally slid off the backs of Scottish Catholic immigrants (most of whom went to Canada anyway) to rest with the numerous Irish. In 1841, for example, the British consul at Boston wrote to the Lieutenant Governor of New Brunswick to try to discourage out-migration: "The strong prejudice which exists in this part of the Union against the labouring Irish tends much to make them discontented."[4] Episcopal or Presbyterian Scots immigrants met no such reaction.

Scots ideals of individual achievement, economic advance, opposition to privilege, and abhorrence of caste happened to be American goals as well. Scots values of self-restraint, hard work, and education were also the norms toward which many reformers sought to push the new nation.[5]

Thus, Scots met virtually no antagonism in Victorian America. Even when they were called "Jock," "Sandy," or "Mac," the term carried no negative connotations, as "Deutscher," "Paddy," or "Mick" often did. The Know Nothing movement of the 1850s produced no Scottish equivalent of "Damn the Dutch" or "To Hell with the Irish." Even the Scots' "faults"—their alleged dour nature, lack of a sense of the beautiful, thriftiness bordering on parsimony, supreme self-confidence, and tendency toward overindulgence—were treated with tolerance.

Often these "failings" were resolved via humor. Consider the number of Scots jokes that burlesqued their meanness (that is to say, stinginess). Who was the least disturbed mouse in Scotland? The one living in the offertory box of the Aberdeen cathedral. How do you take a census in Glasgow? Throw a penny in the street. From this it was but a short jump to an American version: How did the Grand Canyon come about? A Scot lost a dime (and dug until he found it).

The same lightheartedness can be found in the stories that dealt with Scots self-confidence. Historian James Bumsted has recently noted that Canadian Scots have long considered themselves different from, and superior to, their English, Welsh, and Irish cousins.[6] This is not a new concept. In the early eighteenth century, as traveler Edward Burt heard the story, a Spanish ship wrecked on the small island of Barra in the Outer Hebrides, home of the McNeal clan. After deliberation, a council of clansmen decided to confiscate the Spanish cargo. When someone suggested that this might anger the king of Spain, the council observed: "We have nothing to do with that. McNeal and the King of Spain will adjust that matter between themselves."[7] The story continues. In 1847 a Falkirk drover claimed that his accomplishments were more significant than those of the Duke of Wellington at Waterloo. Wellington only had his men scattered here and there around the battlefield, said the drover, "but let him try to put down ten thousand sheep, forbye black cattle, at Falkirk Tryst and it's my opinion he'll make a very confused business of it."[8] A North American example of this trait emerged during the American Revolution, after a Scottish lieutenant led a group of Loyalists to Glengarry, Canada. Afterwards, the lieutenant compared his accomplishment with that of Moses. As he noted, however, Moses had taken forty years and had lost half his men in the Red Sea, whereas he had taken everyone across the St. Lawrence River in only six weeks without a single loss.[9] Truly, the Scots shared "a guid conceit o' themselves."

Parallel with these stories came other versions that dealt with excessive drinking and parsimony. But Scots humor seldom reflected the same harsh edge as can be found in Irish or Jewish stories that burlesqued the same traits.[10]

Traveling Scots encountered little or no prejudice in nineteenth-century America. Visiting New Orleans after the Civil War, Reverend David Macrae found that all prejudice against him vanished (people first thought him a Yankee) when he revealed his country of origin.[11] During the 1890s Texas rancher Thomas Simpson Carson once heard himself termed "that damned Scotsman," but that reaction was an exception to the rule. An 1896 author could find no examples of overt discrimination against Scots.[12]

Because of this lack of prejudice, immigrants to early America created few purely Scottish towns to parallel those established in Ontario, Nova Scotia, Manitoba, or Prince Edward Island. Nevertheless, a distinct Scottish travel network existed, and few Scottish visitors to the States seemed unaware of its existence. The informal network worked well. Traveling through Jacksonville, Illinois, during the 1820s, James Stuart was told that prominent resident James Kerr would be hurt if a fellow Scot passed by without calling. Fifty years later, David Macrae boarded with fellow Scots during his stays in New Orleans and St. Louis. When J. Cameron Lees visited San Francisco in 1888, he made certain to book his passage across the continent through Scots-born travel agent Thomas Mackay, who impressed Lees with his testimonials from the various lords and ladies who had utilized his services. Lees noted that Mackay was "as well known in San Francisco as Mr. [Thomas] Cook is to the British Travellers."[13] Scots Victorian women travelers, such as Mrs. M. A. Pringle of Whytbank and Elizabeth Stirling, followed similar patterns.

Robert Louis Stevenson carefully noted all the Scots he met during his stay in California: a piper who fled from Sacramento with a borrowed dollar; an Aberdonian who took up highway robbery; and a woman who drove him all through the Napa Valley. Stevenson also confessed that when he chanced upon a Greenock resident and exchanged a word or two in Scots, it "pleased me more than you would fancy."[14]

In "The Silverado Squatters" Stevenson elaborated on this emotion:

The happiest lot on earth is to be born a Scotchman. You must pay for it in many ways, as for all other advantages on earth. You have to learn the paraphrases and the shorter catechism; you generally take to drink; your youth, as far as I can find out, is a time of louder war against society, of more outcry and tears and turmoil, than if you had been born, for instance, in England. But somehow life is warmer and closer; the hearth burns more redly; the lights of home shine softer on the rainy street; the very names endeared in verse and music, cling nearer around our hearts. An Englishman may meet an Engishman tomorrow, upon Chimborazo, and neither of them care; but when the Scotch wine-grower told me of Mons Meg, it was like magic.

> From the dim shieling on the misty Island
>   Mountains divide us, and a world of seas;
> Yet still our hearts are true; our hearts are Highland,
>   And we, in dreams, behold the Hebrides.

And, Highland and Lowland, all our hearts are Scotch.[15]

Although the American Scots never established ethnic towns as did the Canadians, they did participate in the various "British Colonies" that arose during the mid-nineteenth century. During this era, Illinois, Kansas, and Iowa created at least six "British Colonies," ranging in philosophical orientation from atheist to Owenite to utopian. All contained a few Scots. These colonies soon boasted yacht clubs, fox hunts, formal dinners, and elaborate banquets. Various visionaries continued to promote similar colonies for years. Immediately after the Civil War, a Scottish laird devised a scheme to send over Highland crofters to the South to replace the former slaves, but that plan failed to materialize. In 1867, however, a Houston firm actually imported eighteen Highlanders to serve as plowmen for farms in Texas.[16]

The "British Colony" that involved the largest number of Scots was Victoria, located southeast of Hays City, Ellis County, in western Kansas. Victoria was founded by George Grant, a Scottish crofter's son who had made his fortune in the cloth business. His ethics and business acumen may be seen in the following tale. Reading of the illness of Prince Albert in the *London Times*, Grant quickly bought up all the nation's mourning crepe, reaping a fortune when Albert died shortly thereafter.

Enticed by American advertisements, Grant toured North America seeking a site for a colony and a country estate. Rejecting Canada because of its climate, he fell in love with the grasslands of western Kansas. In 1871–72 he purchased more than thirty-one thousand acres of railroad lands at the bargain price of eighty-eight cents an acre. Some credited him as the largest landowner in the nation.[17]

Grant was both potential baron and potential philanthropist. Part of his Victoria scheme was to invite poor Scottish crofters to his colony, and he launched a considerable publicity campaign to that effect. The promotional literature spoke of "the champagne air" of western Kansas. "The climate is salubrious," one pamphlet said; "the winters are quite as mild as in Morayshire, snow seldom lying on the ground for more than a few hours."[18] Although a number of Scots, both aristocrats and artisans, responded, mounting criticism at home—especially from the Scottish agricultural press—kept overwhelming numbers from ever emigrating.[19]

A businessman as well as a philanthropist, Grant hoped to make money from his investment. He arranged visits by leading Scots agriculturalists who had skills in steam engineering. His ultimate dream was to introduce high-quality sheep to the region and, especially, to turn his holdings into a model showcase for cattle.

Unfortunately, Grant died prematurely in 1878, well before his dreams had been given a fair chance. This loss of leadership, plus the Kansas droughts of 1873–74 and a subsequent grasshopper invasion, sealed the colony's fate. A few "English lords of Victoria Manor" remained, and a stone Episcopal church that Grant had erected continued to hold services until 1913, but the colony never recovered. A band of Russian Germans who arrived in 1876 proved far better suited to the region and eventually absorbed the remnants of Victoria.

But Grant's Victoria colony did post one success—the introduction of Aberdeen Angus cattle to the state. The Aberdeen Angus Society officially credits Grant with this accomplishment, and in 1943 erected a stone pyramid over his grave in the little churchyard. Ironically, Grant's Aberdeen Angus cattle thrived in western Kansas, but his Scots settlers all eventually moved elsewhere.[20]

The saga of Victoria was writ small in other regions of the Great Plains. So many Scots arrived in the region of Miles City, Montana, that the First Presbyterian Church was virtually a Scottish club for years. Ranchers introduced polo games to the area, and rumor persists that once they even staged a steeplechase. A number of British farmers also tried their hand in Nebraska. In 1872 a land agent termed Nebraska "The English state of the Union," a designation that always included a few Scots.[21] One North Dakota émigré actually "rode the hounds" with wolves rather than foxes as his quarry.

Most of the Scots settlements on the plains were individual rather than communal efforts, as can be seen in the story of Aberdeenshire farmer James Alexander. A veteran of twenty-five years of farming in northeast Scotland, Alexander moved to eastern Nebraska in the early 1870s. He began with confidence that his agricultural training could easily be transferred to the Great Plains, but he found after only one season that this was only half true. Few of his British garden seeds grew well. The swede, oats, barley, and rye never caught on, although he successfully introduced green kale and fall turnips to the region around Crete. But Alexander found real difficulties in breaking virgin prairie for grain crops, and he soon switched almost exclusively to Indian corn. Although earlier British immigrants had generally scorned cornbread, by the 1870s corn had become so popular that Alexander could send samples back to northeast Scotland. Cornmeal, Alexander noted, had become "the staff of life in the shapes or conditions of much cornbread and pancakes."[22] Farming in America, he discovered, took a good deal of adjustment.

In addition to plowmen and farmers, the West also attracted a number of skilled Scottish craftsmen. Generally, these craftsmen did well in America. Historian R. H. Campbell attributes this to the fact that the least skilled Scots migrated chiefly to Australia, whereas the better skilled ended up in the States.[23] But as the major demand for skilled craftsmen lay in the factories east of the Mississippi, immigrant craftsmen did not play as important a role in the post–Civil War West as they had earlier.[24]

Still, pre–Gold Rush California saw Scots working as loggers, carpenters, and trappers.[25] The discovery of precious metals that began at Sutter's Mill and spread to Colorado and Nevada enticed hundreds of Scots into American mining ventures. One of the most colorful was Eilley Orrum, a Scottish Mormon convert who rejected polygamy and moved on to Nevada. There she allegedly used a crystal ball to locate silver and became known as the "Queen of the Comstock lode."[26] A 1912 survey of the Rock Springs, Wyoming, Union Pacific Mines discovered that 3 percent of the work force (eighty-five men) hailed from Scotland. Glasgow-born John Calderwood emerged as the most prominent labor leader during the 1894 Cripple Creek, Colorado, miners' strike. His lengthy essay "The Strike of 1894" is still the chief historical source for this labor dispute. Fellow Glaswegian John Stewart MacArthur probably had more impact on American mining history than any other immigrant. A chemist, MacArthur discovered the cyanide process, a means of extracting gold from discarded mine tailings, and brought the science to Colorado's Crestone Mine, in Saguache County, in 1889. Although it took time to catch on, MacArthur's cyanide process, which is still in use today, literally doubled the world's annual production of gold.[27]

The craft of gardening, more highly developed in Scotland than the States, also had considerable appeal. The city of St. Louis hired a number of Scots gardeners during the late nineteenth century. Famed poet Robert Service once kept body and soul together by gardening for a southern California bordello. The El Camino Real Park and the Golden Gate Park in San Francisco are both credited to the skills of Bannockburn immigrant John McLaren. When McLaren became superintendent of parks for San Francisco in 1887, he faced scrub brush and sand dunes. Through his efforts he transformed this barren region into what is today the marvelous botanical wonder of Golden Gate Park. Recalling his own youth, with its numerous public-garden restrictions, McLaren allowed all types of ball playing and frowned on erecting any statues. His motto: "Trees and more trees."[28] Occasionally, the gardeners took on even wider roles. Yakima, Washington, apple rancher John L. Garretson recalled that their Scots gardener first introduced him to the poetry of Robert Burns.[29]

Granite workers also found seasonal employment in the West. Craftsmen from Aberdeen, "The Granite City," had established an international reputation in stonemasonry, and a number of quarrymen migrated to California and elsewhere as the jobs required. From 1889 to 1892 granite quarries at Aberdeen, Colorado (near Gunnison), flourished. Scots stonemasons also cut granite for the famed Mormon Temple in Salt Lake City. In general the Aberdeen granite industry did not export its dressed and polished stone to America; rather, it exported its quarrymen and masons.

The most notorious incident of this "granite migration" occurred in 1886 when a group of Texas builders hired a large contingent of Aberdeen masons to cut the stone for the new Texas state capitol in Austin. Unbeknownst to the eighteen Aberdeen masons, they were being used as strike breakers, and they soon found themselves blacklisted by the American granite cutters' union. As if that were not enough, the Texas heat proved unbearable. After only a short while three died, and the rest moved on to other regions.[30]

The most extensive western Scottish-American economic links lay with cattle and sheep ranching. During the middle years of the nineteenth century, the Scottish bourgeoisie had reaped the rewards of capitalism. The narrow belt between Glasgow and Edinburgh, rivaling the English Midlands, became one of the most industrialized areas of the world. The Lanarkshire region proved ideal for the flourishing textile industry, and the broad estuary of the Clyde saw a steady stream of ships bearing cotton bales from the American South. In the 1830s, for example, almost one-third of Glasgow's workers had some connection with the textile industry.[31]

The firing on Fort Sumter in April 1861 severely damaged the Scots textile industry. In spite of vigorous attempts to replace southern cotton with Indian cotton, the mills began a gradual decline. But during the conflict itself, the Clyde shipyards built scores of vessels for both North and South. The majority of Confederate blockade runners originated in the Clyde estuary. Dundee's jute industry also flourished during the American Civil War. By midcentury, Edinburgh had emerged as a major banking center of the Western world. "In the course of the first half of the present century," W. R. Lawson noted in *Blackwood's* in 1884, "Scotland was changed from one of the poorest to one of the most prosperous countries in Europe."[32]

Consequently, by the 1870s, the Scottish middle classes had accumulated a significant amount of surplus capital. Aided by the Calvinistic ethic of thrift and the passage of effective limited-liability laws, Scotland became headquarters for an international "client capitalism." *Blackwood's* observed that three-quarters of the foreign and colonial investment companies were of Scottish origin and that even those based in London were run by Scots on Scottish models. Consequently, during the late nineteenth century Scottish bankers and entrepreneurs had the capital to invest in various enterprises in Latin America, tea plantations in India, and land companies in Australia, as well as in the opening of the American West. The Scots seemed especially eager to lend to Americans.[33]

The range of investment was prodigious. Scottish companies invested in Iowa and Minnesota farmlands, Arizona copper mining, Pacific Northwest lumber corporations, numerous railroad and petroleum ventures, irrigation projects, and cattle companies. Mortgage and banking trusts also drew a great deal of Scottish interest.[34] The Scottish Record Office has compiled a list of fifty companies that operated in America during the nineteenth and twentieth centuries.[35]

These ventures were by no means all successful. Many of the mining investments lost money. The City of Glasgow Bank went into receivership in 1881, largely because it sank an inordinate amount of capital into American railroads. The Scottish judge overseeing the case commented that "a Scotch Bank buying and working a rairoad in America is about as startling a thing as one can conceive."[36] But so long as profits remained high—as they basically did until the Panic of 1893—the lure of borrowing at 5 percent and investing at 10 percent proved irresistible. Historian Paul M. Edwards has estimated that the total capital Scots invested in the American West approached almost 6.5 million pounds.[37]

When American cattle entrepreneurs began shipping dressed beef via refrigeration to Britain in the mid-1870s, a number of Scots cattle raisers suddenly became alarmed. In 1877 the

Scotsman sent agriculture writer James Macdonald to the States to investigate the situation regarding western livestock. In a series of articles later published as a book Macdonald carefully assessed the American cattle industry. While he scorned the quality of contemporary American beef, he predicted a great future for American stock raising, depicting the Trans-Mississippi West as a land where one could perhaps reap profits as high as 25 percent on an annual basis.[38]

Within a few years, Scots capital began to flow steadily toward various ranch investments. Perhaps no area received as much Scottish capital as New Mexico, Arizona, and Texas. The first large-scale British joint-stock venture in Texas cattle ranching came with the Prairie Cattle Company, Limited, founded in Edinburgh in 1880. In 1882 it reported a dividend of 19.5 percent, and the next year it paid shareholders almost 28 percent. These high profits set off the infamous "Scottish-American cattle craze."

It was not long before promoters "with ranches in their pockets," began to flood the east of Scotland, especially the Edinburgh, Dundee, and Aberdeen regions. Corporations such as the Texas Land and Cattle Co., Ltd., the Swan Land and Cattle Company, and the most famous, the Matador Land and Cattle Co., Ltd., began seriously advertising their wares. Many a conservative businessman plunged into western American ranching. Investors in Aberdeenshire were confident that their knowledge of animal husbandry would serve them well on America's Great Plains.

These investors had a point. Ever since the earliest days, the raising of cattle had been crucial to the economic life of North Britain. Even in legend, "the Cattle Raid of Cooley" was a pivotal event in Celtic agrarian life. This reliance upon cattle (and, later, sheep) was largely dictated by geography. The glens of the Western Islands and the west of Scotland all fostered early spring grasses and were largely unsuitable for the cultivation of wheat. Similarly, much of the region between the Highland boundary fault and the English border was best suited to pastoral life.³⁹ Traditional wealth had usually been measured in cattle, and Highland black cattle served as the economic base for the Scottish laird and his tenants.⁴⁰

The rise of the eighteenth-century urban centers in southeast Britain transformed the Scottish cattle industry. From c. 1750 to c. 1850 legitimate cattle droving replaced cattle thieving as a Borders way of life. London and the larger urban centers simply could not get enough beef. Drovers swam their herds over sea lochs, or drove them down well-established roads to the great fairs at Smithfield in London or Falkirk in Scotland. As late as 1880 fifteen thousand cattle and twenty thousand sheep were sold at Falkirk.⁴¹ In the eyes of many people Scotland had become a vast grazing area that supplied the English with their beef.

Simultaneously, cattle droving began to emerge as a legitimate profession. As with the fur trade a century earlier, the qualities of ruggedness, adventurousness, and familiarity with the land allowed Scots to excel in this demanding profession. While on the road, armed Scots drovers (and their dogs) lived on oatmeal, onions, ewe's milk, cheese, bannock, and a ram's horn filled with whiskey. When night fell, the drover simply wrapped his plaid around him and slept by his charges.

This life demanded considerable skill. Tradition has it that one man and his dogs could drive from one hundred to four hundred cattle.⁴² For fifty-five years, John Cameron of Corriechoille drove herds to Falkirk Tryst to acquire the reputation as "the most famous drover of Lochabee." He also earned a small fortune along the way. When herding cattle from the Highlands and Islands, a drover often had to swim the beasts across rivers or sea lochs. Drovers moved the herds across the treacherous Kyle of Rhea—the narrow strait separating the Isle of Skye from the mainland—by tying the tail of one beast to the horns of another. The alternative, loading the cattle onto narrow boats, proved equally demanding. These challenges faded only with the 1840s and 1850s when railroads and larger boats gradually replaced the cattle drive.[43] The last cattle swam the Kyle of Rhea in 1906.

Over time, the drovers produced a subculture uniquely their own. Often illiterate, they devised their own means of counting their beasts—and their attitude towards authority was decidedly irreverent. A Scottish visitor to the Mississippi Valley in 1855 once met a ten-year-old drover. "Where are you going, my son?" he asked. "To Minnesota; and I ain't your son; or if I am, I never knew it" was the reply.[44] Drover irreverence, it seems, was international.

Scots farmers also had behind them centuries of familiarity with breeding practices. Highland cattle, or kyloes, probably carried characteristics from neolithic days. Rugged, agile, and alert, the cattle had heavy, shaggy coats that allowed them to withstand the rain, winds, and cold of the north. They are still preferred by some Scottish farmers.[45]

By the middle of the nineteenth century each region of Scotland had specialized in its distinctive type of cattle, easily recognized by professionals. Scottish breeders came up with several well-known varieties: the kyloes, or Highland cattle; the Galloway, or polled (i.e., hornless); the Ayrshire, which were chiefly raised for milk; the Fifeshire, which were known for both milk and meat; the Shetland and Orkney cattle, which tended to be small. Breeder William McCombie of the Tillyfourie region, Aberdeenshire, helped produce the Aberdeen Angus, perhaps the most widely recognized of all the Scottish breeds.[46] Only the Scottish shorthorn rivaled the Aberdeen Angus in popularity.[47] Thus, the Scots' history of cattle raising prepared them to feel comfortable with investment in cattle ranches in the American Great Plains. This confidence stemmed in part from the fact that while American cattle feeding might be haphazard, Scottish cattle feeding had developed into a "science."[48]

A number of Scots crossed the Atlantic to help manage these western cattle operations. For instance, Archie Marjoribanks supervised the family investments in the Texas Panhandle, whereas Thomas Simpson Carson, head of the Scottish Loan Company, managed ranches in New Mexico and Arizona.[49] Coutts Marjoribanks, Archie's brother, ran a ranch in McHenry County, North Dakota.[50] Colin Cameron managed ranches in southeastern Arizona, and John Clay managed the powerful Swan Land and Cattle Company in Wyoming. Clay later became one of the most respected stockman in the entire West.

From a base in Trinidad, Colorado, Murdo Mackenzie oversaw operations of the famed Matador Land and Cattle Company, Ltd., "the mother of British cattle companies in the United States," and later became head of the American National Livestock Association. One observer who saw Mackenzie in action at the Denver Stockyards marveled at his "Caledonian eye for animal" and his "native shrewdness." In spite of all his years in America, Mackenzie would have looked perfectly in place in a Scots cattle byre.[51] Theodore Roosevelt was a good friend of Mackenzie and held him in high esteem. Over the course of his long, successful career, Mackenzie traveled widely in Europe, built homes in Trinidad and Denver, Colorado, sent his children to college, and lived a life not unlike that of a Scottish laird.[52]

Virtually all of these Scottish-American cattle managers placed a priority on improved breeding techniques, but they could do this only when the open-range era ended and fences became common. All the Scots ranch managers prided themselves on their ability to improve bloodlines. One 1875 visitor to a prosperous Scots-run ranch near Portland, Oregon, observed that "pure blood is the rule at Reedville, and it is applied to all animals kept there—to Leicester, Cotswold, and Southdown sheep; and extends to pigs and poultry; possibly (for I did not inquire) to rats and mice."[53]

Headquarters of the Swan Land and Cattle Company, Chugwater, Wyoming. The General Office was in Edinburgh, Scotland. (American Heritage Center, University of Wyoming.)

Not all these enterprises succeeded, of course. The Marjoribanks brothers went broke. But perhaps it is no coincidence that the cattle ranches that Carson, Clay, and Mackenzie managed were among the few to remain profitable in what turned out to be a very risky profession. The remains of the old Swan headquarters in Chugwater, Wyoming, still bear the distinct Scottish architectural motifs that marked the heyday of their operation.[54]

In spite of initial high profits, the cattle-ranching investment boom proved short-lived. The terrible winters of 1886–87 began what the depression of 1893–97 completed. In the words of John Clay, "As the South Sea bubble burst, as the Dutch tulip craze dissolved, this cattle gold brick withstood not the snow of winter."[55] By the turn of the century most Scots investors had turned to the various British Colonies.[56] Still, in 1919, a number of western ranchers reported that they had doubled their capital during the past forty years. The Matador Land and Cattle Company operated until 1951.

Estimates of British investment in western cattle vary, but they are usually put at from six to nine million pounds. Historians also disagree in their overall assessment of this enterprise. W. Turrentine Jackson has suggested that the Scots investors earned enough dividends from the Arizona Copper Companies to overcome considerable losses from ranch investments.[57] Paul M. Edwards thinks otherwise. He argues that in the long run, the losses in mining and railroads just about cancelled out the profits in land mortgages and cattle. W. G. Kerr has suggested that the chief long-term benefits lay less with Scottish profits than with the ultimate rationalization of the cattle industry and the providing of low-priced beef to the entire world.[58] But unquestionably, Scottish investment proved substantial in funding the western cattle industry.

One of the unforeseen consequences of the Scottish interest in American cattle can be seen in the *Letters of a Woman Homesteader*, written by Elinore Pruitt Stewart in 1913. Young Elinore

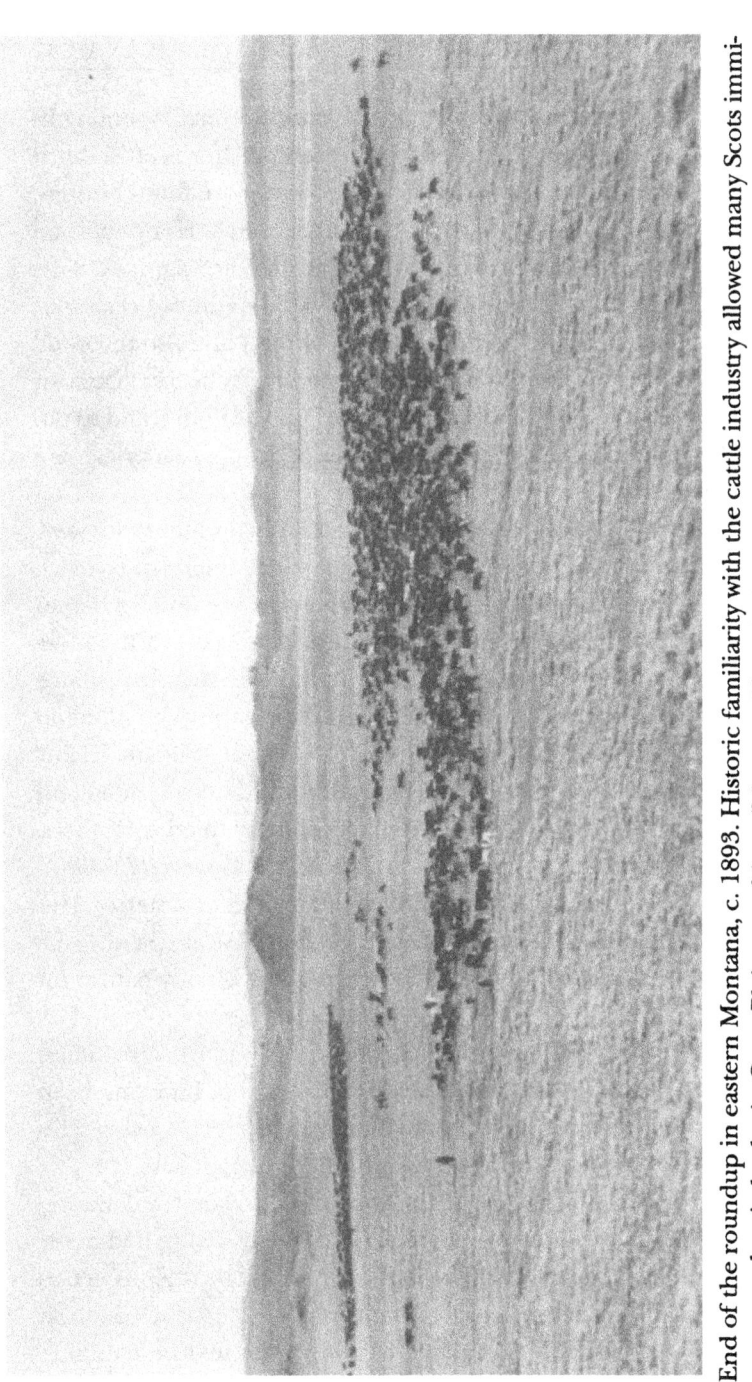

End of the roundup in eastern Montana, c. 1893. Historic familiarity with the cattle industry allowed many Scots immigrants to play vital roles in Great Plains ranching. (Montana Historical Society, Helena. Photo by L. A. Huffman.)

Pruitt arrived as a "grass" widow in southwestern Wyoming in 1909. Eventually she married Clyde Stewart, her Scottish-born employer, filed her own homestead claim, bore four children, and generally helped with all jobs on the ranch. Her published letters recall her husband's love for playing the bagpipes, especially "The Campbells Are Coming." ("Sometimes I wish they would make haste and get here," she wrote.) She also recorded how they gave their cattle names from British history: Duke of Monmouth, John Fox, Bloody Mary, Pope of Rome, and so on. Her letters offer fascinating glimpses of Scottish-American life in frontier Wyoming.[59]

One should also note that this British involvement with western ranching was not always appreciated by American farmers. Adverse reaction to foreign land owners proved much a part of the agrarian protest movements of the latter part of the nineteenth century. Populist agitators denounced British absentee owners in the Dakotas and Nebraska, comparing the situation to the evils of "Irish landlordism." Reformer William "Coin" Harvey claimed that half of Nebraska and South Dakota and one-eighth of North Dakota were owned by titled foreigners. One fictional account, Sara M. Brigham's *Waverland* (1886), stated that the British owned 20 million acres of America. Her character, the Duke of Melvorne, declared: "We are gaining the lands our fathers lost without fighting any bloody battles for them."[60]

Second to cattle, the Scots most affected western agricultural life in the realm of sheep. Sheep ranching also had long been part of Scottish history. Consequently, Scots sheepherding skills were several levels above those of American ranchers.

Although caring for their "four footed clansmen" was an integral part of Scottish agrarian life, sheep raising had never dominated the economy as had the raising of cattle. As late as the mid-eighteenth century, English visitors described Scottish sheep as "dog like" in appearance, with finely textured but thin wool on small wiry frames. Their lack of size could probably be traced to centuries of inbreeding, while the thin wool was largely due to the tradition of keeping sheep indoors during the winter months.[61]

The sheep of the northern Orkney Islands were even more unique. Kept from the land by six-foot-high dry-stone walls on islands such as North Ronaldsay, the sheep lived almost exclusively on seaweed as they followed short-line paths (called *clowjungs*) that may trace back five thousand years. Some of the most ancient ovine stock of Scotland, these black, brown, and white sheep were roughly as tall as a man's thigh, with lambs the size of a small dog.[62]

Social and economic pressures resulting from the onset of enclosures, the end of runrig, and forced emigration from the Highlands eventually caused the Scots to concentrate on sheep raising. From the 1760s forward sheep raising began to fill the abandoned farms of the Highlands; within a few years, it had expanded to encompass perhaps one-third of the Scottish countryside.[63] The process proved slow but relentless. By 1803 the whole of Glengarry had been turned over to sheep raising. Within a few years, sheep had entered the valley of Glencoe. The sheep-farming system of Glencoe, wrote one author in 1818, "had done the work of extirpation of the inhabitants more effectively than the massacre of 1692."[64]

As the sheep advanced north, however, they also improved in quality. Although one could find about forty different varieties by the end of the eighteenth century, two varieties dominated this expansion: the black-faced and the Cheviot. The introduction of the turnip provided an easy-to-grow sheep food, and the Scots discovered simultaneously that the black-faced sheep could winter outside with no ill effects. Improver Sir John Sinclair introduced the white-faced Cheviot, also from the south. For almost three-quarters of a century, these two breeds vied with one another as to which was more suitable to the

Scottish climate. By general consensus the Cheviot proved superior in wool, meat, and fecundity. But the black-faced retained its popularity with northern farmers because of its better ability to withstand the winters.

By the mid-nineteenth century the herds had come to a rough equilibrium. The coarse, heavy-wooled black-face dominated the central Highlands and Islands, for they could live without difficulty on heather swards. The soft, finer-wooled Cheviots ruled the southern hillsides and the lower grounds near the sea farther north. Their domain was more restricted, because they needed grassy swards on which to graze. Each breed could summer on the hills at the head of the glens and winter in the glens themselves. But if the sheep wintered in the glens, the only area where the land could be tilled, that meant the Scottish tenants had to be replaced.[65] As with every major economic shift, the emergence of Scottish sheep ranching had its costs.

No account of Scottish sheep life would be complete without some discussion of the dogs. The few old-timers who remembered the last years of Scottish sheep droving recalled that when the drovers arrived at their inns for the night, their first concern was food for their dogs. On the road they often shared their oatmeal porridge with the animals. Miss Stewart Mackenzie of Brahan, Ross-shire, recalled that a generation earlier she would often ride by solitary collies making their way north. These animals belonged to Scottish drovers who had elected to remain in England for the harvest and had sent the animals home by themselves. The dogs simply reversed the route by which they came, feeding at the inns or farmhouses they had stopped by on the trip south. When the drover returned, he made sure to pay the innkeepers for the food that the dogs had eaten the previous year.[66]

The border collies and Highland sheep dogs soon achieved international fame. Modern sheep growers unanimously agree that sheep dogs are as vital as any human worker to their operations. Medieval documents suggest that the Borders region probably developed the idea that a dog could learn to work at a distance at the sound of a voice or a whistle. Although the sheep dog arrived late in the Highlands—some eighteenth-century accounts recall that shepherds rounded up the sheep by themselves—they came to dominate this part of Scotland as well.

Raising sheep has never been an easy task. The animals are notoriously dull witted, and shepherds wrestled with a variety of their ailments. Sheep pox (*variola ovina*), caused by a virus, devastated the English flocks in the mid-nineteenth century and remained a problem in Scotland for years afterward. Other parasitic diseases, such as sheep scab, mange mite, and the infamous liver fluke appeared with regularity. The ever-present danger of a May "lambing storm" added yet another dilemma to life outdoors.

But raising sheep had advantages as well. The animals' natural fecundity allowed owners to pay shepherds and other workers in stock rather than in cash. Since they had a much shorter life cycle, sheep could be sold far earlier than cattle. Shepherds could lamb in April, wean in sixteen to eighteen weeks, and then sell at Michaelmas in time for Christmas-season lamb.[67] Although sheep did not present the same potential for improvement as did cattle, selective breeding did move the meat to the best joints and shorten marketing time to about two years.[68]

The Scottish sheep industry peaked in about 1870. From that time to the early twentieth century, stability, or even gradual decline, set in. In Argyll, Ross, and Inverness shires, sheep population declined from 2,187,000 in 1874 to 1,608,000 in 1914.[69] The wet summers and cold winters of 1879–80 probably played a role in the decline, especially because they were accompanied by an epidemic of liver fluke. Overgrazing, which had allowed an onset of bracken in the hills that the tramping of the cattle had somewhat controlled in earlier years, may also have been a significant factor in the decline. In any case many farmers lost their breeding flocks and never replaced them.[70] But the decline of Scottish herding meant that a large number of Scots sheep men were available to transfer to the American West.

During the last two thousand years the craft of the sheepherder has changed little. As historian Judith Keys Kenny once observed, by mid-Victorian times sheepherding had evolved into a genuine art form. There were no books from which one could learn sheepherding. Nor were cattle-ranching skills transferable to sheepherding, for a person could not tend sheep from the back of a horse.[71] Few American farmers possessed the necessary skills or the motivation to become shepherds. Thus, the Scots had a real advantage. Brigham Young, for example, always chose Scots shepherds to manage the Mormon communal herds.

The sheep industry in the western United States proved extraordinarily multinational, involving Navajo, Mexican, Hispanic, Norwegian, German, Canadian, and Irish herders, just to name a few. In every region of the West, however, the Scots sheepmen became prominent beyond their numbers. In some regions, such as Wyoming and Idaho, they virtually ruled the enterprise.

Several Scots émigrés established genuine sheep empires. By the 1860s Robert Burnett, who later inherited the title to Crathes Castle in Aberdeenshire, oversaw one of the largest sheep herds in southern California on his twenty-five-thousand-acre ranch. (The land, which he later sold for a tidy profit, now comprises much of downtown Los Angeles.) In 1880 Patrick Healy, who was born in County Kerry, Ireland, teamed with Scotsman Alan Patterson to run sheep in the Buffalo, Wyoming, region; by 1897 they owned one hundred thousand animals. They, too, ranked among the largest sheepmen in the West. Interestingly, Healy and Patterson never kept any type of financial records, dividing the flock as evenly as possible and then playing cards to determine who received which bunch.[72]

Their contemporary, Robert Taylor, a native of Hartwick, Scotland, also owned a flock of one hundred thousand sheep in Wyoming and Nebraska. Most of the Scots sheep men in central Wyoming began herding with Taylor, either as a partner or on a share basis. A savvy rancher—he had once worked as a foreign correspondent for a Scottish newspaper—Taylor spent much effort in crossbreeding his flocks to produce a fine-fleeced, hardy lamb that could withstand Wyoming range life. A frequent fair goer in both Britain and America, Taylor greatly improved Wyoming's wool and mutton production.[73]

If the Estancia Valley of central New Mexico is representative, Scots herders played significant roles in smaller areas as well. William Dunbar from Inverness arrived penniless in the 1890s but owned a twelve-hundred-acre sheep ranch when he died in 1937. During the same era the McGillvary brothers arrived there as herders, each, according to family legend, marrying a local woman from a different ethnic group (Hispanic, Anglo, Indian). The McGillvarys likened New Mexico to Scotland because of the wide-open spaces. Similarly, McIntosh, New Mexico, is named for the McIntosh brothers, William, Donald, and John, who came to herd sheep in the late 1880s. Utilizing the *partidad* system, they also brought in a number of Scots employees who all later became independent flockmasters.[74] William achieved local fame for his Scots managers, his wool barns, his elegant shearing parties (with dancing, pianola, and splended foods), plus a distinct fondness for the bottle. Rumor had it that he would ride into nearby Estancia and get drunk, whereupon the bartender would load him in his buggy and have the horses take him home. Estancia Valley Scots herders occasionally sported kilts while watching over their sheep. Familiarity with sheep raising also offered an entry into local New Mexico Hispanic society. Consequently, there were a number of Scots-Hispanic marriages in the Estancia region, descendants of whom live there to this day.[75]

Scots proved prominent in the Pacific Northwest sheep world as well. HBC physician W. F. Tolmie introduced Scottish sheep into Oregon, as did William McLoughlin. But the real influx of Scottish sheep men in the region did not occur until the 1870s. At first this experiment was not a success, for Scots shepherds strongly disliked the vast herds and open ranges of eastern Oregon and Washington. They had been used to herding flocks in the hundreds, but they suddenly found themselves with herds approaching one thousand. Scots herders also protested the isolation and the fact that they often never saw the owner for a season—sometimes not for an entire year. Consequently, Australian herders replaced the Scots for about a decade.[76]

During the 1880s, however, the Scots returned. The vast public domain provided acres of free fodder, and the eastern Oregon success of British rancher Graham Hewison showed how much profit could be made from sheep.[77] But life on the scattered sheep ranches of the Northwest contained dangers as well. Feuds between ranchers and sheepherders often escalated into open violence, and when Indian resistance broke out, the isolated shepherds were easy targets. Washington cattle ranchers boasted of breeding coyotes and wolves to destroy the sheep. The Klickatat Valley bars carried signs that read: "No sheep allowed. Sheepmen take notice." As early Oregon sheepman John Minto noted, "Indeed, it is safe to say that during the years of expansion of sheep industry over the portion of Oregon west of the Blue Mountains, more lives have been taken and more property destroyed over range feuds, provided by a marauding spirit, than by the racial wars with the natives."[78]

Perhaps the most famous sheep operation of the region was begun by the three McGregor brothers, Archie, Peter, and John, whose parents had moved from the Isle of Mull to eastern

Canada in the 1850s, and who, along with approximately one million other Canadians, crossed to the United States between 1881 and 1891. The brothers began sheep raising on Washington's open range in 1882 and continued for a decade. Astute businessmen, they established credit by being hardworking and fair in their dealings. They also realized that the end of Washington's open range demanded major adjustments in the industry. The company still exists.[79]

If the McGregor Corporation proved the most successful of northwestern Scots sheepherding efforts, the saga of Andrew Little is the most dramatic. Indeed, Little's career is an "Andrew Carnegie" saga writ small. According to legend, young Andrew Little and two sheep dogs arrived from near Moffat, Scotland, to settle in Caldwell, Idaho, in 1894. There he began working for Robert "Scotch Bob" Aikman's sheep ranch. Aikman and fellow Scot Charlie Doane had maintained strong links with their homeland and had aided several Scots in finding work in Idaho.

Like so many other herders, Little took his salary in stock and soon had a small herd of his own. In 1901 he felt sufficiently established to return to Scotland, where he successfully courted a young woman with tales of the Idaho countryside. In addition, seven of his eight brothers followed him to the Boise Basin to join the Scots families of McLeod, Laidlaw, Sproat, Campbell, and McMillan who already lived there.

Little's fortunes grew with those of the fertile Boise Valley. At one time he owned 165,000 sheep, which he ran from the Boise Valley to the Salmon River area. In 1918 Idaho ranked as the world's second largest sheep center, and in Little's peak production year, 1929, his flocks produced a million pounds of wool. When he died, the press termed him the "Sheep King of Idaho, and possibly of the United States."[80] What Andrew Carnegie was to steel, Andrew Little was to western sheep ranching—the ultimate success story.

Andy Little, the "Sheep King" of Idaho. Little's success made him the Andrew Carnegie of western life. (Idaho State Historical Society. Photo 79.95.6.)

Spring lambs on the Andy Little sheep ranch in Idaho, 1906. Scots immigrants played a prominent role in the western sheep industry. (Idaho State Historical Society. Photo 70.164.20.)

It was not long before a regional folklore developed around Andy Little. When he arrived in 1894, the story went, he walked twenty miles to the Aikman ranch to save carfare. On the way he sold one of his two border collies to establish a nest egg. Legend has it that Andy Little never sold a sheep to anyone in the Boise Valley; he would sell only to those outside the region. This he did so that if he ever found an animal without a mark or brand, he knew it belonged to him. One admirer from Scotland allegedly wrote him a letter addressed "Andy Little, USA."

As the Andrew Little story shows, Scotland's famed sheep dogs almost always accompanied the immigrants, especially the Border black-and-white collies. This breed, which originated around 1600, was crossed with several others, and one offspring— the kelpie (Gaelic for water sprite)—began to rival it in popularity in the States. Most western sheep dogs, however, were descended from the black-and-white collies. Usually trained from puppies by older dogs, some pups were even suckled by ewes, literally becoming part of the flock. The test of a born leader, it was said, lay with its ability to keep a band of chickens bunched.[81]

With the dogs came American dog stories, tales often tinged with romance. They begin with accounts of sheep dogs driving wild turkeys into San Francisco in 1879. William Patterson of northern Idaho claimed to own a dog who would bring the sheep to the shearer one by one and, when they were penned for the night, would run to the hills to look for strays. One Oregon herder died of natural causes in the field, but when his friends found him weeks later, his collie had dutifully rounded up the entire herd. Jerry, a border collie in the Umatilla Forest, remained with the flock when Indian clashes caused all the herders to flee. When the men returned, they found that Jerry had increased his flock by rounding up a number of strays from neighboring bands. One Montana sheep man owned a dog, Old Ruddy, who would never take orders and always cut right through the herd. Once, when a potential buyer was watching, the herder cried, "around them now," and just when Old Ruddy was about halfway, "now divide them." One Pacific Northwest herder claimed that he owned a chess-playing collie who usually beat him two out of three. "Ten thousand white ones and sixty black ones. Go round 'em, Shep," a Montana herder allegedly said to his favorite collie.[82]

The man-animal relationship that emerged from this cooperation was deep and meaningful. Dogs would sicken and even die when their masters passed on. One McGregor company herder shot himself when his favorite dog failed to return to camp.[83] Andrew Little discouraged making the dogs into pets—he considered them "hired hands"—but the affection between dog and herder could never be contained by any ranch rules.

Perhaps no one has expressed the canine-human link better than Robert Burns in his "Twa Dogs." The collie Luath is speaking:

> The luntin' pipe, n' sneeshin mill,
> Are handed round wi' richt guid will;
> The cantie auld folks crackin crouse,
> The Young anes ranting thro' the house—
>
> My heart has been
>   sae fain to see them,
> That I for joy hae
>   bark't wi' them.

The legacy of sheep dogs and dog tales is as much a part of the Scots' impact on western life as that of the immigrants themselves.

Since they came from such different regions, usually settled individually, and worked in such a wide variety of occupations, how did the nineteenth-century American Scots create a common identity? The answer is complex. From the onset American Scots suffered an identity problem as to exactly what constituted "Scottish culture." The answer emerged partly as literature (Porter, Scott, Burns); partly as religion (some Catholics, some Episcopalians, some Freethinkers, but mostly Presbyterians); partly as costume (the kilt and other aspects of "the garb of Old Gaul"); partly as music (ballads and bagpipes); partly as language (some Gaelic but mostly Lowland Scots); partly as special foods (haggis, oatcakes); and, of course, "a wee dram," especially significant for a culture that elevated social drinking virtually to an art form.

These items did not, by themselves, an identity make. Consequently, one of the major aspects of nineteenth-century American Scottish culture was the creation of a new self-image. Since Scoto-Americans lacked any real community through which to disseminate these ideas, they had to create one. Thus, the celebration of St. Andrew's Day (November 30) and Robert Burns's Day (January 25) took on a special set of functions in the New World.

As historian Kathleen Neils Conzen and others have noted, nineteenth-century ethnic groups in America found themselves involved in a continual process of "ethnic invention." The process went through several stages. First, the groups had to merge the various Old World regional differences—e.g., the distinctions between Aberdeenshire, Glasgow, Edinburgh, Orkney, Shetland, and so forth and between Highlands and Lowlands—into a single Scots identity. Regional distinctions in accent, dress, and behavior that loomed large in Scotland were completely lost on Americans.[84]

But the blending of the Scots regions into a national identity in America was only the beginning. American Scots also had to demark the chief characteristics of this new Scoto-American identity. The process proved ever fluid. Scots immigrants continually interacted with the host (mainstream American) culture, and the process was never complete.

Initially, one of the chief means by which Scots forged this new identity came with the celebration of St. Andrew's Day. Creating an identity through a saint's day was commonplace all through the century. Each European group had a special day of commemoration. For example, the Hungarians celebrated St. Stephen's Day (August 20), the Welsh, St. David's Day (March 1), the English, St. George's Day (April 23), and the Irish, St. Patrick's Day (March 17). In 1819 Glasgow native John M. Duncan attended the celebration of an early St. Andrew's Day in New York City. His account provides an insight into the way Americans and Scots interacted. Expecting to dine on "barley kale, smoking sheep's head and trotters, sonsy haggis," he ended up consuming a largely American meal that lacked even oatcakes. When he mildly protested, his host insisted that American life had changed their eating habits. When he had served haggis in previous years, he said, the customers shouted to the waiter to remove it. Even an American chef's attempt to improve the taste by adding raisins had come to naught. Duncan complained about the "diluted nationality" and concluded that the whole dinner was a spoiled mixture of "Yankeeism and Land-of-cakeism." He left early.[85]

The disgruntled Duncan missed a good many means by which American Scots kept their identity alive. The New York hotel was draped with Scots flags and medallions, inside and out, and all the "brither Scots" wore broad blue-and-white collars. Bagpipes provided the musical background, in this case backed by a full American orchestra. The entertainment for the evening came largely from the reading of Scottish poems, chiefly by Burns, in a wide variety of first-, second-, and third-generation accents. Then came the obligatory round of toasts: "The day and all that honour it"; "The King of Great Britain and all friendly powers." The pipes, whiskey, poems, songs, accent, and foods all helped create the feeling of auld lang syne.

Over the course of the century the nature of the St. Andrew's Day celebration changed but little. Often hosted by a local

Presbyterian church, it might call forth a special sermon as well as a banquet. "You do not have much to do with St. Andrew in Scotland," a Wisconsin Scot reminded his Aberdeen readers in 1864, but it was different with Scotsmen abroad. The day was necessary here, he noted, to nourish "that noble pride which every Scotchman feels in his ancestral glory and living fame."[86] The St. Andrew's Society also did a good bit of charitable work.

Abraham Lincoln's 1863 proclamation of a national day of Thanksgiving in late November eventually crowded out St. Andrew's Day. It was not long before Robert Burns's Day replaced it. Perhaps the celebration of a saint's day rang foreign to American ears; or perhaps January 25 provided a better time to stage a gala celebration. At any rate, by the last decades of the century the celebration of Robert Burns's Day had emerged as the major disseminator of Scottish culture and "the garb of old Gaul" throughout the region. Numerous reminiscences recall the childhood agony of sitting through yet-another lecture on Robert Burns.

The "Burns ethos," however, harmonized especially well with the American western ethos. The mock heroics of his ballads meshed nicely with western cynicism, and Burns's skepticism about religion (as in "Holy Willie's Prayer") made him free of sectarian bias. Almost Jacobin in outlook, his great poems celebrating democracy ("a man's a man for a' that") and denouncing hypocrisy ("O wad some Power the giftie gie us / to see ourselves as ithers see us") made Burns universally acceptable in America.

Abraham Lincoln, one of Burns's greatest admirers, could quote him by the hour. On January 25, 1865, Lincoln wrote to a Burns committee in praise of the poet's "generous heart and transcendent genius."[87] This respect was shared by a great many others. "I have hope for the human race so long as they celebrate the birthday of Robert Burns," said radical Denver Congregationalist minister Myron W. Reed c. 1893. "I hate to be cruel but think of celebrating the birthday of [railroad magnate George] Pullman."[88]

By 1906 more than sixty American cities celebrated January 25, including San Francisco, Denver, Albuquerque, Seattle, and Lander, Wyoming. A number of Burns's verses were also parodied anonymously ("John Alcohol, my foe, John"), the highest form of flattery.[89] It was not long before the Burns festivities assumed a more or less standard form. The day demanded a wide variety of special foods: shortbread, haggis (Burns's "great chieftain o' the puddin' race"); "howtowdies wi' drappit egge"; "thairums, pies and porter"; and "parritch and milk." The men donned kilts, while the women joined in reels and Highland flings. Bagpipes proved essential and occasionally hornpipes were heard, as singing and music dominated the affair. The songs included: "The Land of Burns," "Flow Gently Sweet Afton," "March of the Cameron Men," "Warrior Bold," "When the Swallows Homeward Fly," "Within a Mile o' Edinburgh," and "Farewell My Home." "Tam O'Shanter" or "The Cotter's Saturday Night" often rounded out the festivities.[90] Writing in 1896, Peter Ross described the Burns Day celebrations as "generally the most thoroughgoing Scotch affairs in the world."[91] In 1901 the *Scottish American* offered advice on "How to Organize a Scottish Society," with a Burns Day at the core.[92] "It was a real important thing for the Scots," recalled one Idaho pioneer. When Burns Day celebrations first began in her area in 1903, few non-Scots attended.[93]

The ceremonial reading of Burns's verse in Scots illustrates the importance of language in the celebration of American "Scottishness," but the Scots immigrants had a problem that most other immigrant groups did not have. Historians generally agree that language is the most important single element in maintaining a separate ethnic identity.[94] Yet Lowland Scots, unlike—say—Gaelic, Spanish, or Dutch, was not exactly a separate language. In general the Lowland dialect was close enough to English so that one could follow the line of argument. A second-generation Scoto-American would not formally learn to speak Scots, for example, as a second-generation German-American or French-American might learn German or French. These young people might speak French or German with an American accent, but they would still master their ancestors' native tongue. But Scoto-Americans could not really do so. One could learn Lowland Scots only by growing up within the culture.

Consequently, one crucial aspect of "Scottishness" did not survive: that of dialect and pronunciation. In 1819 John Duncan complained bitterly that second-generation Scots butchered the dialect; he helped silence a third-generation Scot's reading of Burns by loud applause. But a half-century later, Aberdeen immigrant to Nebraska John Alexander felt otherwise. He criticized his Aberdeenshire fellow travelers for making no effort to modify their talk so that the average Nebraskan could comprehend them. Since the English spoken in Exeter, Fillmore County, Nebraska, served perfectly well, Alexander saw no real advantage in sustaining a North British mode of speech. "Go where we may," he observed, "our dear mother Scotch dialect must go to the wall."[95] At most it might survive as a floating burr that, like a kilt, could be donned for ceremonial occasions. In the American West the accent, which served as the key badge of "Scottishness" in Britain, largely disappeared.

If dialect and pronunciation faded over time, however, Scottish aphorisms, proverbs, and anecdotes remained. Americans loved to quote the aphorisms, even though they did not always seem to understand them fully. The apocryphal story of Robert Bruce watching the spider spin its web seven times became a staple of inspirational lecturers. Many a phrase retained its currency, although not always to the pleasure of grammarians: "Should have went," "et" as the past tense of "eat," and "that" as a substitute for those. The Highland phrase "a far cry" became widely accepted, as did "hey, Mac." Unfortunately, one of George Washington's favorite Scottish maxims, "Many a mickle makes a muckle" did not survive the eighteenth century.

The popularity of these Burns Day celebrations with their dramatic readings varied with the flow of Scots immigrants. Shortly after 1900, the various groups had to incorporate a second generation into the festivities. The Burns Day celebration in Miles City, Montana, for example, slowly shifted from a celebration of Scottishness to a chance for all to become Scots for a day. The ceremonies in Buffalo, Wyoming, died out in the 1920s because Basque immigrants had largely replaced the Scots as the region's sheepherders. Lander, Wyoming, drew six hundred to its 1952 Burns Day celebration, but the next year the day was commemorated only by a "Burns Day sale" at the local supermarket. As Glasgow native Mary Gilchrist of Cheyenne wanted to insure that Scottishness remained prominent in the state, in 1927 she donated twenty thousand dollars to erect a statue of Robert Burns in Gilchrist Park in downtown Cheyenne. Robert Burns still stands there as mute testimony to the importance of Scottish culture in the American West.[96]

If the celebration of Burns Day proved the focal point for creating an American Scottish identity, a number of other organizations played strong supporting roles. The order of the Scottish Clans was formed in St. Louis in 1882, and a number of Wyoming cities boasted Caledonian societies. Over time these groups began to stage Highland games all across the nation.

Like cattle and sheep raising, sporting contests such as the Highland games had long been a staple of Scots culture. When the games transferred to America, they took on a dual function. First, they reinforced Scottishness, and second, they became the origin of American track and field.[97]

In 1800 a charitable organization that later took the name Braemar Highland Society began in Braemar, Scotland. In 1832 the group staged one of the first contests to preserve the music,

The Caledonian Club erected this statue of Robert Burns in City Park, Denver, Colorado, in 1904. (Denver Public Library, Western History Department. Photo 15183.)

games, and clothing of the Highlands. After Queen Victoria began attending regularly, the event received enormous popularity. Filled with contests such as "putting the stone," wrestling, tugs of war, tossing the caber, and footracing, the events combined drama and excitement. The women were included with

THE VICTORIAN WEST: REALITY

Statue of Robert Burns, erected in 1927, in Gilchrist Park, Cheyenne, Wyoming. (Wyoming Division of Cultural Resources. Photo 13581.)

exhibitions of Highland dancing. Of course the bagpipes were ever present.[98]

The first American Highland games appeared in 1836, but they did not become widespread until the Gilded Age. Events included throwing the hammer or the stone and tossing the caber; the pole vault, high jump, long jump, hop-step-and-leap, and hurdles; the tug-of-war; and numerous footraces. Pipers and Highland dancers enlivened the athletics.

During much of the nineteenth century, the games were staged on July 4. The San Francisco Thistle Club, for example, drew five thousand people to Shell Mound Park for their 1889 games.[99] But this tradition faded over time as July 4 became reserved for more solemn observances. "The Fourth of July is an American and not a Scotch holiday," warned the editor of the *Scottish American,* "and a growing sentiment prevails that it should be reserved for Americans."[100] By c. 1890 the games had not only lost their ethnic flavor, they had gradually evolved into American track and field. What began as a Scottish sport had become Americanized.

The game of golf followed along similar lines. This uniquely Scottish import arrived in the East in the early 1880s, but soon reached the West. As the game spread, so, too, did Scots golf professionals. During the fin-de-siècle years, approximately three hundred "Men of Carnoustie" began to dominate the American professional golf world. Not until 1914, for example, did a native-born American win the U.S. Open.

Representatives of this "Carnoustie exodus" were the brothers Smith. Their father, John, served as greenskeeper at a number of Scottish courses, including Carnoustie, and all five of his surviving sons became American golf professionals. The two most famous were probably Alexander and Macdonald. Alexander Smith played in the first organized professional tour in 1899 and won three California Opens prior to 1907. His classic *Lessons in Golf* (1907) reminded readers that "Golf is a science and not a bag of tricks," and he became recognized as America's most prominent golf instructor. His younger brother Macdonald achieved an equal reputation, eventually settling in California, where he worked for several clubs and in 1921 opened a popular golf school. Known for his smooth swing and dour manner, "Old Carnoustie," as he was termed, finished his career as manager of the private range of a Glendale, California, local magnate, from which position he taught a number of professionals. By the turn of the century virtually every American golf course or country club clamored for a Scots professional. As historian Howard N. Rabinowitz has observed, by World War I the Scots golf pro had become as prominent a part of American life as the Irish policeman, the Chinese laundryman, or the Swedish masseur.[101]

From cattle to sheep, from track and field to golf, from St. Andrew's Day to Robert Burns Day, the nineteenth-century American Scots slowly created a new Scoto-American identity. And, as the next chapter will show, much of this new identity resounded with romance.

CHAPTER FIVE

Scotland and the Victorian West

The Romance

In his autobiography *Some Part of Myself* (1980), Texas historian and folklorist J. Frank Dobie recalled his youth in the 1890s in the back country of southern Texas:

> One Christmas we got Porter's *The Scottish Chiefs*. I read it myself and at night as we sat by the fireplace my father read it aloud by the flickering light of a kerosene lamp. What heroes to emulate Bruce and Wallace were! My blood still stirs at the mention of the mere title.[1]

The Scottish Chiefs, which was written by minor Scottish novelist Jane Porter in 1810, probably influenced Sir Walter Scott in the creation of his famous Waverley series. Hoping to "paint the portrait of the most complete heroes that ever filled the page of history," Porter told the story of William Wallace's battle to defend Scotland against Edward I's invasions. Porter drew from the romantic ethos of her day, portraying the doomed Wallace and his equally tragic wife, Lady Wallace, without flaws. When accused of violating the English laws of Edward I, Wallace dismisses them as "tyrants' law." A true Scot, he says, acknowledges no laws save those of God and his country; Wallace refuses to rest "till Scotland be again free." Robert the Bruce is introduced as the successor to Wallace's dream, and in the climactic chapter, "Bannockburn" leads his countrymen to the independence they had so long sought. "So perish the murderers of William Wallace," one soldier cries.[2]

The Scottish Chiefs was translated into numerous languages. Reprinted in 1831, it went through at least ten different editions on both sides of the Atlantic before 1900. Dobie quite possibly read the 1880 version.[3] N. C. Wyeth sketched the illustrations for the 1921 American edition, which is still in print. Scottish culture, it seems, reached the Trans-Mississippi western frontier in a variety of forms.

Most aspects of Scottish culture that traveled west involved some element of romanticism. If Jane Porter led the way, the chief proponent was the famed Wizard of the North, Sir Walter Scott. Immensely popular in his homeland, Scott also sold well in the States, especially in the South. Aristocratic planters saw echoes of his Highland/Lowland tension in their own Backcountry/Tidewater society. When the novelist died in 1832, the *Richmond Inquirer* appeared in a black-bordered edition.

From the 1830s forward Americans made a steady pilgrimage to Scott's Abbotsford home on the Tweed. In fact Abbotsford was second only to Shakespeare's birthplace as a "must see" American tourist venue in the British Isles. U.S. consul to Liverpool Nathaniel Hawthorne visited Abbotsford twice, and ex-Confederate president Jefferson Davis thoroughly enjoyed his 1869 tour. Although one can never measure the influence of any writer, Scott undoubtedly remained very popular with mid-century American readers. After all, Mark Twain did blame him for causing the Civil War, naming the wrecked steamboat in *Huckleberry Finn* the *Walter Scott*.

Antebellum America produced its own romantic counterpart to Scott in James Fenimore Cooper. Scion of an established upstate New York family, Cooper's Leatherstocking Tales nicely complemented Scott's Waverley series. Scott mingled authentic historical figures, such as Rob Roy and Richard the Lion Hearted, with his fictional creations, but Cooper, living in what he felt was a "land without a past," felt obliged to create all his characters from his imagination. Critics often termed Cooper "The American Scott," but he confessed that he wished Scott to be known as "The British Cooper." Virtually every Scottish visitor to the United States gained his or her first impressions of American Indian life from the pages of Cooper. Thus, two of the foremost nineteenth-century novelists helped lay a shared romantic backdrop that linked "Scotland the Brave" and the American frontier West.

The second romantic linkage can be seen in the similarity between western and Scots/Scotch-Irish ballads. Folklorist Albert Friedman once defined a folk ballad as "a short, traditional impersonal narrative told in song, transmitted orally from generation to generation, marked by its own peculiar structure and rhetoric, and uninfluenced by literary conventions."[4] These traditional ballads were less "literature" than "illiterature," since they spread primarily through oral performance. Both Scotland and the American West expressed this ballad tradition in a variety of ways.

When one thinks of Scottish ballads, two regions and two time periods usually leap to mind. The first is the Anglo-Scottish Borders "frontier" from the fourteenth to the seventeenth centuries. From the Borders came the most famous of the ballad classics: "Kinmont Willie," "Hughie the Graeme," "Hobbie Noble," and "Jock o' the Side."[5]

These Borders ballads ran the gauntlet of human activities and emotions: thievery, bravery in the face of danger, heroism, rustling, clever deception, and betrayal. "Jock o' the Side," in folklorist Francis James Child's words, is "one of the best in the world, and enough to make a horse-trooper out of any young borderer, had he lacked the impulse."[6] In the companion ballad, "Hobbie Noble," Hobbie (Robert) Noble, who helped Jock o' the Side escape from prison, is betrayed and sent to a bitter fate. Forged over the centuries and sung in many different forms, the haunting Borders ballads paved the way for the genre of American frontier folk balladry.

The eighteenth century also witnessed an active revival of the Scots ballad tradition. Here the focus lay less with the Borders than with Aberdeenshire, the Moray Firth, and the Highlands, and the themes often revolved around Scots reaction to the English victories over the Jacobites in 1715 and 1746. The Jacobite rebellion provided the local bards with a great deal of material. With a deft turn of phrase, they damned their enemies forever: the hated King William III became "Willie Winkie," "Willie Wanbeard," and "Willie the Wag." When the king died from a fall off a horse at Hampton Court, allegedly because the animal stepped in a molehill, they coined the toast, "To the little gentleman in black velvet." The corpulent Duke of Cumberland, commander of the English armies in 1746, became "this mushroom thing called Cumberland" and "the Butcher." Although the Duke of Cumberland may have won the battle of Culloden, his name has echoed in infamy down to the most recent generation. Another English general, Sir John Cope, whom the Jacobites defeated at Prestonpans in 1745, was similarly satirized by poet Adam Skirving: "Hey, Johnnie Cope, are ye wauking yet? / Or are your drums a' beating yet?" When the first Hanoverian King, George I, assumed the throne, he was similarly parodied as "The wee, wee German Lairdie," and so on. Historian William Donaldson has argued that by the early nineteenth century, the popular song had emerged as the dominant cultural form of the Scottish people.[7]

Borrowing freely from the great British songs of the day, such as those that dealt with Robin Hood, the ballad was one of the central forms of late eighteenth- to early nineteenth-century Scottish popular culture. As such, it differed considerably from the formal, fixed "high art" of the era. A Thomas Gainsborough, Benjamin West, or Henry Raeburn painting was easily recognizable as the product of individual artistic genius. A Mozart sonata had exact, fixed notes. A performer who struck them out of sequence had simply gotten them wrong. But the popular ballad tradition hewed to no such rigid categories. Only rarely could songs be traced back to single individuals. Nor were the ballads in any way fixed so that a performer sang them "wrong." A new locale or a changed set of circumstances could easily call for new verses. Instead of spoiling the performance, the ballad fairly demanded such flexibility. Consequently, one finds endless variations of the 305 ballads that Harvard folklorist Francis James Child collected in his magisterial *The English and Scottish Popular Ballads* (five volumes, 1882–1898).[8]

The ballad tradition crossed the Atlantic with ease. Although a number of items of material culture remained behind, immigrants "packed" the songs with every trunk. In the process many of the tunes became modified into songs of the American West.

There were, of course, changes along the way. British supernatural ballads never made much headway in America, and those that spoke of chivalry often took on a new guise as well. In many cases the American version compressed or skeletonized the original British ballad. Often the original (harsh) message became modified along the way.[9] The cowboy's lament ("The Streets of Laredo"), not exactly a happy tune in its American version, nevertheless bypassed the original lyrics that told of a young man's dying of syphilis, all of which dated from a Scotch-Irish song, "The Unfortunate Rake." No cowboy, when one thinks about it, was likely to be buried to the sound of drums and fifes (or pipes). Another ballad, "The Buffalo Skinners," was originally a British love song, "Caledonia" (an ancient name for Scotland). In the United States "The Twa Brothers," Sir John and Sir Willie, became simply "Two Little Boys." The last line of the Nebraska version reads:

> O, what shall I tell your true love, John,
> If she inquires for you?
> O, Tell her I'm dead and lying in my grave,
> Way out in Idaho.[10]

As folklorists have observed, the American ballads maintained their link to the British originals largely by retaining the *emotional* core of the original, rather than the exact words.[11]

Like their British counterparts, American western ballads dealt with themes that today would probably grace the pages of the tabloids: crime, murder, lost love, lust, family feuds, outlaws, and so on. Consider the ballad of Jesse James, which became the most popular song of its day when it was first written around 1882. The lyrics focus on the same betrayal theme that one met in "Hobbie Noble." Similarly, the most famous line from the chorus—"the dirty little coward / who shot Mr. Howard / has laid poor Jesse in his grave"—has damned assassin Robert Ford, like the Duke of Cumberland, down to the nth generation. The fat abbots whom Robin Hood so harassed bear a strange resemblance to the wealthy bankers robbed by Jesse James, Sam Bass, and even Bonnie and Clyde.[12]

Often the romantic aura that linked Scotland with the American frontier took on tangible form. During the early and mid-nineteenth century a number of Scots travelers actively sought individual salvation in the American West. Charles Augustus Murray, William Drummond Stewart, and the bevy of Scottish gamesters are three of these.

Charles Augustus Murray, second son of the fifth Earl of Dunmore, was born on November 22, 1806. He grew to maturity in Glen Forest in western Scotland. Raised a Roman Catholic and a Whig and "not being under the necessity of working for livelihood," Murray stood as a candidate for parliament twice: for Falkirk Burghs in 1832 and for Marylebone the following year. Both times he suffered defeat. Then, as his biographer phrased it, "Murray sought consolation in travel."[13]

After a harrowing sea journey to the States he landed in New York, where he soon booked passage across the Alleghenies to sail down the Ohio River. Stopping off at Henry Clay's home in Lexington, Kentucky, he met a young German, Mr. Verrunft (termed "V-" in the narrative), who agreed to accompany him to St. Louis. Arriving there in the summer of 1835, Murray assumed the pose of British dandy, flaunting his English rifle, hunting knife, brace of pistols, and Scots valet. At times he wore a kilt.

Since Murray's understanding of Indians derived solely from his reading of James Fenimore Cooper's romantic vision of Indian life, he expressed dismay at the conditions of the tribes he met on the way to St. Louis. Then a chance meeting in Fort Leavenworth, Kansas, with a band of about 150 Pawnees who were relatively untouched by white civilization changed his perspective. Murray found himself captivated by these "genuine children of the wilderness" and vowed to go live with them.[14]

Against all advice, he and V- embarked on this "strange and wild experiment" with enthusiasm, following the Pawnees (with their permission) back to their Southern Plains hunting grounds, a region he described as not unlike the Downs in southern England. Housed with a chief Sa-ni-tsa-rish, whom he came to admire as a "Natural Gentleman," Murray shared the trials and successes of Pawnee life on the Plains for more than a month.

Over this period Murray's romantic view of American Indians underwent a decided shift. Because of the "dog chorus, at midnight, in the Pawnee village," he had trouble sleeping.[15] He found himself dismayed at Pawnee hygiene and especially missed his baths and toothbrush. Pawnee sharp trading practices annoyed him as well, for he found them hard bargainers. Eventually he was forced to trade away his "medicine tube"—a pocket telescope that he had used for hunting in Scotland. But he steadfastly refused to part with his "long blanket"—the family plaid—because it reminded him of home.[16]

Only the hunting of the Great Plains buffalo came up to his expectations. Although he found the Pawnees "very much inferior to our highland deer-stalkers in taking advantage of wind and position of ground," he considered them superior "in following a foot track."[17] After one kill, he gorged himself on fresh liver, "more certainly like a wolf or Indian than a Christian man." One hunting scene reminded him of the glorious twelfth of August in the Highlands, with its "thousands of citizens, cockneys and sportsmen, who were on this day killing (or frightening) their fifty brace on the brown hills of Old Scotland."[18]

Eventually, he, V-, his Scots valet (whom he constantly complained about), and the rest of his party decided to return to the civilization of Fort Leavenworth. Although he once considered the fort the "Ultima Thule," he now eagerly sought it out for its fresh sheets, cooked food, and soap. His earlier romanticism did not return until he had the fort clearly in view. Only then did he find himself momentarily swept by emotion for the life he had left behind: "The buffalo-herds, the howl of wolves, the circles of naked savages round their fires, their yells, their dances, and their songs."[19] On a more practical matter, Murray also invested in a twenty-thousand-acre estate in frontier Wisconsin, on which he made a tidy profit.

After a decade away from the Great Plains, Murray recreated his adventures in his memoirs and in a three-volume novel entitled *The Prairie Bird* (1844) that showed its literary debt to Cooper and Scott.[20] In *The Prairie-Bird,* Murray sketched a romance of two Loyalist families who had migrated to the American frontier. The daughter of one was carried off as a child and eventually adopted by a Delaware chieftain. Another son, Reginald Brandon (modeled on Murray himself) eventually fell in love with "Prairie-Bird." After many harrowing adventures and endless description, the pair became reunited. The reviewer in the London *Times* noted that women readers should enjoy the romance and men the adventure found throughout *The Prairie-Bird*.[21]

The reviewer also assured readers that Murray's residence among the Pawnee allowed him to present a "faithful picture of Indian life." This, however, proved far from the mark. As he ground out a chapter a week from his London town house, Murray confessed that his head remained "full of western legends and tales" regarding Daniel Boone; he also fretted over his Indian character Wingerund's "picturesque drapery."[22] In truth *The Prairie Bird* owed far more to the romance of Scott and Cooper than to Murray's brief sojourn on the Southern Plains.

The romantic journeys of William Drummond Stewart to the West are even more famous. Born December 26, 1795, at Murthly in Perthshire above the River Tay, Stewart was a second son who saw no chance of inheriting his father's title, Lord of Grand Tully and Baronet of Murthly, or the family thirty-two-thousand-acre estate. Thus, in 1812 his father bought him a cornetcy in the military, and he served under the Duke of Wellington at the Battle of Waterloo. In 1821 he retired on half pay and spent about a decade of desultory wandering and hunting in Turkey, Russia, and the Far East.

After these meanderings he met a strikingly beautiful laundress, Christina Stewart (no relation), who soon became pregnant. To his family's dismay, Stewart married her. As they had little in common socially, Stewart arranged a flat for her and their son, George, in Edinburgh. Afterwards he sought further solace on the American frontier.[23]

Murthly Castle in Perthshire. Ancestral home of William Drummond Stewart and in the 1830s–1840s the locus of the first Buffalo Park in the British Isles. (Photo by the author.)

After arriving in New York in May 1832, Stewart made his way to St. Louis. Drawing on his Scots' connections with trader Robert Campbell, he merged easily into fur-trade life. In 1833 he worked his way aboard a fur-trade party heading for that year's Rendezvous.

The Rendezvous were annual gatherings of the Rocky Mountain fur trappers that served as trading opportunities for the trappers and their suppliers. The two- to three-week debauch also exposed fur-trade life at its rawest. A sexual libertine "with strong bodily appetites which he freely indulged," Stewart thoroughly enjoyed this introduction to frontier society.[24] Teaming with a Cree-French *Métis*, Antoine Clement, Stewart lived in the West off and on for the next nine years. Although he inherited the family title in 1838 when his older brother died, he returned to the West in 1843 for one last trip to the Rendezvous, this time in the Wind River Mountains. Ironically, this gathering would also be the trappers' last, since the fur trade had long passed its apogee.²⁵

In attending all these Rendezvous Stewart met with many of the central figures of the frontier West. He knew famed explorer William Clark. He became good friends with trappers William Sublette, Bill Williams, and Jim Bridger, and he shook hands with many an American Indian leader. On the 1836 trip he dined with missionaries Marcus and Narcissa Whitman, where, it is said, he praised her freshly baked bread. In passing, Stewart remarked that the arrival of Euro-American women meant the end of the Wild West. When Narcissa asked him if he mourned its passing, he replied in the affirmative and quoted a verse from William Cullen Bryant:

> ... These
> The unshorn fields, boundless and beautiful
> For which the speech of England has no name
> The Prairies ... ²⁶

Fortunately for historians, in 1837 Stewart happened to admire the watercolor sketches of Alfred Jacob Miller, a young Baltimore artist who had recently moved to New Orleans. Stewart commissioned Miller to accompany him on the thirteenth Rendezvous. Consequently, Miller became the first American artist to paint the Rocky Mountain scenery.

All through the journey, Miller's trail duties were kept to a minimum in order to give him time to sketch. He worked at a steady pace and brought back more than 280 drawings, accompanied by extensive notes, to New Orleans. In his studio he turned the sketches into full-fledged pictures. Miller knew his employer well, featuring Stewart prominently in many a painting. Easily recognizable in the artworks by his white horse, buckskin coat, hooked nose, and black hat, Stewart is painted in a caravan, watching Indian boys play, leaning by a tree, having a meal, and so on.²⁷

Miller's notes, however, show that he genuinely respected the eccentric Scot. He wrote that Stewart was "perfectly competent to take charge" and always referred to him as "Captain." In later correspondence Miller confessed that their joint "wanderings in the west" proved a fond memory and said that whenever he related them to others, everyone expressed envy at his adventures.[28]

Even when on caravan, Stewart lived as a Scottish gentleman. He brought along special cheeses, wine, brandy, and porter; on one occasion his trail cook prepared an elaborate meal of gumbo, *boudon*, tongue, and meatballs.[29] At a breakfast in St. Louis Stewart introduced a variety of rare foods that all the trappers wolfed down. "This breakfast must have cost him upwards of sixty dollars," marveled Miller, "but it furnished him with a capital after-dinner story for Europe, and he considered *that* worth all the money."[30] At the 1837 Rendezvous Stewart gave Jim Bridger a set of medieval armour, and Miller dutifully sketched the old trapper trying to maneuver his horse under its weight.

Miller's paintings of the Mountain West were later exhibited in New York before being sent on to Murthly Castle. In 1840 Miller traveled to Murthly to depict several other scenes. It was there that he painted his famed *Attack by Crow Indians*, which still graces the entrance at Murthly. This image, based on an actual incident, shows Stewart threatened by hostile Crow warriors. Forewarned that the Crows would not attack unless he struck first, Stewart remained calm in the midst of their harassment, thus saving his party through sheer force of personality. Miller also painted a number of religious scenes for him, since Stewart, a lapsed Catholic, had returned to the church in St. Louis after recovering from a severe illness.[31]

Controversial throughout his life, Stewart remained even more so at his death on May 1, 1871. He willed all his property to an American, Frank Nichols, whom he had adopted. (Stewart's own son, George, had died two years earlier, so he was without heirs.) Scots law prohibited leaving the castle or lands to an adopted heir, but "Frank the Yank" legally proceeded to strip Murthly Castle of virtually everything that could be moved, including the tapestries from the walls. He shipped this bounty back to Houston, Texas, where the floods of the early century destroyed most of the collection. Fortunately, Miller's *Attack by Crow Indians* was securely fastened to the wall and remained at Murthly.

Stewart's permanent return to Scotland in 1844 did not end his relationship with the American West. Thanks to his friendship with William Sublette and Robert Campbell, Stewart arranged the first systematic exchange of plants since David Douglas and the earliest exchange of birds and animals. In 1843 Sublette sent him burr oaks, acorns, choke cherry seeds, buffalo berries, sugar maples, mountain currants, may apples, and birch poplars.[32] Campbell hoped that his package of buffalo berries, currants, and gooseberries would remind Stewart of "the mountain life."[33] He had tried to obtain other mountain seeds for Stewart, but to no avail. "You are aware how difficult it is to get mountain men to think of such things," he complained.[34]

Sublette also sent over a number of livestock: antelope, mountain goats, bears, buffalo, and "white swans" (perhaps whooping cranes).[35] Needless to say, this was not an easy task. The antelope were frequently injured in the loading process, and the buffalo often died in transit. "If there should be any animals, birds, [illegible] that you would wish," Sublette wrote in 1844, "let me know and they shall be attended to this spring."[36] In return Sublette asked Stewart for Scottish hogs and Scottish cattle for his own animal park in St. Louis, and at least one shipment arrived safely.

Thus, Murthly Castle and grounds in Perthshire became the first "museum" of western culture outside of America. The bear, deer, and birds seem not to have survived, but several bison did successfully cross the Atlantic to Murthly. Stewart shared his buffalo with his neighbor, Lord Breadalbane, and the animals

Entrance to Murthly Castle in Perthshire. Some of the trees, planted by William Drummond Stewart, were brought back from his visits to the American West. (Photo by the author.)

did well there, too. In 1840 Queen Victoria remarked about the "strange humpbacked creatures from America."[37] *Punch* magazine featured cartoons of the buffalo, and a German traveler noted in 1844 that it had become quite fashionable for British gentry to prominently display them on their estates.[38] The hill behind Murthly where Stewart grazed his beasts is still called "Buffalo Park." Similarly, the giant yew trees, western hemlock, Douglas firs, and Sequoia that today line the Murthly Castle entrance date from Stewart's plantings.[39]

Unlike his fellow Perthshire adventurer Charles Augustus Murray, William Drummond Stewart never wrote a travel account of his years in America. But following the appearance of Murray's *The Prairie Bird* (1844), Stewart did pen two novels based on his experiences, *Altowan* (1846) and *Edward Warren* (1854). Both appeared anonymously, since it was deemed too commercial for a gentleman to write fiction for popular consumption.

Altowan features Watoe, a *berdash* (the book also uses the term *hermaphrodite*), as a central figure. Watoe is heroic in his devotion to the main character, Altowan. Decidedly undistinguished in plot, character, or description of the West, this quasi-autobiographical account speaks occasionally of the "true nobility" that one finds in the American frontiersman and "those wilds, where liberty itself, is still more free."[40]

Edward Warren is only marginally better. Stewart termed this work "a fictitious Auto-biography," and indeed, it seems to adhere to what we know of Stewart's life through other sources. Still, like the other novel, it is eminently forgetable. In the hands of Cooper and Scott the reader was introduced to such memorable characters as Ivanhoe, Rob Roy, Leatherstocking, and Uncas. In the hands of Murray and Stewart one wades through a thousand pages of agonizing prose. *The Prairie Bird* and *Altowan* are totally obscure, and *Edward Warren* is viewed strictly as a period piece.[41] But if Stewart's prose has been justly forgotten, Stewart the adventurer has not. Bernard DeVoto made him the central character of his classic account of exploration, *Across the Wide Missouri*.[42]

In addition to Murray and Scott, the third group of Scottish romantics to visit the American West were the big-game hunters. From the 1830s through the 1880s these gentlemen viewed the Canadian/American Rocky Mountains and the Great Plains as their private hunting preserve.

Although an international phenomenon, the meteoric rise of the "gentleman hunter" had strong links to Scottish history. From c. 1850 forward, the profits from sheep raising on the Scottish estates had begun to decline. Consequently, the lairds replaced the sheep with deer, just as a generation or two earlier they had replaced the crofters with sheep. This transfer was more easily accomplished, however. The lairds simply prohibited hunting on their land for several years, a pause that permitted the red deer and roebucks, neither of which had any natural enemies, to multiply by natural increase. Afterwards, they opened their estates to hunters and fishermen from England or the Continent.

The building of nineteenth-century railroads had made North Britain far more accessible, and the estates did a lively business. The arrival of the double-barreled shotgun made hunting much easier for amateurs as well. The lairds' country houses employed a number of people in this enterprise. Although the wages were seldom high, the outdoor life was not without its pleasures. The gillie emerged as a crucial figure in the economy of Scotland. He denounced the sheep farmers' burning of the heather as harmful to grouse, and he wanted no high vegetation to disrupt the aim of the deer hunter. With good management of the coverts, a laird could reap several thousand game birds and animals from an estate.[43] If a trout stream or salmon river ran through an estate as well, the laird was doubly blessed. "Short of improbable convulsions of nature," wrote one observer in 1875, "Scotland must remain the paradise of the gentlemen who swear by the rifle and the breech loader, to say nothing of the rod."[44]

The rise of the Scottish estates as a hunter's paradise had direct links with the complex social hierarchy of British society. The onset of industrialism had produced a number of nouveau riche. Aping the manners and mores of the aristocracy, these families avidly sought out the blood sports—especially deer stalking—as an indication of high social status. The Scottish tenants, incidentally, did not earn the right to kill game on their own land until 1880.

The ultimate embodiment of this hunting ethos came with the Prince of Wales, later Edward VII. Too fat for golf and too impatient for salmon or trout fishing, Edward relished fox hunting and deer stalking. Consequently, he ordered his estate at Sandringham stocked with partridge, pheasant, wild duck, woodcock, grouse, hares, and rabbits. He also supervised the turning of Balmoral's forty thousand acres into a deer forest and grouse moor. The king was never happier than when he was engaged in hunting. During one carriage drive at Balmoral in 1902, he shot six stags. In addition he and his hunting companions often sought and achieved various "record" kills. On an excursion in 1899 he and six others claimed to have bagged 22,996 partridge, 1,912 pheasants, and 11,396 hares. During three days in 1909 he and his friends shot 2,555 pheasants. In four days in 1906 they brought down 3,534 pheasants and 466 wild duck, plus an unknown number of partridges and rabbits. Other hunters imitated this pattern as best they could. "Dropped over a hundred duck," one sportsman noted in 1896; "lost them in slush and snow three feet deep."[45]

Royal efforts at hunting doubtlessly encouraged a number of wealthy Scots to try their hand in the American West. In 1876 George Wray ventured into the Rocky Mountains west of Denver on a successful elk hunt. Whenever he remained in camp, he read from an inexpensive edition of Shakespeare that he had purchased in a Denver drugstore. His diary reflects the thrill of the Colorado excursion.[46]

A decade later, Scots hunter J. P. Maud went on a similar two-month venture in the American Rockies. Already a veteran of Wyoming and Montana hunts, he concentrated his efforts in the Idaho Rockies. There he found, as he confessed, an *"embarrass des richesses."* His "bag" consisted of bear, three bull-moose, four wapiti [elk] bulls, two black-tail bucks, sundry antelope, lynxes, beaver, and wolverine; his hunting partner caught 185 trout, all over a pound, in a single day. The Rocky Mountains, he noted enthusiastically, were "the spot *par excellence* for sport."[47]

The buffalo on the Great Plains proved especially attractive. On one occasion a Scots hunter named McLeod was trapped on the prairie for four days by passing buffalo, much to his delight. Another hunter, R. Tait Murray of Edinburgh, visited the western section of Kansas in the mid-1870s and left an exceptionally vivid description of his adventures. Finding the Plains "literally alive with Buffalo," he shot his first animal with zest. Yet he discovered that this kill "was greeted with no congratulation—I had, it appears, broken every rule of buffalo hunting." Indeed he had. Murray had placed himself between his party and the herd, making it impossible for anyone else to fire; he had nearly stampeded the herd; and had he not shot a cow buffalo, he might well have been trampled by a wounded bull. Although Murray expressed sympathy for his "noble prey," he concluded that no sport combined more elements of excitement than bison hunting on the Great Plains.[48]

The terrain of the Great Plains and Rocky Mountains shared many romantic attributes with Scotland's Highlands and Islands. By c. 1850 the books by Scott, the popularized visits of Queen Victoria, and the memories of Scots "over the water" had transformed the more inaccessible parts of Scotland into a romantic refuge. In fact it was not long before the Highlands came to represent to Americans all of Scotland.

But the same was true in reverse. At some time during the nineteenth century, the Trans-Mississippi West came to represent America, only more so. Although there were hundreds of American Indian tribes, sporting many distinctive styles of dress, by c. 1880 the Plains Indian, in buckskin shirt and feathered bonnet, had come to represent "the Indian." In 1883 James, Lord Bryce observed that "The West is the most American part of America . . . the part where those features which distinguish America from Europe come out in the strongest relief."[49]

Thanks to the work of numerous artists and photographers, both regions took on an image larger than life. With Waverley novels in hand, tourists sought out the Trossachs and other locations Scott so dramatically depicted. Shortly after midcentury, the Thomas Cook travel agency was providing about five thousand holidays annually north of the Tweed. "The summer tide of tourists has receded from our straths and glens townwards to the last drop," one reporter observed with relief in 1860.[50] As modern art historians have shown, Victorian tourists sought inspiration from their often rugged journeys into the Highlands. Emotions played a major part in their quest, and the three types of landscapes—beautiful, picturesque, and sublime—all called forth different varieties of reaction.

Quite naturally, landscape artists were drawn to these dramatic locations. Borrowing from the prevailing romantic tradition, British artists captured Highland scenery on canvas in an attempt to help preserve Scotland's independent identity. By midcentury Alexander Nasmyth and Horatio McCulloch had emerged as the foremost Scottish painters of landscape. Their colleague, Joseph Farquharson, constructed a mobile studio that he hauled into the glens in order to paint winter scenes. Artist Peter Graham hired a boat to take him near Cape Wrath so that he could paint seabirds and cliffs in a storm. Encouraged by Queen Victoria, English painter Sir Edwin Landseer depicted startling scenes of Highland wildlife and landscape.[51] By the late-nineteenth century, Scottish painter William McTaggart was acknowledged as the greatest landscape painter in all the United Kingdom.[52]

On the other side of the Atlantic, artists were engaged in an identical process. During midcentury, the Great Plains and, especially, the Rocky Mountains had become the ultimate source for romantic inspiration for American-born and European artists.[53] From A. J. Miller to Karl Bodmer, from Charles Russell to James D. Hutton, romantic artists found their ultimate vision in the West.

The best example is probably Albert Bierstadt. The German-born artist's work almost literally invented the Rocky Mountains for many a viewer. Many of his canvases were gigantic, and almost all were heroic. Mark Twain once remarked that his *Dome of Yosemite* (1867) belonged more to Kingdom Come than to the Yosemite Valley.[54]

The life of landscape artist William Keith linked the two worlds. Born in Aberdeenshire in 1839, young William arrived at age twelve in New York with his mother. After an apprenticeship as an engraver, he worked briefly for *Harper's Weekly*. *Harper's* sent him on assignment to California in 1858, and he decided to move there permanently the next year. Locating in San Francisco, he worked as an engineer and gradually moved into landscape painting. Interspersing his time there with study in Germany and France, he made California his permanent home. By the time of his death he was termed "Artist Laureate of the State of California."[55]

Early in his career, Keith met naturalist John Muir, and "Willie and Johnnie" hit it off from the start. In fact Muir guided Keith to some of the most spectacular vistas of the Sierra Nevada, which he later recorded. In 1867 they made an extensive trip from Lake Tahoe to Vancouver, B.C., in preparation for an illustrated publication on western nature that eventually came to naught. "There's naebody like a Scotchman to see beauty," Muir remarked.[56]

Keith's canvases ranged widely, both in subject matter and in size. During his early years as a landscape artist he produced extensive works in the manner of Bierstadt, for "grand scenery" was much in demand. As he confessed in an 1888 lecture at the University of California, "When I first began to paint, I could not get mountains high enough nor sunsets gorgeous enough for my brush and colors."[57] Keith's *California Alps* measured six feet by ten feet. Other paintings included *Seal Rocks, A View Along the Golden Gate, The Crown of the Sierras;* and *The Big Canyon of the Tuolumne.* Later in his career he turned to religious scenes and even more fanciful renditions of the natural world. His productivity may be seen in the estimated two thousand paintings and sketches that burned when his studio caught fire in the San Francisco earthquake of 1906. Hundreds survived, however, and twenty-nine were hung in San Francisco's Pan American Exposition. Although not as well known as Bierstadt, William Keith possessed a vision that reflected a trans-Atlantic romantic mood regarding landscape. One contemporary credited him with having "poetry in his soul."[58]

The wildness of the Scottish and the western American landscapes drew an equal number of photographers. As was the case for the landscape artists, the photographers' quest had a commercial aspect. The hordes of tourists provided a ready market for photographic images that would remind them of their visits. Landscape photographs proved ideal for this purpose, and many a Scottish photographer devoted his time to such endeavors. Francis Frith in Reigate, James Valentine in Dundee, and George Washington Wilson in Aberdeen all employed teams of lensmen to travel throughout the region photographing buildings and natural scenery.[59]

The images of northeast Scotland's most famous photographer, George Washington Wilson, reflect this quest. Wilson journeyed to Orkney, Shetland, the Outer Hebrides, and the remote shires of Caithness and Sutherland for a series of views that seemed to embody Sir Walter Scott's romanticism in visual terms. The most striking of these views, such as Fingal's Cave, he sold as postcards. His views of mist-shrouded Glencoe, sunsets, seasides, snow-covered straths, "sea stacks"—sandstone pillars that arise abruptly from the ocean—and the numerous Highland mountains of his "Ben" series all sold well.[60] By the 1870s his photos were known throughout the British Isles. Not only did his photographs provide thousands of images for the tourist industry, but they were used to illustrate Burns's poetry, Scott's *Lady of the Lake,* and Queen Victoria's *Leaves from the Journal of*

Our Life in the Highlands. Some of his images are today recognized as the classic features of Scottish scenery. One commentator credited Wilson with doing "more for opening up Scotland generally than Sir Walter Scott has done for the Trossachs."[61] In all, Wilson left a legacy of c. forty thousand images.

A number of photographers played similar romantic roles in the American West. Timothy O'Sullivan, C. Jack Hillers, and Andrew J. Russell all traveled west either with the railroad or with the early government survey parties. San Francisco photographer Carleton E. Watkins and his English pupil Eadweard Muybridge made stunning sixteen-inch by twenty-one-inch views of Yosemite Valley that delighted the Paris Universal Exhibition in 1867. An unnamed Highland laird purchased twenty-six Watkins prints as a souvenir of his c. 1870s visit to California and displayed them in his great house in a majestic solid-oak screen that now resides in the California Museum of Photography in Riverside. Glasgow-born John James Riley also produced thousands of stereo views of California. A. C. Vroman in New Mexico and L. A. Huffman in Montana made the same type of heroic images for their regions.

The most famous photographer of the American West was probably William Henry Jackson. Born in rural Vermont, Jackson spent most of his one-hundred-year life-span involved with photography. Beginning in 1868, from an Omaha base, Jackson took the first photographs of Mesa Verde and Yellowstone Park and some of the earliest scenes of the Grand Canyon and the Colorado mountains. Like Wilson, he also established a popular "image factory," Jackson Photograph and Publishing Company, to share his discoveries. Many of his forty-thousand images have also become classics.[62] What Wilson did for Scotland, Jackson did for the West: each captured majestic scenery in romantic photographic images that have lost little power a century later.

If William Keith linked the Scottish and American romantic art worlds, so did Alexander C. Gardner link the two worlds of photography. Born in 1821 in Paisley, Scotland, Gardner grew up in a middle-class household. Apprenticed to a jeweler, he mastered that craft and then moved to Glasgow, where he served as a reporter for the *Sentinel*. Along the way he learned photography as well.

Like many of his generation, Gardner became involved in utopian reform movements aimed at bettering the condition of working men. In 1849 he visited the Scots colony of Clydesdale, Iowa, near the town of McGregor, on the Mississippi River. This settlement was organized around the principles of Robert Owen. Gardner returned to Glasgow for several years, but in 1856 he planned to move permanently to Iowa. When he and his family arrived in North America, however, they learned that the community of Clydesdale had collapsed because of illness. Gardner consequently moved to New York City, where he worked for famed photographer Mathew Brady. Recognizing Gardner's skills in photography and bookkeeping, Brady appointed him manager of his Washington, D.C., photographic studios, where he served until 1863.[63] He photographed many Civil War scenes for Brady's Studio. In 1862 Gardner quarreled with Brady over the question who held the copyright for battlefield images— the photographer or the Brady Studio. The next year he established his own studio in Washington, just around the corner from Brady's. Many of Brady's best image makers, including Timothy O'Sullivan, joined Gardner, and each photographer received individual photo credits when Gardner published his classic *Photographic Sketchbook of the War* (1866). His later work included photos of important Indian delegations to Washington, key Reconstruction politicians, a "Rogues' Gallery" of Washington criminals, and a set of illustrations for a special 1868 edition of Burns's *Tam O'Shanter*.

In 1867 Gardner took his camera equipment to the prairie states when he assumed the position of official photographer for the Union Pacific Railroad as it laid track, at about a mile a day, to meet the Central Pacific line coming from California. Although he sometimes photographed railroad scenes in the eight-by-ten or eleven-by-fourteen format, he more often used the relatively new stereoscopic camera. Eventually, in 1867, he published *Across the Continent on the Union Pacific Railway, Eastern Division*. Gardner's western images included shots of forts, American Indians, rail-line construction, and geological features from Kansas to Texas to California. One art critic has suggested that the real romantic hero of his western photographic venture was the railroad itself.[64]

Although the novels, ballads, visitors, artists, and photographers helped link romantic Scotland with the romantic West, they paled beside the realm of fin-de-siècle popular culture. One sees this most clearly in the widespread appeal of stage performers Harry Lauder and Buffalo Bill. Each, in his own way, was a peddler of romance to his own country and to interested parties abroad.

Born on August 4, 1870, in Portobello, near Edinburgh, Harry Lauder began work in the flax mills of Arbroath at an early age. Later he worked in the mines, supplementing his meager wages by singing at local gatherings. Gifted with a magnificent voice, he reached the West End stage in 1900. Soon he became the talk of London. Lauder's skills may be seen in the observation by drama critic James Agate that the only stage personalities who could make themselves felt *through* the curtain before it went up were Sarah Bernhardt and Harry Lauder.[65]

Turn-of-the-century vaudeville was probably the most popular form of entertainment. From 1907 forward Lauder made at least one American tour almost every year for twenty years—about forty in all. His agent Will Morris discovered that Lauder could fill houses from New York to San Francisco, from Eugene to Salt Lake, and from Denver to Butte. As Lauder himself admitted, "the exiled Scots in the States had more to do with my success than many people imagined."⁶⁶ Indeed, the Scots of many a western community paid handsomely to see Harry Lauder perform his magic. "Wherever he stays," a reporter noted in 1909, "Scotsmen rally 'round him, and the rest follow."⁶⁷

At five feet three inches and 170 pounds, Lauder boasted a stage walking stick, kilt, tam-o'-shanter, Balmoral bonnets, tartan ties, and all manner of Scottish costume. He "worked" his audience with a combination of song and Scots patter, always in a dialect that proved less regional than "Scotland in general." Lauder drew on both folk ballads and his own compositions to perform "She's Ma Daisy," "Stop Yer Ticklin', Jock," "I Love a Lassie," "The Saftie of the Family," and "Roamin' in the Gloamin'." Virtually alone among vaudeville performers of his day, he used no double entendres or risque comments.

During his 1915 tour Lauder crossed the United States preaching the gospel of preparedness for war. In one San Francisco gathering, he spoke to a crowd of twenty thousand. Much to his agent's dismay, he took his message to German-dominated American cities as well, meeting both Theodore Roosevelt and Woodrow Wilson along the way. Lauder's preparedness crusade took on poignant reality when his only son died in France. He continued his war work by entertaining the troops and by establishing a fund to aid Scots war veterans afterward.⁶⁸ His popularity never diminished, and when he visited America during the 1920s, he dined with Presidents Warren Harding and Calvin Coolidge.

After World War I, Scots intellectuals began to attack Harry Lauder and his "Stage Scot." They scorned his affected accent, his mannerisms, and his humor, complaining that Lauder had "made the Scot a figure of fun throughout the world."⁶⁹ But such carping missed the genuine appeal that Lauder had for thousands of émigrés across the globe. Compared with Robert Burns for his sincere humanity, Lauder could arouse the deepest emotions of his audiences.[70] All through his performances he appealed to Scottish "nationalism" in a subtle, affirming manner. The Doig family of Montana fondly recalled their Scots-born grandmother's loyalty to Lauder. On certain weekdays she would nap after dinner with an alarm clock by her bedside so that she might tune in Harry Lauder on the radio (presumably from a Canadian station). Lauder must have had people like her in mind when he told an Oregon *Journal* reporter in 1920 that "the Scotch are hardy and as hard as the granite of our Scotch hills."[71]

Harry Lauder's humility also shone through in his ability to poke fun at himself: "I gave all his stage hands a postcard of myself with: 'Sae here's my picture, laddies, and when I come again next year I'll sign them for you.'"[72] In Butte he willingly descended a mine shaft; at other times he boasted that he could earn his living mining today. The extent of his appeal can be seen in the inclusion of his voice in a "Great Voices of the Twentieth Century" record series.

Scottish people may have formed the core of his audiences, but Lauder did not become the most popular vaudevillian of his day solely by appealing to them. They were too few in number to sustain him for his more than forty visits to America. Instead, Harry Lauder utilized his Scots theme to strike universal, romantic chords about Scotland that reached out to touch all Americans. His renditions of "I Love a Lassie" and "Roamin' in the Gloamin'" could be understood by everyone.[73] From a base in Highland mythology, Harry Lauder approached the universal. As historian Harold Orel put it, Lauder "may have been responsible for making permanent in the popular imagination more images of Scottish life than the work of an entire tourist board."[74]

Similar claims could be made for Lauder's American contemporary, Buffalo Bill. William F. Cody was born in Scott County, Iowa, in 1846. He spent his youth on the plains as herder, stage

Sir Harry Lauder carried the myth of Scotland to England and to western North America. (Sketch by Bateman from the National Galleries of Scotland, Edinburgh.)

driver, army scout, and pony-express rider. But he made his name working as a buffalo hunter for the Kansas Pacific Railroad. His task was to supply meat for the crews constructing the KP line. During one year he killed 4,280 buffalo, whereupon he earned his sobriquet.

Blessed with good looks, a shrewd business head, and a sense of showmanship, Cody began performing locally on a small scale. Two of his hunting clients, New York *Herald* editor James Gorman Bennett and author E. Z. C. Judson (who wrote as Ned Buntline) suggested that he come east in 1872 for a New York play, *Buffalo Bill, King of the Bordermen.*

This move launched his career. Soon Buffalo Bill was publicized as the personification of western virtues—honesty, integrity, and marksmanship—although in real life he proved a hard drinking womanizer. His Wild West show, complete with Deadwood Stage, horsemen of every stripe imaginable, Annie Oakley, and authentic American Indian performers (including the famed Sitting Bull), became the most popular manifestation of western life for the fin-de-siècle era. A clever showman, Buffalo Bill delighted in portraying "The Western Experience." As part of his show, Bill, with the spotlight on him, would turn to his horsemen and say: "Wild West, are you ready? Go!" The Buffalo Bill show became the romance of the West personified.[75] During his lifetime authors penned about 1,700 books (mostly dime novels) to glorify his exploits. It is no exaggeration to say that Buffalo Bill's was the most widely recognized American name of his generation.

A number of modern western scholars have piled scorn upon Bill's performances. These critics argue that Cody contributed to negative stereotypes and clichés about American Indians and did not treat his Indian performers fairly.[76] Oklahoma historian L. G. Moses, however, strongly disagrees. The show Indians themselves always spoke well of Bill, and star Native performers, such as Sitting Bull and Red Cloud, often had equal billing on the posters with Cody.[77] In addition, no U.S.–government officials ever found reason to prohibit Bill from employing any Native performers, although they often tried to do so.

Moreover, Moses maintains, Bill saw his role as that of a cultural broker. His Indians performed Native dances, staged races, and demonstrated great feats of horsemanship. As Cody's manager "Arizona John" Burke noted, it was Bill's "honorable ambition" to instruct and educate the public "to respect the denizens of the West by giving them a true, untinselled representation of a page of frontier history that is fast passing away." As Cody himself said to an Aberdeen reporter, when the show Indians returned home to their reservations they told their tribes about their adventures, and that would "bring the white and red races closer together."[78] Cody's "Myth of the West" had a unifying dimension to it: it would help heal longstanding Native-White antagonisms.

During the last decades of the nineteenth century William F. Cody brought his Buffalo Bill's Wild West show to the British Isles. In 1887 he gave a command performance for Queen Victoria, much to her delight. During this visit his advertising posters introduced a phrase that soon passed into common parlance in Britain. The Wild West show would perform twice a day, "rain or shine." Like his mother, the Prince of Wales also admired Cody's shows. As Harry Lauder's friendship with American presidents aided his career, so, too, did the approval of the British royal family insure that millions would come to see Buffalo Bill.[79] Outside Germany, no nation welcomed Bill more heartily than did Britain.

The phrase "rain or shine" was still in use when Cody brought his show to Scotland, as he did twice, in 1891 and in 1904. Each time, the Scots received him with great enthusiasm. A persistent legend maintains that several Indian performers were so charmed by the area that they married local women and remained in the northeast of Scotland, where their descendants still live today.

On July 20, 1904, Bill took his show to Scotland in what was advertised as "positively the last visit to Great Britain." The week in Glasgow played to overflow crowds on a daily basis.[80] From August 8 to 13 about 140,000 watched the Edinburgh performance at Gorgie Road near Gorgie Station. When Bill's troupe marched down the west end of Princes Street, one reporter noted that Edinburgh "had never witnessed a stranger cavalcade."[81]

Beginning in Montrose on August 15, Cody took the show to Aberdeen for three days and then spent one day each in nearby Peterhead, Fraserburgh, and Huntly. Moving this entourage proved no small task, and Bill needed almost three-quarters of

Wild West show program, 1886. William F. Cody (Buffalo Bill) and the Wild West carried the myth of the American West to Scotland and around the world. (Denver Public Library, Western History Department. Photo F29537.)

a mile of railroad cars, nineteen coaches of the first train providing living quarters for the staff of more than eight hundred people. The remaining carriages housed the gigantic canvas tent, the various stagecoaches and props, and about five hundred horses. The food for the animals and staff, mostly drawn from local suppliers, demanded the highest organizational skill. Refrigerated cars filled with eggs, milk, and meat were regularly replenished, and the chefs kept an "emergency" wagon filled with one day's supply of tinned foods, soups, and milk in case the supply line ever broke down.

The performances at Aberdeen's Central Park, covered in detail by the local press, revealed this intricate organization. The keynote to the 2:00 P.M. and 8:00 P.M. renditions lay in their "incessant movement." No sooner did one act leave the arena than another entered from the opposite side. Aberdeen audiences thrilled to a reenactment of Custer's last stand, a holdup of the famed Deadwood stagecoach, a trick-riding exhibition by several American women, a pony-express demonstration, a group of riders performing the Virginia reel on horseback, trick shooting, wild-horse roping, bucking broncos, an Indian raid on an emigrant train, and a series of tableaux and war dances by the more than one hundred American Indian performers.

By 1904 Cody had modernized and internationalized his troupe. He displayed the skills of Carter "The Cowboy Cyclist," who performed an aerial "leap through space." Cody's most dramatic spectacle, however, came from the riding performance by the International Rough Riders. This troupe of skilled horsemen hailed from Japan, Russia (which caused a bit of tension in 1904 because of the Russo-Japanese War then underway), Mexico, and Arab lands. In addition it included African-American riders and a band that dubbed themselves the "United States Cavalry."

The local reporters were treated to a behind-the-scenes tour of the operation. Former American reporter Frank Small, now

THE VICTORIAN WEST: ROMANCE 149

Bill's publicity manager, swapped tales with his Scottish counterparts as he carefully pointed out the man who had fired the first shot in the Spanish-American War, various Native dignitaries, two men who would be feuding were they back in the States, and so forth. The Scots reporters responded in kind with extensive coverage, so much so that the Great North of Scotland Railway Company put on special excursion trains to bring in the country people. More than twenty-three thousand Scots witnessed the first day's performance—in spite of rain—and Cody marked this down as a first-day record for attendance. Five thousand were turned away.[82] In all, the three-day stay produced the greatest crowds Bill had ever had in his British tours. Statistically, more than half of Aberdeen's residents "were thrilled and stirred" by the performances.[83]

In many ways this 1904 tour was eminently symbolic. The appeal of the American West proved universal. Newly purchased British automobiles brushed up against ancient horse-drawn buggies. Scots whose complexions "betoken a healthy country life" rubbed shoulders with city bankers and elegant ladies who lived in country homes. One reporter commented that most of the young men with wives and bairns in tow had been raised with Buffalo Bill stories in their youth: "What boy of Britain has not read of attacks by Red Indians on the prairie emigrant trains crossing the plains?"[84]

Scotland suddenly had a new set of heroes. Reporters noted that the Rough Riders, the trick shooters, and Buffalo Bill would give the boys on the street a good deal to talk about over the winter.[85] Scots spectators had thoroughly enjoyed their glimpse, however brief, of America's "Wild West."

As the popularity of Lauder and Cody illustrated, the legends of Scotland and the American West had an appeal far beyond their own regions. In fact, by 1900 they had emerged as two of the world's great mythologies. The stories of Scotland and the West were, indeed, wonderful stories, and they each possessed the immediacy that a story holds when it links with human experience. By treating both the heroism of conquest and the heroism of defeat, Scottish legend and Western legend became infused with wonder. They each illuminated honor, valor, endurance, suffering, hope, and tragedy—the very stuff of epic poetry. Like the Homeric epics of ancient Greece, these legends reached out to the universal, asking questions that concerned truths about life in general. Such truths are complex. They defy both bureaucratic formulations and literal, exact historical readings. Ever fragmenting and ever fleeting, they must be expressed in mytho-poetic terms, and Lauder and Cody did just that.

Without romance, the story of the American West is simply that of American history set in a western locale. Similarly, without romance, the story of Scotland is largely that of North Britons living in a very demanding climate. But with romance, these two histories rank among the most fascinating of the modern world. To paraphrase Kiowa author N. Scott Momaday, Scotland and the American West each must be seen to be believed. And each must be believed to be seen.

CHAPTER SIX

Varieties of the Scottish-Western Experience

Historian Bruce LeRoy concluded his 1976 study of Scots in the Pacific Northwest with a set of fifty capsule biographies of people who had made an impact on Pacific Northwest history. He also began compiling a list of three-hundred other important figures as a guide for further research.[1] One wishes that every region of the West had someone duplicating this effort. Only then will the story of Scots in the West approach completeness.

Ever mobile, the canny Scots settled in every western state and territory. Assessing the economic status of such a group is impossible, but one may put forth the cautious generalization that the Scottish-Western interaction proved fruitful for both sides. The careers of Andrew Little, William Keith, and John Muir served as goals toward which others might strive. Although there were many who slipped through the economic cracks, the dominant theme of Scottish western immigration from c. 1790 to c. 1917 remains advancement—not always great wealth, perhaps, but advancement. As Frank Emerson, governor of Wyoming, observed in 1929 when he dedicated Cheyenne's statue of Robert Burns: "Especially among the flockmasters do we find the thrifty Scots in leading places. In business and professional circles, and in many other places of importance we also find the countrymen of Robert Burns as real leaders."[2]

To be fair, however, one should begin this chapter with a discussion of Scots who failed economically. Doubtless there were many who fit this category. The wealthy Scots who remained in Britain certainly thought so. One wonders what happened to the émigré Andrew, "the man of music," of whom Thomas Carlisle observed: "He can fiddle, he can dig, and to beg he is not ashamed."[3] An 1828 letter from James Joseph Hope-Vese of Cragie Hall reveals a similar concern: "What a curious society they must have on the other side of the Atlantic since all the scoundrels from this country fly thither."[4]

Unfortunately for the historian, scoundrels seldom leave the necessary materials to track them down. The trails of Wyoming prostitute "Puss" Newport, the Scots vagrants, and the largely anonymous Scots miners and sheepherders all come to dead ends. One finds only glimpses of the Idaho Scots herder who achieved local notoriety because he never bathed or changed his clothes. Another Boise herder was so articulate that locals guessed he once had been an academic before alcohol drove him into other lines of work. For reasons not easily explained, a surprising number of western hermits, such as David Douglas Gowan, "keeper" of the Tonto Natural Bridge in Arizona, also claimed Scottish background.[5] We know that Alexander Sinclair Sutherland died destitute in a Wisconsin county almshouse in 1869 and that George Sim lived out his life in San Francisco just above the poverty level. Economic success also eluded the Scottish Mormon converts from the John Thomson/David MacNeil clans.[6] All in all, however, failures generally leave fewer historical tracks than successes.

Historians of Scotland remind their readers that there was not one but "many" Scotlands. The same caveat holds true for the Scottish-Western connection. The tales of emigration to the West are as varied as the tellers themselves. This chapter will relate six stories to illustrate the varieties of the Scottish-American experience in the West.

THE RELIGIOUS CONNECTION: THE LATTER-DAY SAINTS AND THE MENAUL BROTHERS

Virtually all Scots/Scotch-Irish emigrants maintained some link with organized religion, though they spread across the entire religious spectrum. Probably the majority retained their Roman Catholic, Episcopal, or Presbyterian heritage, but one can find evidence of a number of defections. Both William Keith and the Alexander Gardner families began as Presbyterians but ended as active members of the Church of the New Jerusalem (Swedenborgians). Scots Presbyterian Hugh Duncan eventually adopted Arminianism and became a Methodist minister in Montana. Freethinker William David Schacter wrote satirical essays for the British rationalist magazine *National Reformer* from a mining camp in Colorado. John Alexander Dowie brought over many of the ideas of Edward Irving's Catholic Apostolic Church to the States—specifically, spiritual healing, prophecy, and a renewed concern that the world was ripe for God's judgment. Dowie introduced spiritual healing to the San Francisco area in the late 1880s and then went on to found his own religious denomination in Zion, Illinois. Consequently, generalizations about the faith of Scots immigrants must always be made with caution. All one can say for certain is that the theme of organized religion remained a central aspect of Scots life from the sixteenth century forward.

Perhaps this accounts, in part, for the Scottish response to Mormon missionaries. In 1839 Scots converts Alexander Wright and Samuel Mulliner began the first LDS mission to the land of

John Knox. Within a decade they and their missionary brethren had helped distribute about five thousand copies of the British edition of the *Book of Mormon*. The British church weekly paper, the *Millennial Star,* boasted a circulation of twenty-five thousand by the early 1850s. As Elder George D. Watt wrote from Edinburgh in 1840, "The Saints in this place are a good people. The people of Scotland are slow to believe and embrace the truth, but after they have embraced it, they are firm, yea, they would lay down their lives for the truth."[7]

From 1840 to 1900 about ten thousand Scots joined the Church of Jesus Christ of Latter-day Saints.[8] According to historian P. A. M. Taylor, the Scots formed about 18 percent of all British emigrants to Zion during this time period.[9] The Mormon challenge to openly debate Scottish ministers as to the nature of the true faith also gave them considerable publicity. A conference in Edinburgh once drew 1,500 observers.[10]

If one can judge by the spate of anti-Mormon pamphlets, the arrival of LDS missionaries caused great consternation among Scottish churchgoers. In 1842 a Clackmannan mob even burned an effigy of LDS founder Joseph Smith, Jr. Pamphleteers used terms such as "fanatical superstition" and "humiliating impostures." So did Scottish visitors to Utah. When William Fraser toured Salt Lake City in 1885, he found himself arguing theology and Scripture with Scots converts. "I denounced their system," Fraser wrote, "and expressed my astonishment that any person brought up in Presbyterian Scotland and taught the Chief End of Man, would ever turn a Mormon."[11]

Scottish critics of the Saints often lumped the movement with that of the Catholic Apostolic Church founded a decade earlier by Edward Irving. A former schoolmaster at Heddington and Kirkcaldy, Irving assisted at Glasgow's St. John's Cathedral before moving to London to expound his radical positions on imminent millennialism, miracles, and the need for an elaborate ritual. Mormonism reflected these themes as well.[12]

Who were the Scots converts to Mormonism, and why did they emigrate? These questions are easier posed than answered. London reporter Henry Mayhew concluded in 1851 that the British converts "chiefly consist[ed] of farmers and mechanics of a superior class," and historians have tended to agree.[13] Scots Mormons also seemed to come from the more industrial areas rather than the countryside. Historical attempts to determine whether these conversions were primarily spiritual or economic have not been conclusive.[14]

One can say with certainty, however, that Mormon missionaries had considerable appeal in Edinburgh, Glasgow, the Lowlands, the north coast, and Aberdeen from 1840 to c. 1900. *The Edinburgh Review* might ridicule both Smith and the new faith—blaming the conversions on the spread of free libraries and popular education—but still they joined.[15] "The promised land of the Mormon," complained one pamphlet writer, "is in the far West of America. . . . Mormons allure the ignorant with the promise that Christ will appear in the west of America."[16]

Mormons bolstered their religious appeal with an extremely well-organized system for transporting converts to Utah. The Latter-day Saints believed that God had commanded His people to enlist in a "gathering" to Zion in order to build the Kingdom of God in Utah. Scots migrants, who usually moved in groups, first gathered in Liverpool, the main port of embarkation. From there they sailed to New York, where they transferred to train and, perhaps, wagon until they reached the Salt Lake Valley. Regular steamship travel in the late 1860s simplified this process considerably. From 1840 to 1900 British emigration laws and modes of transportation altered considerably, but the Mormon system of Atlantic travel from Liverpool to Utah remained steadfast.[17]

Although there were exceptions, the land of Deseret (Utah) often proved kind to Scots immigrants. By 1890 Utah boasted almost 3,500 Scots, a very visible minority that generally mingled easily with the rest of the population rather than establishing separate LDS towns, as did the converted Swiss or Icelanders. Thus, kilts, bagpipes, and Burns Day celebrations proved important in keeping the Utah Scots' identity alive. One finds Scots names all through Utah, from Bryce Canyon (named after Ebenezer Bryce from Glasgow) to Glencoe to Ben Lomond. Nineteenth-century Scots immigrants played many roles in pioneer Utah. John and Margaret Blythe are credited with introducing the first grapevines and peach trees in northern Arizona at Moenkopi. Other immigrants served as superintendent of the Utah common schools, as business managers of the LDS publication *Deseret News,* as gardeners in Pioneer Park, and even as members of the First Presidency. Perhaps the most successful LDS convert, in a financial sense, was industrialist David Eccles, who had amassed an estate of 7 million dollars at his death in 1912.[18] The 1920 census showed a preponderance of Scots in the central Salt Lake Valley, and Salt Lake City still boasts popular bagpipe bands.

Although the nineteenth-century Scots Mormons proved exceptionally visible, the majority of Scots and Scotch-Irish maintained links with the Presbyterian faith. Writing in 1856, religious observer Robert Baird claimed that American Presbyterianism owed its foundation exclusively to the Scots "exiles" and the Scotch-Irish.[19] Although Baird's observation may have held true for most of the eighteenth century, by the mid-nineteenth, Presbyterianism in the United States, in its northern and southern versions, had largely become a mainstream American denomination. Unlike the Canadian church, American Presbyterianism shed its predominantly ethnic character.

Having said this, however, one must acknowledge the prominent role that émigré Scots played in the American Presbyterian Church during the nineteenth century.[20] An Idaho Scots woman confessed that she had never known a Highlander who was other than Presbyterian. Princeton University drew heavily upon Scots theologians to bolster its traditional Calvinism, as did the San Francisco Theological seminary, a key Protestant seminary west of the Mississippi. Even today, a number of Presbyterian students take their advanced degrees at Scottish universities.

If the foremost nineteenth-century American Presbyterian theologians had one foot in Ulster or Scotland, so, too, did a number of ordinary parish ministers. The saga of the family Menaul will illustrate this aspect of Scots Presbyterianism in the American West.

Originally from the Highlands, Matthew Menaul acquired a tract of land in County Tyrone, Ulster, in the early nineteenth century. He and his first wife had two sons, John (b. 1834) and James (b. 1842), who were known from their youths as "bible pounders."[21]

As a young man John came to America, where he attended Lafayette College in Pennsylvania, studied theology for two years at Princeton Seminary, and studied medicine for one year at the University of Pennsylvania. After ordination in 1867 he married Harriet McMechan and sailed to West Africa as a missionary. For three years, the Menauls worked at the Corsico Mission, where Harriet Menaul died. Broken in health, John and his two young daughters returned to the States. In 1870 the Presbyterian mission board sent him as a missionary to the Navajos in Fort Defiance, Arizona.

Menaul recovered his health, met fellow missionary Charity Ann Gaston at Fort Defiance, and married her. The Menauls then moved to Laguna Pueblo, where they remained for fourteen years, from 1876 to 1890. Afterwards, they moved to Albuquerque, and until 1904 they were engaged in work with the Hispanics of the Southwest. Menaul then retired and moved to Oklahoma, where he died in 1912 at age seventy-seven.

John Menaul was one of the relatively few missionaries spoken well of by secular observers. George Wharton James and John Hanson Beadle both praised his Indian work.[22] In general

Protestant missionaries made few converts among the Pueblo Indians in the Southwest, most of whom had merged their Native belief patterns with Spanish Roman Catholicism. Although there were a handful of converts in Jemez, Laguna was the only pueblo where the Protestants made the slightest impression. This was largely due to the teaching skills of John Menaul.

Menaul drew from both his Scottish and his African experience to place his emphasis on reading and books. In 1877 he imported a hand printing press to Laguna, and, if his second annual report is to be believed, he printed almost four thousand pages on it within the next eight months.[23] These publications were mostly in Spanish, but he also translated and printed sections from Scripture and reworked hymns into the Keresan tongue of Laguna. He did at least two editions of *McGuffey's First Reader* in Laguna as well.

In his writings Menaul linked the situation of American Indians to those of the Africans, East Indians, and Chinese. These groups were not eager to receive the Christian message, he noted, even though "we owe the Indian a debt which can only be paid in this way." He viewed his missionary efforts "more of the nature of an influence than a work; more like the constant drip than like the sledgehammer blow," even as he admitted that his work at Laguna was recognized as the most advanced of that at any Presbyterian Indian mission.[24]

Menaul's career in the States enticed his younger brother James, who had first worked as a farmer, to follow. He, too, attended Lafayette College. From there he went on to study theology at Western Theological Seminary and then pastored a small Centerville Presbyterian church in Butler County, Pennsylvania.

In 1881 the Board of Home Missions sent James to pastor the Presbyterian Church in Albuquerque, which he headed until 1888. In 1889 James assumed the position of Synodical Missionary in charge of all Presbyterian missionary work for the territories of Arizona and New Mexico. While in this position, he conceived the idea of taking over a former Presbyterian–U.S. Government Indian contract school and turning it into a school for Spanish young people. He approached the Presbyterian General Assembly with this scheme in 1895 and received a go-ahead. In 1896 the school began as the Albuquerque Industrial Training School for Spanish Boys; it was renamed the Menaul School upon his death the following year.

As was the case with his brother, virtually everyone spoke well of James Menaul. "He was a man of genial, friendly temperament, sagacious in dealing with men and possessed of a keen Scotch-Irish wit which stood him in good stead in the buffetings inevitable in a frontier town," wrote one admirer. Another friend, Miss M. E. Disserte of Zuni, said that she and James once "sat discussing [a theological treatise], its pathos, humor, and theology with that mutual understanding and enjoyment which only those of Celtic ancestry can fully enter into."[25]

Wherein did the Menauls' success—however measured—lie? In 1892 John Menaul noted, "In working for these people [Indians] and in supporting those who are working for them, a great deal of patience is needed." For Menaul, any advance would come only through books. From his first *La Solana* ("*The Sunlight*") for children to the 1,409,000 pages he printed in 1891, John Menaul placed his faith in the printed word. So prolific was his press that eventually his Spanish-language pamphlets were used by missionaries in Mexico, Cuba, Puerto Rico, and the Philippines. Indeed, when he left Albuquerque, he donated the press to the Menaul School so that Spanish boys could learn the printer's trade. As for James, who once said, "I can work better than I can tell about it," the Menauls' solutions to missionary problems lay with reading, formal education, a tolerant attitude, and the old standby of "Scotch-Irish wit."[26]

THE WOMEN'S VOICE:
MRS. M. A. PRINGLE AND LADY ABERDEEN

Bruce LeRoy complained vigorously that few Scottish women left behind sufficient records to illuminate their roles in Pacific Northwest history. Unfortunately, this holds true for other sections of the West as well. Diaries and memoirs of Scots women, either as travelers or as immigrants, are rare.

If the experiences of Idaho Scots female émigrés can be taken as representative, virtually all of the women managed domestic households. The 1880 Idaho census listed all the Scottish women as either "keeping house," "helping father," or "helping mother."[27] In pioneer conditions this proved challenging indeed. Teenager Nellie Allen from Keith scrubbed the kitchen floor twice every day, tended sheep, and milked cows. After her marriage she raised chickens and "bum" lambs (lambs whose ewes had rejected them). One year, she raised thirty-six bums, using a five-gallon coal-oil can with holes cut out for nipples. Another year, when she went out to feed her bum lambs, she discovered that they had disappeared into the main herd. Dismayed, she picked up her milk bottles, approached the herd, and called out to them. One by one they came out of the band. "It's really something . . .," she recalled. "They knew I was their mother."[28]

On a number of occasions Scottish young women would hire out as domestic help. Nellie Allen, from Banffshire, served her Idaho neighbors, the Regan family, for five years, attending to the four children born to Mrs. Regan during that time. So trusted was she that Mrs. Regan asked Nellie to marry her husband if any disaster should befall her. Nellie also worked at a dairy, where she rose at 4:00 A.M. and milked ten cows daily. Prior to her emigration she had worked for a family in Aberdeen, where she had to address the children in her care as "Master Edward" and "Miss Margaret." But when she moved to America, she insisted upon much more democratic procedures. She even refused to respond to a maid's bell. "I loved America from the minute I came," she recalled. "Everything was so much nicer, so much better for me."[29] For the older Scottish women, however, several of whom had hired maids in Britain, the western pioneer ordeal proved disastrous. Betty Hitt's mother died of Rocky Mountain spotted fever in 1908 while working on a Ditto Creek ranch, eighteen miles from Mountain Home, Idaho. "It must have been just really living hell for her to be out here just slaving like that," Hitt said, "when she had had a comparatively easy life all her life."[30]

The world of western Scottish women frequently revolved around church life, children, and various social gatherings, such as "the Robbie Burns." The women were also expected to carry on the Scottish cultural traditions. Fathers frowned on those who planned to marry non-Scots. But the restrictions often had their costs. Andrew Little's wife lacked little in material goods, but she confessed in her old age that she had led a very lonely life.[31]

Among the few women's travel diaries at the Scottish Record Office in Edinburgh is that left by Mrs. M. A. Pringle of Whytbank, who visited the United States during the summer of 1903. Fortunately, Mrs. Pringle left a lengthy record of her impressions of the American West. Arriving in San Francisco via Honolulu, Pringle toured the Spanish missions of the area with mixed feelings. Although she admired the architecture, she viewed the Spanish authority over the Natives as "a form of bondage." Similarly intrigued by San Francisco's Chinatown, she described the city of thirty thousand as "no longer America but Shanghai or Hong Kong." From California she took a train to Salt Lake City and spent several days amidst the Saints, where she observed "root beer [was] the strongest thing sold."

Although scornful of Mormon religious services, which she attended, she had nothing but praise for the famed Mormon

Tabernacle choir of two hundred mixed voices. Still, she confessed that she could never completely concentrate on the music because she kept wondering "how many of the women belonged to one man."[32]

Mrs. Pringle spent many hours each evening recording her daily activities. But her diary might best be described as narrative rather than analysis. Thus, the historian is grateful for the extensive writings of another Scottish woman traveler, Lady Aberdeen, which are both descriptive and analytical.

Born in London, Ishbel Marjoribanks came from a family of anglicized Scots who owned a summer shooting estate in Glen Affric (Guisachan, Scotland). She moved to the beautiful country estate of Haddo House, north of the city of Aberdeen, upon her marriage to Lord Aberdeen. The family had long maintained a connection with the American West, for an earlier Lord Aberdeen, serving under the Robert Peel administration, had helped negotiate the 1846 treaty that drew the U.S.–Canadian border at the 49th Parallel. In 1846 Lord Aberdeen, who felt national honor was at stake, had been prepared to go to war to defend the Columbia River boundary until Peel argued before the House of Commons that a single month's military expenses would cost more than the whole territory was worth.[33]

Ishbel's Lord Aberdeen, owner of the largest estate in northern Scotland, followed his ancestors into the diplomatic service. He was first stationed in Ireland and then served as governor general of Canada for most of the 1890s. He later returned to Ireland for a second term.

In each of these assignments Ishbel proved a force in her own right. Brilliant and eccentric, she set up a Haddo House Association for the education and recreation of her Scots tenants. This eventually evolved into the "Onward and Upward Association," an organization dedicated to improving the lives of girls and mothers who lived in the rural districts of northern Scotland. Lady Aberdeen also began a periodical with the same name as the organization, and, later, a children's magazine entitled *Wee Willie Winkie.*

Lady Aberdeen moved easily in the international evangelical Christian circles of her day. Henry Drummond, popular Scots Presbyterian minister, was both a good friend and "sub-editor" of her journals. She met famed Chicago evangelist Dwight L. Moody, Canadian religious novelist Ralph Connor, and Hull House pioneer Jane Addams among many others. Evangelical without being the least denominational, she quoted with approval Massachusetts Episcopal Bishop Phillips Brooks's sermon on the meaning of existence: "The true meaning of life is service, service, service."[34]

As a result of their station in life, the Aberdeens traveled a good deal. In mid-June of 1887 they landed for the first time in the western United States, where Ishbel found herself charmed by American culture. Two large deputations of immigrants, the Scots and the Irish, met the Aberdeens at the boat and later hosted a large reception in their honor. At the party they met a Mr. Duncan, born and reared in Aberdeenshire. Upon shaking hands he remarked, "It would be like the thing, my Lord, if I were meeting you somewhere between New Deer and Haddo House."[35] From San Francisco they took the train to Denver, where they engaged in a public Jubilee Celebration in honor of Queen Victoria's half-century on the throne. The British Colony of Denver hosted them, and Ishbel noticed that the Americans joined in the celebrations with no ill feelings of any kind. This contrasted sharply with the July 4, 1876, British-American celebration in Hays, Kansas, where Americans turned "God Save the Queen" into "God Shave the Queen" and a fight broke out.[36]

When Lord and Lady Aberdeen moved to Canada in 1893, Ishbel carried her credo there as well. She traveled all through the land to urge the formation of a Canadian Nursing Organization, which later became the Victorian Order of Nurses. She also transferred *Wee Willie Winkie* to Canada. After a visit to the infant Scottish crofter settlement at Killarney in 1890, she persuaded a group of Winnipeg women to launch the Aberdeen Association for Providing Literature to Settlers, actually a reading society for Canadians in isolated regions. In the course of her official duties she traveled all across the Canadian provinces. Her energy was prodigious, and her legacy can be seen in her leadership of the Canadian National Council of Women as well as the International Council of Women (an early League of Nations), of which she was president for over forty years. During the early 1930s friends nominated her for the Nobel Peace Prize.[37] When she died in 1939, she was genuinely mourned.

Lady Aberdeen also had another, direct connection with the West, since two of her brothers were involved in various ranching enterprises. Archie Marjoribanks (pronounced Marchbanks) managed a cattle ranch in the Texas Panhandle, while Coutts Marjoribanks was involved with a similar ranch in McHenry County, Dakota Territory. Both brothers thus qualified as remittance men, one of the most controversial of all the British frontier groups.

REMITTANCE MEN

Remittance men were usually second and third sons of titled British aristocracy who, for various reasons, found themselves excluded from the usual occupations reserved for such sons— the military or the clergy. Thus, families often sent them stateside, either to manage cattle ranches and/or simply to get them out of the country. These sons lived from month to month on their "remittance" checks from home, until the time when many inherited their titles and left the West for good. Colorado locals once termed a valley south of Canon City as "the Valley of the Second Sons."

Generally well educated, usually arrogant, and often contemptuous of their American comrades, the remittance men gained the reputation of being high livers and hard drinkers.

They often had a difficult time adjusting to western democracy. According to legend, one approached a Wyoming cowboy to ask if his "master" were at home. The reply: "The son-of-a-bitch hasn't been born yet." Remittance men possessed a peculiar set of British academic skills that allowed them to give the Latin names of local flora and fauna and quote Shakespeare, but they proved decidedly impractical when confronted by loose door hinges or broken wagon wheels. In the parlance of the time they were "handless men."

Canadians generally treated the remittance men with scorn and contempt. Some British Columbian storekeepers placed signs in their windows warning them away. Although Canadian historian A. G. Bradley acknowledged that there were exceptions, he concurred in 1903 with "the rule which, I fear with truth, sets down the gentleman emigrant as a failure."[38]

Not everyone agreed with this assessment. Alaskan Scots émigré Robert Service wrote two poems in their defense. In the "Rhyme of the Remittance Man," the speaker scorns his "purse-proud brothers," while in "The Younger Son," the narrator observes that "he's building Britain's greatness o'er the foam."[39]

Arizona historian Larry A. McFarlane agrees with Robert Service. His study of two such remittance men (one being Coutts Marjoribanks) discovered that they often became active members of their local communities. They joined school boards and regional cattlemen's associations, imported British cattle, and generally tried to become good citizens. A North Dakota school district is named for Coutts, and a plaque at the North Dakota International Peace Garden commemorates Ishbel's visit to Coutts's Ranch in 1887.[40]

Good citizens though they might have been, neither Archie nor Coutts made a financial success of his ranching experience. Seeking to profit from the western cattle boom, the Aberdeens purchased stock in the Rocking Chair Ranch in Texas. Archie agreed to manage the holdings. Even though he introduced bloodhounds to protect the stock, he could never control the rustling that made the ranch unprofitable. Eventually, the Aberdeens sold the ranch and Archie returned to Britain.

Coutts faced similar difficulties in McHenry County in northern North Dakota. In addition, sister Ishbel worried about Coutts's excessive drinking in that isolated setting. Thus, when he was preparing to depart North Dakota, Ishbel conceived the idea of turning him into a titled Canadian landlord. Accordingly, the Aberdeens purchased a homestead in the Okanagan Valley of British Columbia and brought Coutts and a friend to Canada to manage it.

Since the mountains surrounding the valley reminded Ishbel of her Inverness-shire home, she named their new ranch Guisachan, Gaelic for "place of the fir." No fir trees grew there at the time, so she imported dozens of Highland seedlings. Unfortunately, the "place of the fir" never proved congenial to their growth. The Aberdeens also purchased another nearby cattle ranch named Coldstream in the region Lady Aberdeen described as a "lovely woods of birch and fir with a little burn running along. It was just like Scotland; father compared it to Balmoral."[41]

Urged on by émigré real-estate agent George Grant Mackay, previous owner of the island of Raasay, Lady Aberdeen hoped to revolutionize the economy of the Okanagan Valley. She and her husband enticed a number of northeast Scots farmers to emigrate there, and they also introduced a variety of new crops. They began extensive planting of apple, pear, and plum trees as well as several berry plants: strawberries, raspberries, and blueberries. All were irrigated from nearby mountain streams. As part of their fruit operations, they established a local jam factory in Vernon that they hoped would compete with the famed British firm of Crosse and Blackwell.[42] Viewing the valley as an ideal home for Scots farmers of proper social standing but little capital, the Aberdeen's Okanagan efforts combined hard economics with moral enthusiasm.

Unfortunately, Coutts proved more typical of the image of British remittance man than Lady Aberdeen might have wished. His managerial skills were not up to the challenge of the valley. His love of fancy parties with "grand entrances," his hard drinking, and his tastes, as seen in his order for gold Japanese wallpaper for the ranch house, proved far too extravagant. In 1892, when Lady Aberdeen's financial advisor arrived to inspect the property, he found the operation a disaster. The two thousand cattle at Coldstream had dwindled to eight hundred, and a foreman told him that the ranch, which had once been praised as the finest in British Columbia,[43] had now become "the laughing stock of the country."[44]

In 1894 Coutts's father, Lord Tweedmouth, died and Coutts finally came into his inheritance. With that he fled Canada. The West remained in his blood, however, and he eventually returned to live in the Okanagan Valley.

Although Coutts never became the wealthy "Lord of Okanagan" as planned, Lord and Lady Aberdeen's venture forever changed this little British Columbia valley. Under the Aberdeens' impetus, the valley evolved from a large-scale ranching region to an irrigated area of small fruit farms. Because of the climate, the soft fruit was phased out in favor of apples, still the mainstay of the economy. Although Guisachan eventually became a log ranch and Coldstream turned into a suburb, Lord Aberdeen (one should include Lady Aberdeen as well) was termed "the Father of the Dry Belt in British Columbia."[45]

"LORD" OGILVY AND THE ARISTOCRATIC/MILITARY TRADITION

A central adage of immigration history notes that "dukes don't immigrate." Certainly that rings true for most of the Scots discussed in this book. With the exception of Charles Augustus

Murray, William Drummond Stewart, the Marjoribanks brothers, and Lady Aberdeen (only one of whom remained) virtually all the Scottish settlers in the West came from middle- or lower-class backgrounds. Consequently, the saga of Lyulph (pronounced "Lyuf") Ogilvy, who lived most of his adult life in Colorado, is unique.[46]

The Ogilvy family owned Cortachy Castle, near Glamis Castle in Angus, and a townhouse in London where Lyulph was born in 1861. The family social position may be seen in the following anecdote. Once when Lyulph and his older brother returned from a term at Oxford, the neighborhood children were all assembled by the side of the road to cheer their journey home.[47] Their ancestral castle, the "Bonnie House O'Airlie" (the title of a song), also proved home to an eerie legend. A badly treated young drummer boy allegedly cursed the family by instructing his spirit to haunt the castle. Whenever people heard echoes of his music, an Ogilvy would soon die.[48]

Lyulph's father, the Earl of Airlie, had become friends with William Henry Seward, Lincoln's secretary of state, and Seward had urged him to explore the American West as the site for possible ranches. The earl had young Lyulph's interest at heart in this venture, for, as a second son, Lyulph would not inherit the family estate. Thus, in the late 1870s the two Ogilvys joined Lord Dunraven's British community in North Park, Colorado, and they purchased 3,500 acres near Greeley for a ranch. Unfortunately, the earl visited Mexico afterward, where he contracted dysentery, dying in the Windsor Hotel in Denver in 1881. Presumably, the ghostly drummer alerted the Scots to his passing.

After a brief sojourn home, eighteen-year-old Lyulph decided to return to America and moved briefly to Oregon. Since Americans knew nothing of British titles, they termed him "Earl," "Baron," or, most commonly, "Lord." As the second son of a lord, his real title was the Honorable Lyulph Corlchrist Stanley Ogilvy. Since no one could pronounce his forename, he usually signed himself "L. Ogilvy." As his family sent him regular funds, for years Ogilvy led a stylish life that included buffalo hunts, fine horses, elegant resorts, and considerable travel.

Unlike the stereotype of the remittance man, however, Ogilvy reflected a more gracious aristocratic upbringing that allowed him to move easily among both cowboys and the American upper class. He impressed the cowboys with his horsemanship and heavy drinking, and he impressed "proper" society with his elegant manners and with parties where he "made champagne pour around like a river."[49] "He is popular in all circles," the *Denver Times* remarked in 1900.[50] Much of this popularity can be traced to the legends that surrounded his various escapades.

Ogilvy boasted that his ancestors had fought for Charles I, Bonnie Prince Charlie, and Mary Queen of Scots. Consequently, a number of stories revolved around his love for military action. In 1898, when the Spanish-American War broke out, Ogilvy enlisted in Company D, Colorado Infantry. Fearing that he would never see action, he shifted to Torey's regiment of Rough Riders, a band raised largely in Wyoming, where he impressed the soldiers by regularly breaking the ice in the horse trough to bathe. The Rough Riders moved to Jacksonville, Florida, but the war ended before Ogilvy saw action.

His appetite had been whetted, however, and when the Boer War began the next year, "the Baron of Greeley" volunteered to escort a boatload of mules from Galveston to Capetown. Suspicious of the martinet tradition of the British army, Ogilvy enlisted in Brahant's brigade of Colonial Rough Riders, a group that engaged chiefly in guerrilla warfare for about twenty months.[51] From South Africa Ogilvy wrote his friend the state veterinarian, and some of his correspondence made its way to the Denver *Times:*

> I enjoyed the fight pretty well but it was not as exciting as I expected. I thought one would have hot and cold thrills

up and down one's back like in *The Red Badge of Courage,* but I found that was all rot.⁵²

Ogilvy's brother died in the Boer War, and the *Times* reported that the ghostly music of Airlie sounded again.⁵³ Luylph Ogilvy's bravery won him both a captaincy and the British Distinguished Service Order. Later, at age fifty-three, he volunteered for service in World War I and served from 1914 to 1915 as a lieutenant of Scottish horse. In 1940, at age eighty, he again volunteered for World War II. In his own words, he could never avoid "a scrap."⁵⁴

The saga of Lord Ogilvy also involved a number of Colorado Legends. His son, Jack, who became a professor of English at the University of Colorado, has attempted to separate fact from fiction regarding his father's life but with little success.⁵⁵ Lord Ogilvy tales evolved to become an essential part of Front Range folklore, in part because of American fascination with having a real Scottish aristocrat in their midst.

Here are some examples. An expert horseman from his youth in Scotland, Ogilvy drove with wild abandon. Once he killed a horse and destroyed a buggy while attempting to jump a shallow draw. On another occasion he tipped a buggy and a six-horse rig, and when the irate stable master demanded five hundred dollars in damages gave him one thousand dollars instead. In Denver he staged a mock funeral for himself, rising from the coffin to petrify the undertaker. On another occasion he placed roosters in vacant rooms in the Windsor Hotel so as to awaken the patrons at dawn. On yet another he staged a party for his favorite racing horse. In probably his most notorious exploit, Lord Ogilvy drove a team of horses through the lobby of Denver's Windsor Hotel.

But Ogilvy's importance to Colorado extended far beyond the realm of folklore. Because of his financial independence, he always purchased the latest agricultural equipment for his ranches. He bought the first steam tractor in Colorado, and when he drove it home, he popped the trusses on every bridge along the way. His observation: they needed rebuilding anyway. Over the years he purchased a number of ranches, the most famous being the Crow Creek Ranch, at the junction of Crow Creek and the Platte River. In addition he helped build one of the first canals in Colorado, the Ogilvy Ditch, which diverted water from the Cache la Poudre River for agricultural purposes. (It is still in operation.) He also constructed, with his own money, the Platte and Beaver Canals in Morgan County, the Traveller's Canal in the San Luis Valley of southern Colorado, and part of the North Platte Canal near North Platte, Nebraska. The Ogilvy ranch prospered, in part because it was well situated to receive sheep being driven across Colorado to the Nebraska feedlots. In addition he introduced alfalfa to the region and pioneered in breeding Polled Angus cattle, Shropshire sheep, and thoroughbred horses. In 1898 the Denver *Republican* credited him as "having contributed more time and money to improve the stock of the country than almost any other stockman in the West."[56]

In 1902 Lord Ogilvy gave up both drinking and the glamorous life when he married Edith Gertrude Brothroyd, the daughter of a local English family. The newspapers described her as a "typical Colorado girl" who had graduated from State Agricultural College in 1895, where she had been active in the literary societies and president of her senior class. They had two children, a daughter who died in 1915 and a son, Jack. Edith died in 1907.

After his marriage Ogilvy's life took a turn as dramatic as the various legends surrounding his exploits. His family cut off his funds, perhaps because he had married an American commoner, and he lost his farms to creditors. After moving to Denver he was forced to work at the Union Pacific Freight Depot as a night watchman for $1.50 a day. In 1909, however, Harry Tammen, once a bartender at the Windsor Hotel but now co-owner of the fledgling Denver *Post,* offered him a job as an agricultural writer, insisting that he use the byline "Lord Ogilvy."

For the next three decades "Lord Ogilvy" wrote on agriculture for the *Post,* one of the first full-time western correspondents to do so. A regular visitor to the state and local fairs, he encouraged young 4-H'ers and soon knew many farmers and ranchers by name. Moreover, he brought a lifetime of agricultural experience to the subject. As one observer noted: "His knowledge of agriculture and livestock was second to that of no one in America. To accompany him to a stock show, to hear him talk of cattle and horses, was like listening to a reading of Homer."[57] A gentleman in the best sense of the word, Ogilvy could always find something to praise in a show animal. When he died in 1947 at age eighty-five, Colorado lost one of its most colorful citizens.

ROBERT LOUIS STEVENSON AND THE IMPACT OF CALIFORNIA

Like most British citizens, the Scots have traditionally held their writers in the highest esteem. Statues of Robert Burns or Sir Walter Scott grace as many a High Street as do those of William Wallace or Robert the Bruce. Burns's cottage in Ayrshire and Scott's country house in the Tweed Valley rank among the most visited of tourist sites. When Jefferson Davis toured Scott country in 1869, he marvelled at how Scott's fictional descriptions were viewed as actual history by contemporaries.[58]

Scott, apparently, never contemplated crossing the Atlantic, but Burns once seriously considered emigrating to British North America. But in 1879, their most famous (although at the time unknown) literary successor, Robert Louis Stevenson, did make the journey, first to New York and then to California.

It would be no exaggeration to mark Stevenson's 1879–80 stay in the American West as pivotal to his entire career.[59]

Stevenson traveled to America for one reason: his love of Frances (Fanny) Osbourne. Stevenson had met Osbourne, at the time a married woman, at an artists' colony at Grez in the Barbicon region of France. A refugee from both the profession of law and the cloying influence of his family, the Bohemian Stevenson fell in love with Osbourne immediately. Originally from San Francisco, she and her son, Lloyd, had fled to Grez to escape her pleasant but irresponsible husband. Only when he withdrew his financial support in 1878 did she return to the States.[60]

Completely infatuated, Stevenson waited until early August 1879 when Osbourne cabled him in Edinburgh, presumably asking him to come to California. Boarding the *S.S. Devonia* in Glasgow, Stevenson arrived in New York on August 18. In *The Amateur Emigrant,* he depicted in detail the "humble hostelry" where he spent a few days. In *Across the Plains,* he described his adventures amidst a crowded emigrant train, which he rode across the country from August 19 to August 30.

Eight months later, on May 19, 1880, a local Presbyterian minister married Osbourne and Stevenson. After a brief honeymoon Stevenson, Fanny, and her son, Lloyd, took a train to New York to sail to Scotland and meet his parents. Although many Scots have since criticized Fanny, often with good reason, Stevenson always held his talented, strong-willed wife in high regard. Two years before his death, he termed his marriage "the best move I ever made in my life."[61] Not only did Fanny nurse him through his many illnesses, she also supported him in all his writing endeavors. The acquisition of a wife and family proved the most notable legacy of Stevenson's California stay.

When the still-married Fanny met Stevenson at the San Francisco train depot, she discovered that his health had virtually collapsed. They spent the next two to three weeks recovering together on an angora goat ranch a few miles from Monterey.

Afterwards he moved alone to Monterey while she continued divorce proceedings. He lived there until December 1879, writing a number of works, including essays on Thoreau, "The Pavilion on the Links," and *The Amateur Emigrant*. Critic Jonathan Raban has termed the latter, a slim volume of travel memoirs, "quite simply, the best account ever written of the great European adventure in the nineteenth century, the passage to America, the New World."[62] In addition Stevenson began a novel entitled *Arizona Breckenridge, a Vendetta in the West*, which he would later discard.[63]

Poverty dogged Stevenson all through his early stay in Monterey. In fact so desperate was he that his cronies at the local Simoneau's restaurant secretly contributed two dollars a week to enable the editor of *The Monterey Californian* to hire Stevenson as a part-time writer. Stevenson never knew where the money came from.[64] This small stipend literally kept him from starvation through a very difficult period.

Around Christmas Stevenson moved to San Francisco, where he lived for three months at 608 Bush Street, a cheap hotel that charged him forty-five cents a day for food. His descriptions of San Francisco in "A Modern Cosmopolis" reveal his frame of mind. He depicted life there "in a circle of hell unknown to Dante—that of the penniless and dying author." He was saved from further collapse only by a telegram from his father promising him a yearly stipend of 250 pounds sterling.

With this new funding Stevenson cabled his publisher to halt the publication of *The Amateur Emigrant*, which had already been set in type. He did so out of respect for his family, because Stevenson's father, a wealthy Edinburgh businessman, was embarrassed that his son had traveled to the American West Coast as a common immigrant. A complete *Amateur Emigrant* did not see the light of day until 1896.

During this period in California Robert Louis Stevenson, at the age of twenty-nine, came very close to dying. The exact nature of his illness is disputed, but there is little question that he almost crossed the line. Two kindly California ranchers found him exhausted and starving on a local Monterey hillside and took him in. During the winter of 1879–80 in San Francisco, Stevenson squarely faced the question of his own mortality. It was then that he penned the most famous of all his poems, a copy of which he sent to London with his own epitaph.[65]

"Requiem" reads:

> Under the wide and starry sky,
> Dig the grave and let me lie.
> Glad did I live and gladly die,
> And I laid me down with a will.
>
> This be the verse you grave for me:
> *Here he lies where he longed to be;*
> *Home is the sailor, home from the sea,*
>   *And the hunter home from the hill.*

Literary scholar Anne Roller Issler has argued that a second legacy of Stevenson's California sojourn was his turning into an invalid.[66]

Stevenson's months on the West Coast have been thoroughly documented. In fact "Stevenson in California" has emerged as something of a local industry. Modern travelers can visit the Silverado Museum, opened in 1969 in St. Helena, which boasts eight thousand items of Stevensoniana, and can tour the Stevenson House in Monterey where he once lived. Appropriately, the first monument to him was erected in Portsmouth Square in San Francisco in 1897. Over the years a number of the author's works drew upon his experiences in a country that, he later confessed, "was to me a sort of promised land."[67]

The short essay he wrote there, "The Silverado Squatters," draws on a theme that would often reappear in his later prose: the exile's bittersweet vision of his native land. One finds a number of references to Scotland in this account of his honeymoon in a miner's cabin on Mount Saint Helena, the towering peak at the end of the Napa Valley. For example, he compares the fogs from the Pacific, which he dreaded, to those he had once observed in the Hebrides. His Jewish hosts, the Kelmars, caused him to reflect on why "the races which wander widest, Jews and Scotch, should be the most clannish in the world." He also analyzed the dilemmas of "The Scot Abroad." After a lament, "Oh why left I my hame," Stevenson concluded, "The happiest lot on earth is to be born a Scotchman."[68] According to his biographer, Ian Bell, the dilemmas of an exile occur with regularity in a number of his later works.[69] The Scottish National Library exhibition in honor of the centenary of Stevenson's death made this point as well.

Son of an engineer father, Stevenson always reflects a keen awareness of place in his prose. Indeed, one can trace on a map the exact path that Allan Stewart and David Balfour took from the west of Scotland to Edinburgh in *Kidnapped*. Similarly, his descriptions of the landscapes of St. Helena reflect precision in both geography and botany. His sketch of "The Old Pacific Capital" of Monterey depicts the polyglot ethnic composition that characterized many a frontier western community. His "New Pacific Capital" similarly describes San Francisco.

Some of the people he met in Monterey and San Francisco would appear in his later book, *The Wrecker*.[70] But a person writes from his imagination as well as his physical location, and nowhere are these two themes more perfectly blended than in *Treasure Island*, a book that has never gone out of print.

Literary critic J. R. Hammond once ruefully observed that adults are loathe to accept the fact that *Treasure Island* has no existence outside the author's imagination.[71] Happily, this may not be entirely true. Although there is no precise treasure *island*, there may, indeed, be a treasure *peninsula:* Point Lobos on the Monterey Coast.

If one looks closely at Stevenson's map of *Treasure Island,* it is virtually identical to the features of Point Lobos, now a California state park about four miles south of Monterey. The Big Dome could easily be "Spyglass Hill," while Bird Rock might well be "Skeleton Island." Stevenson himself wrote in an 1884 letter to Sidney Colvin that "the scenery is California in part, and in part *chic,*" but the resemblance to Point Lobos is too strong to be ignored. Moreover, Stevenson and a Chinese friend once hunted for buried treasure in the area.[72]

Since he was born in 1850, Stevenson obviously never met any of the eighteenth-century brigands he wrote about. But when he lived in Monterey and San Francisco, he could easily have listened to tales of California highwaymen such as Tiburcio Vazquez and Black Bart. Most literary critics see Stevenson's bold pirates as the unconventional alter ego of a sickly Edinburgh lad. But they could just as easily be based on the vivid firsthand tales of brigands and outlaws that he heard in California. When filtered through the genius of his imagination, these rascals live again in *Treasure Island* and the pirate crew of the *Hispaniola.* Even the name he gave his ship recalls his stay in Hispanic California. Thus, some of Stevenson's most memorable lines and settings harken back to his sojourn in the American West.

JOHN MUIR AND THE POPULARIZATION OF THE IDEA OF WILDERNESS

As the nineteenth century drew to a close, the most famous Scottish-American was probably Andrew Carnegie. In the twentieth century, however, Carnegie's stock has plummeted disastrously. Indeed, Carnegie and his ilk have recently had to shoulder the blame for some of America's worst problems: the waste of natural resources and the pollution of the land. In the 1990s, if one were asked to name the most famous Scottish-American, the reply would surely be "John Muir." As the environmental movement has emerged as the most popular of all crusades, Muir's reputation has grown accordingly.

Born in 1838, Muir spent his first eleven years in the tiny town of Dunbar, Scotland. There, he tells us in *The Story of My Boyhood and Youth*, he' became "fond of everything that was wild."[73] And Muir found wildness everywhere: by the riverbanks, in the Dunbar Castle grounds, and especially by the shores of the North Sea. In addition the schools of his day thoroughly indoctrinated him in Latin, French, and English grammar along with thrilling tales of William Wallace and Robert the Bruce, "with which every breath of Scotch air is saturated." For Muir the saga of biblical history was mingled with that of Scottish history. Young John had to memorize all the New Testament and three-quarters of the Old by age eleven. The punishment for failing to do so, he dutifully recorded, was a sound whipping.

In 1849 his father moved the family to the then-wild frontier of Wisconsin, where Muir grew to adulthood surrounded by an equally pristine natural world. The Muirs arrived in Wisconsin before the railroad had reached his region, and the family farm on Fountain Lake in Marquette County had no neighbors for a four-mile radius. Consequently, John admired the flowers and made friends with the farm animals. He also grew to respect the deer, foxes, and other wildlife, especially the giant flocks of passenger pigeons: "Oh, what bonnie, bonnie birds."[74]

A brilliant tinkerer, Muir enrolled in the University of Wisconsin in Madison, where he was first introduced to the writings of the American transcendentalists. Afterwards he walked from Kentucky to Florida, in large measure to examine the virgin forests along the way. From there he made his way to California, the state with which his name will always be associated.

During his early years in California Muir herded sheep, helped run a sawmill, escorted visitors, and worked at odd jobs. Finally, in 1880, he married Louise Wanda Strentzel, and soon his inherited farm in the Alhambra Valley of California became famous for its horticultural innovations. He did so well with the produce there that he was able to devote the rest of his life to natural history. An acknowledged amateur in the fields of geology, glacier study, and forestry, he nevertheless gained considerable respect for his discoveries and theories. During the 1880s he wrote several articles for *Scribner's* and *Century* in which he extolled the majesty of the western landscape. In these and other related essays, Muir literally created the genre of wilderness journalism.[75]

All the men and women who crossed his path acknowledged Muir's presence. Not only did he enjoy debate, he possessed the ability to penetrate to the heart of an issue in just a few words. Moreover, he had a marvelous eye for the precise phrase. He once described sheep as "hoofed locusts." In 1871, while hiking in the Sierras, he stumbled upon a "living glacier." Of cities he observed, "All are more or less sick; there is not a perfectly sane man in San Francisco." Of wilderness he said, "Man needs beauty as well as bread." In the midst of a fight to dam the Hetch Hetchy Valley for San Francisco's water supply, he argued: "Dam Hetch Hetchy! [You might] as well dam for water-tanks, the people's cathedrals and churches, for no holier temple has ever been consecrated by the heart of man." Perhaps his most famous aphorism was his invitation to the American public: "Come to the mountains and see."[76]

Muir's commitment and his literary skills enabled him to become the premier nature spokesman of his day. In 1889 he joined with *Century* editor Robert V. Johnson in a crusade to save the Yosemite Valley from erosion caused by the overgrazing of sheep. Their campaign to turn the region into what is now Yosemite National Park passed Congress in 1890. Other parks that Muir advocated—Sequoia, General Grant, and Mount Rainier—followed in succession. His personal friendship with Theodore Roosevelt, with whom he camped in Yosemite in

1905, was instrumental in Roosevelt's setting aside several thousand acres of forest reserves. Muir has even been termed the spiritual father of America's National Park System.[77]

In 1893 John Muir helped to found the Sierra Club. Until the 1960s this venerable nature organization served as the major—sometimes the sole—voice for conservation issues. Even Muir's failures, such as his inability to stop the damming of the Hetch Hetchy Valley, were celebrated; this lost battle so alarmed the West Coast that there has been no repetition in the twentieth century.

At the core of Muir's environmental accomplishments lay his vision of the interconnectedness of all life. Growing to maturity in a world of Darwinian materialism and rapacious utilization of natural resources, Muir's forging of a new relationship between humankind and nature represented a genuine intellectual breakthrough. Some have termed it a "Religion of Nature."[78]

Muir's "Religion of Nature" placed its emphasis on the majesty of creation, with little or no concern for Jesus as a redeemer. Indeed, if a redeemer existed, it was nature itself.[79] Through his writings, Muir advocated a oneness with the natural world, both animals and plants. Although as a young adult he occasionally hunted, he later gained fame for his renunciation of hunting and his advocacy of the rights of animals. He spent much effort in devising new concepts of community and harmony that would include *all* living things.[80] As he wrote in 1872, "A Burns may step outside the selfish circle of his species with sympathy for a suffering daisy or to claim the mousie as a fellow mortal but in the smug highwalled realms of the civilized such souls are rare."[81] Because the natural world revealed the handiwork of the Creator, Muir argued that nature was holy in and of itself. Thus, one should always treat it with awe and reverence.

Historians have spent a good deal of ink trying to analyze the exact sources of Muir's nature ethic. Some credit his reading of the transcendentalists while he was at Madison. Others see its origin in his childhood familiarity with Scottish gillies and their land/game management techniques. But the most common view is that Muir's new vision of man/nature was a reaction against the Presbyterian doctrine of his Dunbar youth and the religious rigidity of his father Daniel's faith, usually termed "dour Calvinism."[82]

Historian Mark Stoll suggests, however, that to interpret Muir's conservation ethic simply in terms of a rejection of Calvinistic Christianity is far too simplistic. Mainstream Christian thought speaks of a man-nature dualism, to be sure, Stoll notes, but it contains a respect toward nature as well. Even the idea that humankind should dominate nature and the natural world has always put forth a corollary: that humans should dominate not for the *individual* pursuit of wealth but for the *common* good (the Kingdom of God). Herein lies the biblical concept of stewardship of resources. Even more significantly, from Neoplatonist times forward Christian thought has contained a romantic mysticism, wherein nature reveals the hand of God in sublime form. Thus, when one is close to nature, one is close to God as well.[83]

Since Muir's essays are replete with biblical analogies, his critics often find it difficult to link this "God language" and his rejection of Scotland's "dour Calvinism." But perhaps these critics have used the wrong model. Around 1848 John's father, Daniel Muir, who might best be described as a religious seeker, left the Scottish Presbyterian Church and joined the Disciples of Christ church in Dunbar. It was this conversion that drew him to the Wisconsin frontier. Indeed, the elder Muir often preached in Wisconsin for the Disciples. Although Muir's writings reveal dismay with his father's narrow, biblical literalist outlook, Muir the younger proved far more indebted to the Disciples' point of view than he ever realized.

The denomination that came to be known as the Disciples of Christ or Christians was founded in Kentucky/Ohio/Pennsylvania in the early nineteenth century by the father-and-son team of Thomas and Alexander Campbell. Both Scotch-Irish graduates of the University of Glasgow, Thomas came to the States for his health c. 1808 and Alexander followed soon after. The Campbells began as Presbyterians but rejected this faith for a "restoration of the ancient order of things." They pledged to discard all "man-made" church ordinances (synods, presbyteries, general assemblies, titles such as reverend, conferences, missionary societies, lengthy creeds, and so forth) and to adopt the "watchword principle" forged by Thomas c. 1809: "Where the Scriptures speak, we speak; where they are silent, we are silent."

This ecumenical appeal drew converts from a number of frontier denominations: Baptists, Methodists, and other "New Light" (i.e., evangelical) groups, such as the sect founded by contemporary evangelist Barton W. Stone. The issues that most concerned the Campbells were baptism by immersion, weekly communion, and the nature of Scriptural authority. Alexander Campbell proved an excellent promoter of these principles. He combined a stress on logic and reason on the one hand with a deep-seated emotionalism on the other. He was also quite effective in debate, and in 1827 convinced an Edinburgh University graduate, Walter Scott, to become an evangelist for the emerging Disciples movement. Scott helped the cause considerably when he devised the famous "five finger exercise" that stressed faith, repentance, baptism, remission of sins, and the gift of the Holy Spirit.[84] By the 1830s the movement had grown considerably, primarily through the merging, in Lexington, Kentucky, of the Campbellites with the Stoneites, resulting in the Disciples of Christ. Originally numbering around 13,000, by mid-century the Disciples claimed 120,000. Disciples evangelists found success both in Scotland and along the American frontier.

The Disciples faith that Daniel Muir adopted (and one which young John must have heard endlessly discussed) was not "dour Calvinism." Rather, it emphasized a New Testament biblical literalism; an Arminian (i.e., free-will) position on salvation; a combined simple rationalism/strong emotionalism; an ecumenical goal of uniting all Protestant churches that only reluctantly evolved into another denomination; and a love of the art of debate. All these positions—save the emphasis on biblical literalism—can be clearly seen in John Muir's later career.

Muir's ecumenical views began with the universal message of the New Testament and moved to the realm of nature, but they remained no less all inclusive for the shift. Muir's appeal to "Come to the mountains and see" strangely echoed the altar call of the frontier Disciples revivalist who asked sinners freely to accept the offer of God's grace. One modern scholar has compared Muir's more polemical writings to a Hebrew prophet's denunciation of wickedness in high places.[85] Muir himself drew on biblical phrases at virtually every turn. On one occasion he even likened himself to John the Baptist: "Heaven knows John Baptist was not more eager to get his fellow sinners into the Jordan than I to baptize all of mine in the beauty of God's mountain."[86] After visiting Yosemite for the first time, he said of the experience: "We were new creatures, born again."[87] Thus, John Muir's nature ethic probably derives less from a rejection of his Calvinist, Presbyterian youth than from an amplification of his father's Disciples of Christ view of the world.

Today it is hard to find a more famous Scoto-American than John Muir. In 1989 the State Legislature of California designated April 21 as John Muir Day, an act that insures an annual celebration of his ideas. There are more sites named for Muir in California than for any other person, including a Muir Grove, Muir Gorge, Muir Pass, Muir Trail, Muir Woods State Park, a Muir Wilderness area, and a National Monument. A recent bumper sticker proclaimed: "Muir Power to You."

John Muir's fame is growing in Scotland as well. The town of Dunbar has recently restored his birthplace as a potential tourist site, and Scottish authorities have also set aside a 1,700-acre wildlife preserve on the Firth of Forth under his name. A prominent British nature organization has adopted the name "The John Muir Trust."

Muir's writings are available today in many formats, and from 1979 to 1990 at least sixty-seven books and articles were written on various aspects of his life.[88] Originator of the environmental concept of "deep ecology," John Muir drew on both his Scottish youth and his Wisconsin boyhood to call for awe and reverence in the face of nature. Almost alone among his generation, he saw virtue in wilderness. He also drew on another traditional Scottish theme that can be found in both Enlightenment and Romantic thought: the dream of shared, universal knowledge. Born in Dunbar, Scotland, John Muir today has become a "secular saint" for America, and, to a lesser extent, for the world.[89]

CHAPTER SEVEN

The Western Canadian Alternative

Unlike those in the United States, the Scots in Canada have always retained a high public profile. From the sailing of the *Hector* (the Canadian "Mayflower") from Ullapool in 1773 to the Highland Clearances of the 1840s—"nothing now remains but to have them removed to Canada" wrote one observer—to the late twentieth century, Scottish immigration has played a crucial role in Canadian history.[1] In 1841 Robert MacDougall wrote one of the few Gaelic travel books—*The Emigrant's Guide to North America*—for Highlanders contemplating the move. The thirteen volumes of the *Dictionary of Canadian Biography*, which carry the story to 1920, "are simply full of Scots."[2] Historian J. M. Bumsted has argued that Scottish immigration to Canada remained roughly stable throughout much of the nineteenth century—around 3,000 a year. One hunded and seventy thousand arrived between 1815 and 1870; 80,000 between 1870 and 1890; and 246,000 between 1900 and 1918. This consistent influx of settlers kept memories of the old country alive for each generation. By 1870 at the latest, the Scots had established themselves as the third largest ethnic group in Canadian society. By 1911 one observer boasted that Scots held about half of the nation's top positions.[3] Even today, many Scots who have never set foot in the United States have made numerous trips to Canada.

Unlike the States, nineteenth-century Canada never developed any melting-pot ideal. Their preferred metaphor of national identity became a mosaic. Thus, Canadian Scots found it easier than those in the States to retain their ethnicity. As a result, assimilation into the dominant culture varied considerably from province to province. During the late eighteenth and early nineteenth centuries, whole clans settled in Nova Scotia (New Scotland) and Cape Breton Island.[4] The region today is studded with Highland place-names. Even after five generations of settlement, Gaelic remains the preferred language for thousands of Cape Bretonites. The last all-Gaelic newspaper *MacTalla* (*Echo*), which survived until World War I, was published not in Inverness but in Sidney, Nova Scotia. In 1930 a Scots writer observed that "there is no part of the Empire more Highland than Cape Breton."[5] Ontario also produced a vibrant Scottish subculture.[6] In 1990, when Canadian writer David Craig began searching for stories of the Highland Clearances, he discovered a history of family legend and artifacts throughout all of eastern Canada.[7] In 1949, when the St. Andrew's Society of Detroit held its one-hundredth anniversary celebration, virtually all the pipers, bands, and Highland dancers hailed from either Ontario or the Prairie Provinces.[8] As Ged Martin and Jeffrey Simpson have recently observed, few places have as much in common as do Canada and Scotland. To a large degree, they wrote, "the history of the one is the history of the other."[9]

Although the impact of Scots on eastern Canada has been fairly well studied, the story of the western migration has been less highly profiled. Yet because the Prairie Provinces and British Columbia contained relatively few people, the power of a strong personality—often touted as a Scots characteristic—could reach a great distance. Historian J. M. Bumsted's figures for Scots in the Canadian West read as follows:

TABLE 3.
Total Scots in the Canadian West

Year	Prairie Provinces	British Columbia
1871	—	—
1881	10,415 (16.7%)	3,892 (7.8%)
1901	72,905 (16.9%)	31,068 (17.3%)
1921	305,774 (15.6%)	104,965 (18.6%)

Source: J. M. Bumstead, *The Scots in Canada* (Ottawa: Canadian Historical Association, 1982), 17.

Even though declining slightly over time, as late as 1941 Scots still composed almost one-seventh of the western Canadian population.[10]

The story of Scottish settlement in the Canadian West begins with Thomas Douglas, Fifth Earl of Selkirk. Born in 1771, Selkirk reached his maturity during the heady days of the French Revolution. His idealism also drew on the Scottish Enlightenment, whose principles he absorbed while attending the University of Edinburgh (where he knew Walter Scott). A man of catholic interests, Selkirk wrote books and essays on numerous themes: national defence, the fur trade, American Indian civilization, and poverty in Edinburgh. No armchair theorist, he mastered Gaelic so as to understand the Highlands better and also inaugurated a modest scheme to alleviate Edinburgh's worst social problems. In 1799, much to his surprise—for he was the seventh son—he succeeded to the family title. Afterwards he had the resources to enact some of his ideas on a grand scale.[11]

During the course of his education Selkirk had read McKenzie's *Voyages* and been deeply impressed. Later he sought out other books on the fur trade, even adding one to their number. By chance his interest in North America coincided with his longstanding concern over the plight of the Highlanders. In 1802 Selkirk established a pioneer Highland colony on Prince Edward Island, which, if it was not quite a success, was not a failure either. Then, in 1811, he purchased title to 120,000 square miles along the Red River of the North from the Hudson's Bay Company for what became his most celebrated venture. Terming the area "Assiniboine," Selkirk selected Miles MacDonnell as governor and oversaw the 1812 arrival of thirty-six Scottish and Northern-Irish workers in one of the grandest colonial ventures in the Canadian West. The new colony sited itself a mile below the North West fur-trading post of Fort Gibraltar in Manitoba and soon became known as the Red River settlement.[12]

On one hand the little settlement at the confluence of the Red and Assiniboine Rivers produced an object lesson in Enlightenment humanity. But it also produced a clash of cultures and economics. The fur traders of the rival North West Company viewed Selkirk's settlement and the Hudson's Bay Company's management of the situation with a jaundiced eye. They interpreted Red River as a bald attempt to cut off their supplies of furs and block them from their traditional lines of communication. Consequently, in June 1816 a group of North Westerners, led by Cuthbert Grant, a Scoto-Indian mixed-blood, murdered twenty-two settlers in the now-infamous "Seven Oaks massacre." Lord Selkirk arrived the next year with troops to restore the settlement. While tension remained for years, further dangers to the colony came primarily from other sources: frosts, grasshoppers, and especially floods. Although the community contained a number of ethnic groups from the onset, the Scottish immigrants predominated. In 1821 Scots comprised more than 50 percent of the population of Red River (221 of 419).

That same year the North West Company and the Hudson's Bay Company united, thus closing more than two decades of bitter rivalry. The union not only ended all danger of raids on Red River, it began to alter the nature of the community itself. The largely mixed-blood trappers began to consider the settlement as their own. After retirement from trapping they moved there in large numbers. By 1836 the population had grown to five thousand; by 1845 it had reached seven thousand. With this growth the Scots component of the Red River community lost its dominance. In 1845 it had dropped to a mere 5 percent (four hundred of seven thousand). It remained at that level when Manitoba became a province in 1870 (seven hundred of twelve thousand).[13]

With the Red River experiment Lord Selkirk forged the model that would be followed all through the century for Scottish settlement in the West. If kith and kin emigrated together, departure from Scotland did not necessarily mean exile. But, as time would show, it proved far easier to sustain Scottish group loyalty in eastern Canada—Prince Edward Island, Cape Breton, and Ontario—than in the vast regions of the Canadian West.

If the Scots component of Red River faded over time, the number of Canadian Scots mixed-bloods in the region rose. Cuthbert Grant was appointed "Warden of the Plains" by the Hudson's Bay Company and eventually established the community of Granttown at White Horse Plains, west of Winnipeg. On the west bank of the Red River, mixed-bloods and Orkney farmers steadily carved out small homesteads. Other Scoto-Indians assumed leadership roles, notably Captain William Kennedy, an explorer, trader, legislator, and negotiator of Indian treaties. Alexander Ross, who lived there with his Native wife and mixed-blood children, always thought that Red River might serve Canada as its "city on the Hill" (on the plains?)—a model to imitate regarding national race relations.

During the 1860s Scots-born politicians John A. Macdonald and George Brown led the movement for confederation; both of the first two Canadian prime ministers were childhood émigrés. In addition about one-fifth of Canada's industrialists in the 1880s were of Scottish birth, as were many of the timber magnates and bankers. Scots also served as the first veterinarians of the West.[14] Most of the great railway entrepreneurs, from surveyors to builders, were also Scots, Donald A. Smith and George Stephen of Moray Firth being perhaps the most famous. When the last spike was driven in 1885 at a spot named Craigellachie, British Columbia, an observer noted:

> His [Lord Strathcona's] presence recalled memories of the Mackenzies, Frasers, Finlaysons, Thompsons, MacTavishes, McLeods, MacGillivrays, Stuarts, and McLoughlins, who in a past generation had penetrated the surrounding mountains.[15]

In a real sense the laying of the Canadian Railway track *created* the west country. Outside of slow and ineffectual river communication, no real settlement was possible without effective transportation. Until the arrival of the railroad in the 1880s, neither the government nor private individuals made any concerted effort to open the Canadian West to European settlement.

From the 1870s forward, however, Canada's dreams of populating its West fit well into Britain's plans to resettle displaced crofters from the Highlands and Islands. In 1886 the Canadian high commissioner agreed to provide financial aid to this scheme for "so desirable a class of settlers as the Scotch crofters."[16]

Since life on the prairies in Victorian Canada proved largely male, a considerable demand arose for women settlers as well. Shetland author Jessie M. Saxby wrote to encourage middle-class Scots women to immigrate to the Canadian West, as did Edinburgh native Elizabeth Mitchel. Western Canada, they suggested, offered both economic opportunity and a chance for social advancement. "There is so much *room* here" became their major message. Each individual, especially the women, counted, because "there were so few of them."[17] Moreover, most

Victorians believed that the mere presence of women would cause men to behave better. Thus, the appeal for women settlers would help civilize the barbaric West.

Because of the demand for settlers, a minor "recruiting war" erupted between the various public and private agencies. Agents from the Canadian Pacific Railway, the Canadian National Railway, the Canadian national government, and the various Canadian provinces sometimes worked with, and sometimes against, one another in the quest for settlers. In addition they jostled with agents from the American western states and the American railroads.

The Canadians generally won the recruiting war for Scots with ease. Historian Marjory Harper has counted 16,000 immigrants from northeast Scotland who left for Canada in the middle of the nineteenth century. During a later period, 91 percent of all emigrants from the port of Aberdeen listed Canada as their destination. Canadian adverts continually emphasized the theme that their provinces were "more like home" than the United States. From 1910 to 1914 about 170,000 Scots emigrated to Canada.[18]

Canadian agents based in Scotland raised recruiting to the level of high art. They commissioned booking agents in all the major cities and in many remote parts of the land. From a Glasgow base they sent speakers out on a steady tour of the farming regions of the Lowlands and northeastern Scotland. Since the Canadian prairies demanded agricultural skills, the various recruiters began to turn away from the crowded British cities to concentrate on Scotland's richer farm regions. The culmination came in 1907 when agent John MacLennan, a Gaelic-speaking Canadian from Alberta, established a permanent office in Aberdeen. For over a decade he regularly sent hundreds of agricultural Scots to Canada.

MacLennan proved a master of his trade. He met with from twenty to thirty visitors a day in his downtown office. He obtained posters, pamphlets, and leaflets, which he distributed at numerous local gatherings at hotels, working men's clubs, annual hiring fairs for farm workers, livestock markets (held weekly), and summer shows. He hired billboards and sent out a traveling display of Canadian produce and natural resources to every local fair. Its message, "You need Canada—Canada Needs You," was also echoed in the regular adverts placed in area newspapers. On occasion he helped fund visits by Scottish journalists or representatives of local farm organizations.

MacLennan's message bore fruit. During his first year in Aberdeen he replied to more than 100 letters a week. During January 1910 he responded to more than 320 a week. During a 1909 speaking tour he drew an audience of 400 in Insch and 1,800 in Elgin. The *Aberdeen Journal* suggested that Canada's interest in the area reflected a recognition of the superior quality of settlers from northern Scotland.[19] Local pride notwithstanding, the *Journal* had a point. The small farmers, farm workers, farm wives, and maid servants all possessed skills that were immediately applicable to the recently opened Canadian prairies. One Canadian Pacific Railway agent in the early 1920s actually journeyed with his Black Isle recruits to northern Saskatchewan to make certain they were properly settled. Moreover, as Harper has noted, the emigrants from northeast Scotland seldom left without some modest financial means. The region was losing "the backbone of the rural population," complained the Aberdeen *Herald*.[20] About 20 percent of the 1.2 million British people who arrived between 1901 and 1914 were born in Scotland. Canadian recruiting agents could be found touring northeast Scotland until the 1930s.

Once the railroad opened up the Canadian prairies, a number of private organizations made similar attempts at settling Scottish immigrants. The huge Scottish-Canadian Land and Settlement Association, Ltd., the Dundee Land Investment Company, the Scottish Ontario and Manitoba Land Company, and the

Dundee Investment Company all tried to establish various "Scottish colonies."[21] In 1888 the Canadian Pacific Railway proclaimed that "millions of acres" of rich land awaited the landless and touted Assiniboia as a virtual utopia. Their brochure depicted the climate of Calgary as benefiting from warm Chinook winds that kept the "ground free from snow in the winter, except for a day or two at a time."[22] Comments that most Métis children who lived on the Red River shared "the blood of men who fought with Lochiel near Inverness on the 15th [sic] April 1746" rounded out the appeal for Scottish immigrants. In large measure the publicity worked, and Manitoba, in the words of one historian, "became the El Dorado of many a Scots lad."[23]

In the early 1880s Lady Gordon Cathcart of Cluny Castle in the Western Isles attempted to establish a settlement of Island crofters in Manitoba. By then Lady Cathcart had attained a modest reputation as an idealistic heiress with concern for the plight of the crofters on her estate, even going so far as to offer one hundred pounds to any family willing to immigrate to Canada. At her urging a crofters' delegation from Benbecula, in the Outer Hebrides, visited Manitoba in 1881 and reported back favorably. Given this impetus, Lady Cathcart teamed with the Canada Northwest Land Company and funded the passage of eleven families (one came independently), so that in 1883 fifty-one people arrived in what would be named New Benbecula, Manitoba. Her plan, as the *Manitoba Daily Free Press* reported, hoped "to combine sound finance and genuine, clear-eyed philanthropy."[24] Encouraging reports enticed forty-six additional families the next year. By 1885 the community numbered 239. The experiment aroused sufficient interest that Professor G. G. Ramsay made a trip to Canada to report their story for *Macmillan's Magazine*.

Ramsay's assessment proved quite positive. He praised the émigrés' Canadian sod houses, with their thatched roofs woven from the abundant prairie grasses. He noted that all households had planted oats, barley, and potatoes and kept cattle for butter, cheese, and milk. Because of their farm skills, the men found that they could always get work at harvest time. The young women similarly discovered that they could always find temporary work as servants. Anticipating Frederick Jackson Turner's famed frontier thesis by eight years, G. G. Ramsay marveled how land ownership could transform Gaelic culture. The Highland settlers began life with "charm of manner" but without the "energy of the lowlander." Yet, after a brief period of land ownership, "all this seems to disappear in Canada."[25] Other travelers gathered comments from the settlers to confirm their impressions. "If they saw me owning soil like yon in Aberdeen," said former Banchory blacksmith John Murray, 'They'd a' tak' their hat aff to me." "How can we thank Lady Gordon enough?" said a New Benbecula resident. "She has made lairds of us all."[26]

Later historians, however, have been far more critical of Lady Cathcart's efforts. Hugh MacPhee has noted that she encouraged her crofters to emigrate just as the famed Napier Commission began its investigation into landlord-crofter relations. Although the seventeen letters from Benbecula émigrés that were included in the Napier report presented to Paliament praised her beneficence, it is somewhat suspicious that all were written in clear English rather than the crofters' native Gaelic.[27]

The Gaelic poem composed by Manitoba resident Donald Mackinnon from Balivanich, Benbecula, presents a very different picture of life in Canada:

> A thousand liars, well rewarded
> Went about with books
> Extolling the North West
> and the excellence of Manitoba.
>
> In our cheerless houses in the cold morning
> There is hoar frost on the blankets;

water and ale, whey or milk,
all like frozen glass.

When there is a blizzard in the bleak land
One needs the fur of every animal for clothing.

Woollen tweed will not protect us;
The wind whips our flesh off.

In Scotland on a May morning
I would go barefooted to the moors;
There was no need of the ugly Moccasin,
Nor were we clothed in furs.
If I survive until Spring
I shall leave the 'Land of Promise.'
I'll go to Dakota;
Land and gold abound there.[28]

Present-day Benbecula crofter sentiment lies far closer to Mackinnon's view than to Ramsey's. It recalls Lady Cathcart as a grasping evictor, unsympathetic to the Catholic faith of her tenants. One historian has termed her "a notoriously implacable proprietrix."[29] Modern scholars have concluded that in spite of the benevolence involved in all the landlord-assisted emigration schemes, the ultimate goal was to free the estates of people to increase financial profit.[30]

The Canadian West hosted a number of these quasi-utopian Scottish resettlement schemes. Between 1888 and 1889 Killarney, Manitoba, and Saltcoats in the Northwest Territories (now Saskatchewan) were each begun with high hopes, both from the crofters—who had resisted group emigration for a generation—and from various officials of the Canadian government. As historian Wayne Norton has shown, however, the emigration scheme was "flawed in conception and rushed in implementation."[31]

Killarney proved marginally successful, but the community established at Saltcoats failed miserably. When the forty-one crofter families from the Isles of Lewis, Harris, and North Uist arrived in Saltcoats in 1889, they met a variety of bureaucratic blunders, including a shortage of supplies. After a winter of genuine suffering the community faced several years of drought, hail, and early frosts. By 1894 forty-eight families had abandoned their homesteads. Only a Donald McIver determined to meet his obligations. A decade later the Imperial Colonization Board, which had overseen the experiment, washed its hands of the whole affair by selling the land to a Minneapolis businessman.

Well-intentioned though it was, the Saltcoats crofter resettlement plan failed for several reasons. Foremost, perhaps, was the initial stretch of bad weather, always a concern for agriculture at that latitude. But some of the blame should be placed on the crofters themselves. Many had primarily been fishermen in the Western Isles, and they did not take easily to the demands of breaking virgin Canadian prairie soil. Moreover, the men discovered that they could earn modest wages by working as day laborers for the railway, cutting wood in winter, or hiring themselves out during the harvest season. In addition members of the community often quarreled among themselves. Consequently, after fourteen years, the Saltcoats residents disbanded and the former crofters disappeared into Canadian society.[32] The failure of these prairie colonies also basically spelled the end of government-assisted crofter emigration schemes.[33]

In spite of such failures numerous private agencies continued to set forth a vision of western Canada as a solution to Highland and Island social problems. A c. 1912 Canadian Pacific pamphlet virtually promised social advance to any Scot willing to journey to the Canadian West.[34] In the 1920s Benedictine priest Andrew MacDonell urged his South Uist flock to form a group settlement in Manitoba.[35] A January 28, 1927, *Stornoway Gazette* article still praised Alberta as the "land of opportunity" for

Highland Scots. As late as 1936 the Duchess of Atholl funded the passage of twenty-eight children to the Prince of Wales Fairbridge Farm School on Vancouver Island. There these (mostly) orphans joined nearly one hundred other young people who had been sent there from similar situations with the hopes of turning them into potential farmers.[36] In short, the Earl of Selkirk's experiment at Red River had many echoes.

Scottish farmers not only settled the southern Canadian plains, they emigrated to the cosmopolitan western cities as well. Many immigrants from industrialized Glasgow and commercial Edinburgh also sought their fortunes in urban areas. In fact so many Scots landed in Vancouver that one reporter suggested in 1933 that one needed to be born "in Aberdeenshire or thereabouts" in order to work for the police force. Aberdonians were found in all walks of Vancouver life: medicine, commerce, law, trade, and the churches. The people of northeastern Scotland, an Aberdeen reporter concluded, "are helping to mold the character of this western city."[37]

The link between Scotland and the Canadian Northwest received yet another boost when the Canadian Bank of Commerce transferred a twenty-seven-year-old teller from Victoria, B.C., to Kamloops, B.C., in 1901. The teller was Robert W. Service, son of a Scottish bank teller of the same name who had emigrated from the Lancashire region to Canada on a tramp freighter in 1895. From Kamloops young Service moved on to Whitehorse and Dawson, Yukon Territory. Although he soon resigned his position with the bank, he remained in Dawson for several years, working chiefly as a free-lance writer. During his stay he witnessed firsthand the decline of Klondike gold-rush society, which he decided to try to capture in verse.

His first collection of poems appeared in 1907 as *Songs of a Sourdough* in Canada and *The Spell of the Yukon* in the States. The

Recruiting poster for western Canada, 1903. The Prairie Provinces tried their best to attract Scottish immigrants to try their luck in the Canadian West. (Provincial Archives of Alberta. "A" Collection, Photo A7538.)

volume sold over a million copies, an enormous print run for a book of poetry, and a sequel, *Ballads of a Cheechako* (1909), did almost as well. Reporters soon dubbed him "The Poet of the Yukon" and "The Canadian Kipling." Modestly claiming that he was simply an "inkslinger" or "rhymer," not a true poet, Service nevertheless reached an enormous audience. From 1907 to the mid-1920s he was probably the most popular household poet in both the United States and Canada.[38] Afterwards he moved to France, where he lived until his death in 1958. Although he turned out a steady stream of works, none approached the appeal of his earlier volumes.

Service's easily memorized poems of the Yukon and the Klondike drew heavily from the Scots/Scots-Irish/Irish tradition of folk balladry, which he must have absorbed during his youth in Britain. In this largely oral world the bard assumed the mantle of public historian, the person who recorded the crucial events of the day for posterity. Without a bard to record his deeds, the old saying had it, a great leader would soon be forgotten.

This broadside tradition of balladry usually began with an invitation. "Come all ye fair and tender maidens," the poet might say, or "Come all ye noble patriots and listen to my song." The invitation theme is nicely reflected in the opening lines of Service's "The Cremation of Sam McGee."

> There are strange things done in the midnight sun
>   By the men who moil for gold;
>
> The Arctic trails have their secret tales
>   That would make your blood run cold;
> The Northern Lights have seen queer sights,
>   But the queerest they ever did see
> Was the night on the Marge of Lake Lebarge
>   I cremated Sam McGee.

The balladeer's theme of invitation is raised to even greater heights in the opening lines of Service's "The Shooting of Dan McGrew":

> A bunch of the boys were whooping it up in the Malamute saloon;
> The kid that handles the music-box was hitting A jag-time tune;
> Back of the bar, in a solo game, sat Dangerous Dan McGrew,
> And watching his luck was his light-o'-love, the lady that's known as Lou.[39]

It would take a hard heart, indeed, not to want to read those poems to conclusion. And, it should be noted, Service's two most famous protagonists bore the names of "McGee" and "McGrew."

Since the world of religion has always been central to the Scottish experience, it is not surprising that the kirk and the clergy played important roles as they followed, and in some cases led, the Scots to the Canadian West. In Red River during the 1820s Church of England chaplain John West complained that neither the Gaelic-speaking Highlanders nor the American Indians could understand his sermons. While he tried to minister to the numerous Scots settlers, they usually rebuffed his efforts.[40] In the 1850s Red River had a major confrontation over issues of faith. The repeated requests from the Gaelic settlement in Killarney, Manitoba, for a minister who spoke the old language reflected this concern.

As historian George Bryce has shown, Baptist, Methodist, and Roman Catholic Scottish clerics were very active in the Canadian West.[41] Yet the two churches that played the most central roles were probably the Presbyterian and the Episcopal. Religion was as important as race and the Scots influence proved vital in the "churching" of the Canadian Prairie West.

Churches have seldom been given their due in the story of the settlement of the Prairie West. But both south and north of the 49th parallel, they often served as the "glue" that kept an ethnic community together. In the more crowded urban areas of Toronto or Chicago, an immigrant community could support a variety of institutions: bakeries, restaurants, mutual-aid societies, even newspapers. But in the vast region of the Great Plains, the church had to assume all of these social roles.[42] No institution played a larger part in reinforcing ethnicity in the plains than did the ethnic church.

The various divisions among Presbyterian factions in the States were not duplicated in Canada; initially all Canadian Presbyterians united in a single denomination. Although Scots were crucial to the development of American Presbyterianism, one would not say that either the Northern, Southern, or Cumberland Presbyterians in the States were a "Scots Church." This proved to be very different in Canada, where, as historian John S. Moir has noted, the Presbyterians began as an ethnic church and never really lost that dimension.[43] George Bryce's compilation of 390 Presbyterian clergymen who served in western Canada from 1871 to 1910 revealed only a handful who lacked a Scots or Scotch-Irish surname.

On the Canadian frontier the Presbyterian clerics virtually served as "Scottish shepherds." "I never take a trip away from home," one wrote in 1884, "but Scotch immigrants from Highland glens and Lowland straths are met with, and they prove to be excellent settlers." One of Presbyterian T. N. Richmond's duties in Winnipeg in the 1890s was to meet Scottish settlers on arrival and give them aid as they sought places of settlement.[44] Missionary aid from the Church of Scotland proved a major funding source for Canadian Presbyterian home missions, and

Scots theological students often tested their skills in a temporary Canadian pulpit during the summer. Missionary letters are replete with tales of Scots immigrants who sought out the ordinances of the Canadian church: men who returned to services after years of indifference; an Edmonton woman from Logierait, Scotland, who drove sixty miles in November to have her child baptized; another emigrant, handicapped by age, who devised a homemade sled of rope, hay, and an old tray so that she could attend services. The novels by Ralph Connor, especially *The Sky Pilot*, reflect the central role of the church in western Canadian life.

Although the ethnic dimension was central to Canadian Presbyterianism, over time the church took on a wider set of responsibilities. Joining with the Anglicans, the middle-class, generally well-educated Presbyterian clerics also saw themselves as engaged in a great crusade to save the Canadian West for "British civilization." Thus, by 1895 home missionaries were preaching the gospel in six languages. Often they concentrated especially on those other ethnic groups, such as the Hungarians, who also had a Reformed tradition in their past. Theological boundaries slipped considerably in the vastness of the prairies, and most settlers, whatever their affiliation, welcomed a visit from a Presbyterian cleric.

The western clerics viewed the presence of the church as the chief counter to barbarism. Scorn, indifference, and occasional threats of rotten eggs made the plains ministers well aware of the fragility of "civilization" in their region. Judging from the accounts in the *Home and Foreign Missionary Record*, civilization contained a number of aspects: sacredness of life; sacredness of marriage and the rights of property; control of liquor; and the closing of gambling halls, base playhouses, and houses of ill repute. But the most prominent symbolic element that decided whether a community passed muster or not was its observance of the Christian Sabbath. "There is no heathen so low as the heathen with a white face," one minister warned, and the solution was to keep the Sabbath intact.[45] As events transpired, however, most prairie communities reached a compromise. On weekdays and Sunday Victorian respectability reigned supreme, more or less, in western Canada. But especially on Saturday nights, the towns became the property of the wilder elements.

"Personality," Ralph Waldo Emerson once said, "never goes out of style." The late-Victorian Canadian West boasted three Scottish religious personalities who had major impacts on their regions. One was Presbyterian and two were Episcopalian.

The Presbyterian was John Robertson. Born in Perthshire, Robertson served as superintendent of Presbyterian Home Missions in western Canada from 1881 to 1902. In addition to his numerous travels, Robertson enlightened readers of the *Home and Missionary Record* with tales of adventure from the Great Northwest. Although he occasionally denounced the "infidel views and lax morals" of the region, he concentrated primarily on depicting social progress, especially the increased respect for rights of property and for the sacredness of life. The census of 1891 showed that the Presbyterian Church of Canada had become the nation's largest Protestant denomination, and Robertson's career—as the driving force behind the church in western Canada for over two decades—formed an important part of this story.

The Episcopalians Robert McKay and John Maclean were born in northeast Scotland. Each came from a Presbyterian background but converted to the Episcopal Church at university, probably as a reaction to the Great Disruption of 1843, which split the Presbyterians. After ordination McKay was appointed bishop of Rupert's land and, from a base in Winnipeg, presided over the church in western Canada for forty years. His diocese originally contained two million square miles. Maclean, in turn, became the first bishop of Saskatchewan, a post he held until his death in 1886, at which time he was proclaimed "the central figure of our community."[46]

Given the vast distances and sparseness of population, these well-educated, peripatetic Scots clerics had considerable personal influence. For example, like many pioneer clergymen, they estabished institutions that long survived them. McKay revised and reorganized St. Johns College in Winnipeg and also served as first chancellor of the University of Manitoba. Maclean, in turn, established Emmanuel College at Prince Albert in 1879, intending it as a teaching center for Native clergy. Robertson helped establish Knox College, Winnipeg. Presbyterian George Bryce founded Manitoba College in the same city and also had a part in the establishment of the University of Manitoba in 1871. Thus, kirk and education overlapped considerably in this "brick-and-mortar" era of the Canadian West.[47]

The church was not the only bastion of Scottish culture in the Canadian West. One could find overt manifestations of "Scottishness" in a wide variety of areas. Former Highland farmers cursed their oxen in Gaelic, and local entertainment always demanded the pipes and a Scottish reel. Men donned the kilt for numerous ceremonial occasions, especially weddings, funerals, Burns Day dinners, and St. Andrew's Day celebrations. Canadian Scots soldiers usually disliked the kilt, but the "ladies from hell" (as they were termed by the Germans) wore it bravely during World War I. Transported Highland games, performed from Nova Scotia to Vancouver, also provided a fine opportunity to parade things Scottish. There is general agreement that the Canadian national sport of ice hockey had its origin in the ancient Gaelic game of shinty.

During the early twentieth century, the Canadian railways discovered the appeal of Scottish customs to tourists. They hired pipers to dress in kilts and play traditional tunes at stations along the way west. Later, the brilliant novels of Margaret Laurence, depicting life in her fictitional Manawaka (Keepawa), Manitoba, also reflected Scots themes.

Scots names retain a high profile in western Canadian life. On the map one finds Calgary ("clear running water" in Gaelic), Banff, and a host of other towns that betray their origin. Among Canadian citizens the surnames MacLeod or MacDonald imply "Scots" just as Boudreau or Chevalier imply "French" or Goldberg and Epstein, "Jewish." One does not find this immediate Scottish connection with American Scottish surnames. For example, *Montana Magazine* editor Charles Rankin discovered that no one identified his name as Scottish until he moved to Helena. In the South a name such as McLelland or McGregor is perceived as an American surname. In the Southwest MacDonald is seen as a Navajo surname, for the father of a former Navajo tribal chairman took it from a song ("Old MacDonald Had a Farm") when asked for his last name by a teacher.

Although Scottish culture is woven all through the Prairie Provinces, it is nowhere more prominent than in the Okanagan Valley of British Columbia. As noted in the previous chapter, Lord and Lady Aberdeen planted some of the first fruit trees there in 1892; in 1895 they subdivided the property into units of ten to one hundred acres each. These they sold to prospective fruit ranchers, many Scottish themselves. Lord and Lady Aberdeen also introduced the first irrigation system into the valley. Although they eventually lost money on the venture—in fact, their Scottish estates financed much of their Canadian programs—the Aberdeens prided themselves on shaping the future economy of the Okanagan region. They took credit not only for the shift from cattle to fruit but also for encouraging wealthy Scottish immigrants to the region.

But the Scots immigrants brought more to the Okanagan than simply their wealth or their farming skills. They also brought with them their love of mystery and romance. Even in the decidedly unromantic late-twentieth century, Americans and Canadians have looked to Scotland for an aura of mystery. How else can one explain the popularity of Alan Jay Lerner and Frederick Loewe's *Brigadoon,* a fantasy tale of two hunters who stumble upon a mysterious Scottish village that appears only once a century? This musical has charmed audiences ever since it was first performed in 1947 and remains a perennial favorite among high-school and college drama students.

Equally enticing was the greatest discovery of its day: the Loch Ness Monster. Prior to 1933 Loch Ness ranked as only one of Highland Scotland's striking lakes. That year, however, the government commenced construction of an improved road on the west side of the loch. The constant noise and commotion, so it is said, drew the monster from its deep sea lair and a wave of sightings alerted Fleet Street that a major story was in the making. Over the years the story has grown steadily. Today, if one mentions Loch Ness outside the Highlands, the first reaction is certain to be: "the monster."[48]

Loch Ness is the largest body of fresh water in the United Kingdom. About twenty-three miles long and a mile wide, it is over seven hundred feet deep, about twice the depth of the North Sea. This depth has served to discourage swimmers, and it has earned the grim reputation as the loch that never gives up its dead.[49] Monster supporters maintain that this is why no one has ever found a carcass.

From 1933 to the present day Loch Ness has attracted millions of visitors who hope against hope for a glimpse of Scotland's most famous resident. The visitors range from the stern Englishman who left after an hour, threatening to sue for "false advertising," to engineer Tim Dinsdale, who has spent his entire life searching the lake for ultimate proof of the monster's existence.[50]

The literature on "Nessie" or "The Great Orm" is enormous. The official Loch Ness Monster Exhibition Centre at tiny Drumnadrochit also contains examples of numerous photographs, all suitably blurry. While other Highland lochs, Loch Morar and Loch Shiel, have traditions of similar sightings, knowledge of their stories remains confined to locals. Only Nessie has achieved an international reputation.

The settlers of the Okanagan Valley in British Columbia, many from Lady Aberdeen's birthplace of Inverness-shire, brought these ideas with them. In Lake Okanagan, virtually alone among North American lakes, one can find a similar "Great Orm." It, too, received its first publicity in the 1930s. The publicity surrounding the Loch Ness Monster gave new life to its Canadian counterpart—named "Ogopogo" after a popular song of the day—and it has received a great deal of interest ever since.

Ogopogo has often been seen but, unlike Nessie, has never been captured on film. No photos of the lake surface show anything of interest either, but the 1938 discovery of the living fossil coelacanth, a five-foot-long fish thought to have died out seventy million years ago, has given believers hope. If the waters off Madagascar could produce a living fossil, what might these deep-water Canadian lakes contribute? Some have suggested that the creatures might even be hatching from eggs laid in preglacial times.[51]

The parallels are uncanny. The Loch Ness tale stretches back to St. Adamnan's biography of St. Columba (c. 565 A.D.) and even, perhaps, to the Celtic Highland lore of the water horse or water kelpie. Similarly, American Indians of the Columbia plateau have termed the Okanagan creature "Naitaka" and have allegedly tried to pacify it by sacrificing small animals before crossing the lake. As Loch Morar and Loch Shiel have tried to usurp the fame of Loch Ness, so, too, have Lake Simcie in Keswick, Ontario, and Lake Winnipegosis, Manitoba, come forth with their various creatures, "Igopogo" and "Manipogis." Vancouver Bay also boasts an ocean-going sea monster named "Caddy."[52] One should not be surprised to learn that the chief historian of Ogopogo, journalist Mary Moon, was the daughter of a well-known Scottish novelist. Finally, there is a persistent legend that as the Okanagan Valley was initially settled by Highland farmers, one approached the lake and asked a local resident, "What kind of beasties do ye hae in this loch, laddie?"[53] The Scottish links to the Canadian West come in a number of guises.

The question, "Why were the Scots so drawn to western Canada?" has often been asked, but no reply has been completely satisfactory. In 1911 writer John Murray Gibbon wryly observed that the best passport for any Canadian immigrant was to speak with a Scots accent. But he also put forth his own explanation of the Scots' success in Canada: "They were able to adapt themselves to any circumstance, they had faith in themselves, and they stuck together."[54] To this one might add the generous experiments of the philanthropists, the community role of the clergy, the promotion efforts of the Canadian Railroads and land companies, and the vast richness of the land itself. When combined, the attraction proved irresistible.

EPILOGUE

Words on the Land

Somewhere around the era of World War I, the Scots and Ulster Scots lost their fascination with the North American West. By this time the less-skilled immigrants from southern and eastern Europe had largely excluded the Scots from many of the occupations of the previous two generations. Perhaps Scotland's own industrial stagnation and decline sapped a spirit of adventure as well.[1]

Simultaneously, America lost some of its fascination for Scotland. The rise of the militant Glasgow labor movement at "Red Clydeside," with its loud boasts of coming radical social changes, did not sit well with the conservative tone of America in the 1920s. From 1920 forward Scots continued to immigrate to the States, of course, but they became just one of many immigrant groups. Their impact on the American West was much less noticeable in the twentieth century, although one can still find a strong Houston-Aberdeen oil link. By about 1925 over a century of creative interaction had largely drawn to a close.

Why did the Scots have such an impact on the nineteenth-century North American West? This is not an easy question to answer. One might fall back on the "Scottish character," with its boasts of pragmatism, honesty, logic, and democratic ethos. There may be some truth to this. An 1843 letter from Glasgow émigré William Wilson to his mother thanked her profusely, because "I never knew I was so well raised till I came to America."[2]

Yet the crucial factor was probably the Scots emphasis on formal education. Although the Scottish educational system remained a bewildering mixture of parochial, state, charitable, and private schools until the end of the nineteenth century, it also had few rivals in any European country. As early as the mid-eighteenth century the majority of Scots could read and write. Except possibly for Switzerland, Prussia, and New England, no other region in the Western World could make this claim. The ability to read, write, and cypher was not commonplace among most nineteenth-century immigrant groups. When William Wilson traveled on an immigrant ship to St. Louis, he observed that only the two Scots on board "knew more than how to handle the chopping axe."[3] When Nellie Allen arrived in Boise in 1913, her employer asked her if she could make mayonnaise, a food she had never heard of. "Well, na, I have never made mayonnaise," said Nellie, who had quit school at twelve, "but I can read."[4] Angus McDonald founded his first school in Montana in 1850, and his mixed-blood children and grandchildren could all read and write, which was not all that common on the Flathead reservation at the turn of the century. As a great-great granddaughter recently observed, "We McDonalds have always been what we have been because we have been educated."[5] Growing up in 1940s Montana, Ivan Doig recalled the great respect for education that permeated his primarily sheep-herding Scottish community. Historian Rosalind Mitchison has credited the discipline of regular work and widespread literacy as the two qualities best instilled by the Scottish educational system.[6]

But there were other factors as well. A sense of adventure, a self-confidence, a familiarity with harsh landscape, a work ethic, an individualism that combined nicely with group loyalties, and, often, a set of industrial or agricultural skills set Scots apart from many of the other immigrants. And these talents were sorely in demand in nineteenth-century America.

In 1950 an anonymous author concluded a U.S. Information Agency pamphlet with the observation that it was impossible "to determine the exact extent of Scottish influence—except to say that it is large, and has become part of the bone and sinew and the character of America."[7] Certainly this was true for the American West as well. Although they were never a statistically large group, Scots pioneered in the West as explorers, fur traders, gardeners, farmers, clerics, miners, cattle-ranch managers, and, especially, sheepmen. In several of these areas they had few equals.

The dream of "rational" economic success, as reflected in the lives of George Smith, Andrew Little, David Eccles, Robert Dollar, and Andrew Carnegie, had echoes in the accolades accorded to "romantics" such as George Keith, Alexander Gardner, and John Muir. Thanks to the popularity of Harry Lauder and Buffalo Bill, the dramatic histories of Scotland and the American West entered the realm of myth, from which they could never be dislodged. From the 1790s to World War I, the Western American-Scottish interaction proved extensive, indeed.

Where are the western Scots today? Two recent books, *We the People: The Atlas of American Ethnic Diversity*, and *The Atlas of Contemporary America*, have tried to determine just that. The authors have discovered that Scots today live in countless locations across the West. They are especially concentrated in the Salt Lake Valley, Montana, eastern Oregon, Idaho, and western Washington. There is no western city of any size without them. Interestingly, the largest number live in Orange County, California, and in other cities along the southern California coast.[8] "You can see more kilts in an hour [in Santa Monica]," wrote one visitor in 1974, "than you will encounter on Princes Street [in Edinburgh] in a month of Sundays."[9]

One way to tell exactly where the Scots settled in their moves west is to chart the number of Scottish place-names scattered across the American landscape. There are eight Aberdeens, seven Glasgows, and eight Edinburghs in the United States, mostly west of the Mississippi.[10] One finds Aberdeen, South Dakota; Aberdeen, Washington; Glasgow, Montana; and Edinburgh (pronounced "Edinberg"), Texas. Nebraska boasts towns named Kelso and Campbell. Wyoming and New Mexico all contain small valleys named Glencoe. (Like the original, New Mexico's Glencoe echoes a tragic conflict, the infamous Lincoln County War of the 1870s.) A hamlet named Inverness, California, overlooks the narrow Tomales Bay in Marin County. Scores of towns beginning with "Mac" or "Mc" also dot the West, from McIntosh, New Mexico, to McCall, Idaho, to McAllister, Montana. The list could be extended. The northern tier of states, interestingly, contains more obviously Scots names than, say, those of Scandinavian, French, or German derivation. As any United States atlas will show, the Scots have permanently left their mark on the western landscape.

Such western place-names may or may not evoke Scottish memories among locals today. But since the early 1960s there has been a revival of Highland games that are clearly intended to do so. Golden, Colorado, began what are now the "Colorado Highland Games" in 1963; Tulsa followed in 1979; and Albuquerque joined in 1987. A 1994 listing cites twenty-seven western locations for such contests, the majority in California.[11] Since 1989 the state of Idaho has boasted an "official Idaho tartan plaid." The state of New Mexico is considering a similar official state tartan (perhaps with a cactus motif?). The College of Northern Idaho is justly proud of its recently inaugurated

Scottish Studies program, and a bookseller who retails only Scottish materials operates from Winters, California.

In areas of the West where Scots are relatively few in number (e.g., Colorado, Oklahoma, and New Mexico) promoters usually expand their Highland games to include the Irish and/or all "Celts." In the Southwest this broadened appeal has borne fruit, for many contemporary Hispanic surnames can be traced to Celtic roots in the Iberian peninsula: Gallegos, for example, originally meant Gaelic; Maldonado reputedly came from MacDonald; and Tapia derives from the Celtic word for sod. The St. Andrew's Scottish Society of New Mexico, founded in 1962, invites in people who are "Scottish by birth or descent or [have] an interest in Scotland." With pipes, drums, and Highland flings, the modern Highland games feature a "Scotland in America" theme that reflects a decidedly romantic Highland/Celtic mythology. The Colorado Scottish Festival, for example, bills itself as: "A Bit of Brigadoon in Your Own Back Yard."

Why the revival of romantic Scotland in America? There are, perhaps, two main reasons. First, the recent move to celebrate ethnic diversity in the States has awakened a self-consciousness in many groups that had hitherto considered themselves almost completely "melted." Consequently, Americans of Scots and Scotch-Irish background have once again renewed the process of creating a Scoto-American identity. In its latest version this identity has combined both the specific and the universal. One needs neither a Scottish surname nor a precise blood quantum to become involved. Having *any* Scots ancestor—no matter how distant—allows an interested person to find a clan, wear a tartan, and participate in the celebration. The Longs Peak Scottish/Irish Festival in Estes Park, Colorado, founded in 1976, claims to be one of the largest gatherings of its kind, with crowds approaching one hundred thousand over a three-day period. In the late twentieth century the "Scots" have emerged as the most inclusive of all of America's ethnic groups.

Young women dancing at the Highland games in Salt Lake City, Utah. Recently, the Highland games have emerged as a popular form of ethnic celebration in a number of western states, including New Mexico, Kansas, Washington, California, Colorado, and Utah. (Utah State Historical Society. Photo B-239, #6.)

Second, the rise of the New Age movement has fed into this enthusiasm. Characterized by an eclectic search for spirituality and one of the nation's most rapidly growing nonconventional faiths, New Agers almost invariably surround themselves with

Celtic lore. Indeed, any display of Celtic iconography today is virtually certain to refer back to a quasi-mystical, largely imagined Irish/Scottish past. The popular acclaim given to the blockbuster films *Rob Roy* and *Braveheart* draws from the same source.

Finally, the recent upsurge of Scottish themes is reflected in a number of literary studies. After the exploratory phase, the literary history of the American West from c. 1850 forward manifested only a marginal Scottish dimension. Unlike the Jews or the Irish, the Scots penned relatively few autobiographical/ fictional accounts of their immigrant experience.[12] There are a few exceptions to this statement. California immigrant Robert Brownlee wrote an autobiography that was not published until 1986. Jessie Macmillan, a single woman homesteader in southern New Mexico, also kept a diary that later broke into print.[13] Son of a Scottish sea captain, John L. Sinclair became a well-known regional novelist in the Southwest.[14]

In general, however, the Scottish literary upsurge in the North American West had to wait until the era of the Second World War. This is true for Canada as well as for the United States. North of the 49th parallel, Scots author Hugh MacLennan is generally credited as Canada's great literary pioneer.[15] Born in Glace Bay, Cape Breton Island, in 1907—a culture almost entirely Highland Scots—MacLennan grew to maturity in Halifax in a Presbyterian, Anglophile family. After a Rhodes Scholarship and a Ph.D. in classics from Princeton, he returned to Canada to teach and write. Through numerous essays and novels, including *Barometer Rising* (1941), *Two Solitudes* (1945), and *Return of the Sphinx* (1967), MacLennan began to compose what literary critic Edmund Wilson once termed "a Canadian way of looking at things."[16]

Although Hugh MacLennan is acknowledged as the writer who put Canadian literature on the map, he ponders the Scottish dimension of his nation's past in a number of perceptive essays. His somewhat quirky view of Canadian-American relations derives largely from his reading of the historic Scottish-English interaction, aspects of which he believes lie buried in the Canadian collective unconscious.[17] In "Scotchman's Return" (1958) MacLennan writes of his initial visit to the Highlands, comparing the panorama of his ancestral Kintail with that of Northwest Canada:

> But this Highland emptiness, only a few hundred miles above the massed population of England, is a far different thing from the emptiness of our North West Territories. Above the sixtieth parallel in Canada, you feel that nobody but God has ever been there before you, but in a deserted Highland glen you feel that everyone who ever mattered is dead and gone.[18]

Upon returning from this visit, however, Hugh MacLennan concluded that perhaps those Canadians of Scottish descent had become truly at home in the northern half of the North American continent.

While MacLennan spoke for Scots scattered all across Canada, the clearest voice of a distinctly Scottish-Western writer probably belongs to Margaret Laurence. Her family, a branch of Clan MacDuff, emigrated from the Lowlands to Manitoba in the 1870s. She was born Jean Margaret Wemyss in the small town of Neepawa, Manitoba, in 1926. After university, she moved with her engineer husband to Africa, where she became reacquainted with the concept of tribalism. Upon her return to Canada in 1957 she began to write the first of her five books dealing with the fictional town of Manawaka, Manitoba. *A Stone Angel* (1964) was followed by *A Test of God* (1966); *The Fire-Dwellers* (1969); *A Bird in the House* (1970); and her most ambitious epic, *The Diviners* (1974).

In a perceptive essay, critic Colin Nicholson has noted that the Scottish heritage of Margaret Laurence's fiction was both "there and not there." In *The Diviners* Laurence's fictional heroine, the orphan Morag Gunn, first visits the Highlands. After peering across the Firth to Sutherland, presumably her ancestral home, Morag decides that she does not need actually to set foot there. Her real home, she concludes, lies in Canada, where she was reared. As for Scotland: "The myths are my reality."[19]

Margaret Laurence treats great themes in her fiction: survival, hard work, human dignity, and suffering. These derive both from her Scots ancestry as well as from the reality of multicultural Manitoba in the 1930s. Morag Gunn's illegitimate daughter, Piquette Gunn Tonnerre, illustrates this confluence to perfection: Piquette is half Scots, half *Métis,* and all Canadian. Nominated for the Nobel Prize in 1985, Margaret Laurence died in Ontario in 1987.[20]

Since Canada has steadfastly refused to accept the national ideal of a melting pot, Canadian-Scots writers reflect an active link with Scotland that is only mildly echoed across the border. South of the 49th parallel, the story of the Highland Clearances is only dimly recognized. In truth the average American has scarcely heard of this tragedy. Consequently, Scottish-American writers reflect much less a sense of belonging to a "wronged people."[21] One sees this clearly in the works of Ivan Doig and Norman Maclean, two writers who have drawn upon their Scottish-American heritage with exceptional skill. Both originally hail from Montana, and each has brought the best of Scots universalism to the realm of western American literature.

Ivan Doig has dazzled readers with his prose in a number of books, especially *English Creek* (1984), *Dancing at the Rascal Fair* (1987), and *Bucking the Sun* (1996). Critics argue that his best book is *This House of Sky: Landscapes of a Western Mind* (1987), a nonfiction memoir that mingles tales of his Scottish upbringing with the vast spaces of midcentury Montana.[22] No author has better described the generations of Scots settlers who migrated to this region.

Norman Maclean's posthumous *Young Men and Fire* (1992) has been well received, but his reputation rests with his novella, *A River Runs Through It* (1978). This memoir relates a partially fictionalized account of his younger brother's tragic murder, probably over a gambling debt. But most of all, the book sympthetically treats his Presbyterian minister father, the art of fly-fishing, and the wonders of early twentieth-century Montana. Behind the entire work one finds the Scottish themes of water, majestic scenery, and predestination. The ending can hardly be improved upon:

> Eventually, all things merge into one, and a river runs through it. The river was cut by the world's great flood and runs over rocks from the basement of time. On some of the rocks are timeless raindrops. Under the rocks are the words, and some of the words are theirs.
>
> I am haunted by waters.[23]

The shades of Robert Burns and Sir Walter Scott would not turn their backs on this upsurge of Scottish-Western writing. From Alexander Mackenzie's *Voyages* to Margaret Laurence's Manawaka series to Ivan Doig's *This House of Sky* to Norman Maclean's *A River Runs Through it*, the North American West has often spoken—in Robert Louis Stevenson's phrase—with a "strong Scots accent of the mind."

Notes

PREFACE

1. Some of these were: Ferenc M. Szasz, "Jefferson Davis's 1867 and 1871 Visits to Scotland: Cultural Symbols of the Old and New Souths," *Northern Scotland* 14 (1994):147–54; "Scots Poet William McGonnagal Visits America, 1887," *Scotia: Interdisciplinary Journal of Scottish Studies* 17 (1993):25–32; "The Scots and Abraham Lincoln," *Northern Scotland* 16 (1996):127–40; and "The Wisconsin Scot Reports on the American Civil War," Part I, *Milwaukee History* 17 (Summer 1994):34–50, Part II, *Milwaukee History* 17 (Autumn/Winter, 1994): 88–103; "Peter Williamson and the Eighteenth-Century Scottish-American Connection," *Northern Scotland* 19 (1999):47–61.

CHAPTER 1. HISTORIANS AND THE SCOTTISH-AMERICAN CONNECTION

1. James Logan, as cited in *The Scotch-Irish in America: Proceedings of the Third Congress at Louisville, Kentucky, May 14–17, 1891* (Nashville: Publishing House of the Methodist Episcopal Church, South, 1891), 1320.

2. Hunter Dickson Farish, ed., *Journal and Letters of Philip Vickers Fithian, 1773–1774: A Plantation Tutor of the Old Dominion* (Williamsburg: Colonial Williamsburg, 1957), 29, 94; Edward Miles Riley, ed., *The Journal of John Harrower: An Indentured Servant in the Colony of Virginia, 1773–1776* (Williamsburg: Colonial Williamsburg, 1963).

3. Kerby A. Miller, *Emigrants and Exiles: Ireland and the Irish Exodus to North America* (New York: Oxford University Press, 1985), quoted, 165–66.

4. John Witherspoon, "An Address to the Natives of Scotland Residing in America," attached to *The Dominion of Providence over the Affairs of Men* (Philadelphia: R. Aitken, Printer, 1776), 61. Copy, Scottish National Library, Edinburgh.

5. George A. Shepperson, "The American Revolution and Scotland," *Scotia* 1 (April 1977):1–17.

6. John Kenneth Galbraith, *The Scotch* (Boston: Houghton Mifflin, 1964).

7. David Dobson, *Scottish Emigration to Colonial America, 1607–1785* (Athens: University of Georgia Press, 1994), 166. See also Duncan A. Bruce, *The Mark of the Scots: Their Astonishing Contributions to History, Science, Democracy, Literature, and the Arts* (Secaucus, N.J.: Birch Lane Press, 1996), 23.

8. Raymond A. Mohl, ed., "'The Grand Fabric of Republicanism': A Scotsman Describes South Carolina, 1810–1811," *South Carolina Historical Magazine* 71 (1970):181. Mohl has edited a number of similar accounts of Scots travel to other regions.

9. The only sketches of Smith and Mitchell are found in the *Dictionary of American Biography* (New York: Charles Scribner's Sons, 1928–58) [hereafter DAB]; Frederick Voss, *We Never Sleep: The First Fifty Years of the Pinkertons* (Washington, D.C.: Smithsonian, 1981); Saul Englebourg and Leonard Bushkoff, *The Man Who Found the Money: John Stewart Kennedy and the Financing of the Western Railroads* (East Lansing: Michigan State University Press, 1996); Joseph F. Wall, *Andrew Carnegie* (Pittsburgh: University of Pittsburgh Press, 1989), is the best biography. See also Joseph F. Wall, ed., *The Andrew Carnegie Reader* (Pittsburgh and London: University of Pittsburgh Press, 1992).

10. William P. Breed, *Presbyterians and the Revolution* (Philadelphia: Presbyterian Board of Publication, 1876); James G. Craighead, *Scotch and Irish Seeds in American Soil* (Philadelphia: Presbyterian Board of Publication, 1879); Samuel S. Green, *The Scotch-Irish in America* (Worcester, Mass.: American Antiquarian Society, 1905); Peter Ross, *The*

Scot in America (New York: Raeburn, 1896); John W. Dinsmore, *The Scotch-Irish in America* (Chicago: Winona Publishing, 1906).

11. Herbert B. Casson, "The Sons of Old Scotland in America," *Munsey's Magazine* 34 (1906):599–611.

12. *The Scotch-Irish in America: Proceedings of the Third Congress at Louisville, Kentucky, May 14–17, 1891*, 98.

13. *The Scotch-Irish in America: Proceedings of the Third Congress at Louisville, Kentucky, May 14–17, 1891*, 85, 101, 124.

14. Ross, *The Scot in America*, 411.

15. See also the four-volume study by W. J. Rattray, *The Scot in British North America* (Toronto: Maclean and Co., 1888).

16. Henry Jones Ford, *The Scotch-Irish in America* (Princeton: Princeton University Press, 1915).

17. George Fraser Black, *Scotland's Mark on America* (New York: The Scottish Section of "America's Making," 1921), 24.

18. Eric Richards, "Varieties of Scottish Emigration in the Nineteenth Century," *Historical Studies* 21 (October 1985):473–94.

19. Rodger Doyle, *Atlas of Contemporary America* (New York: Facts on File, 1994), 32.

20. T. J. Wertenbaker, *Early Scotch Contributions to the United States* (Glasgow: Jackson, Son and Co., 1945), 23. The next year Wertenbaker published *Princeton, 1746–1896* (Princeton: Princeton University Press, 1946), which also explored these connections.

21. John Clive and Bernard Bailyn, "England's Cultural Provinces: Scotland and America," *William and Mary Quarterly* 11 (April 1954): 200–13.

22. George A. Shepperson, "The American Revolution and Scotland," 1–17; "The Free Church of Scotland and American Slavery," *Scottish Historical Review* 30 (1951):126–43; "Frederick Douglass and Scotland," *Journal of Negro History* 38 (1953):307–21; "Harriet Beecher Stowe and Scotland," *Scottish Historical Review* 12 (1954):40–46; Robert Botsford, "Scotland and the American Civil War" (Ph.D. diss., University of Edinburgh, 1955); Helen Finnie, "Scottish Attitudes toward American Reconstruction, 1865–1877" (Ph.D. diss., University of Edinburgh, 1975).

23. Bernard Aspinwall, "The Scots in the United States," in R. A. Cage, ed., *The Scots Abroad: Labor, Capital, Enterprise, 1750–1914* (London, etc.: Groom Helm, 1985), 80–109; "The Scottish Religious Identity in the Atlantic World, 1880–1914," in Stuart Mews, ed., *Religion and National Identity* (Oxford: Basil Blackwell, 1982); *Portable*

Utopia: Glasgow and the United States, 1820–1920 (Aberdeen: Aberdeen University Press, 1984).

24. Ian Charles Cargill Graham, *Colonists from Scotland: Emigration to North America, 1707–1783* (Ithaca, N.Y.: Cornell University Press, 1956). That same year, the Irish were the subject of a similar study by Carl F. Wittke, *The Irish in America* (Baton Rouge: Louisiana State University Press, 1956). See also R. J. Dickson, *Ulster Emigration to Colonial America, 1718–1775* (Belfast: Ulster Historical Foundation, 1976).

25. Douglas Sloan, *The Scottish Enlightenment and the American College Ideal* (New York: Teacher's College Press, 1971).

26. Andrew Hook, *Scotland and America: A Study of Cultural Relations, 1750–1835* (Glasgow and London: Blackie, 1975). See also Susan Manning, *The Puritan Provincial Vision: Scottish and American Literature in the Nineteenth Century* (Cambridge: Cambridge University Press, 1990).

27. Duane Meyer, *The Highland Scots of North Carolina, 1732–1776* (Chapel Hill: University of North Carolina Press, 1961). Bernard Bailyn, *Voyagers to the West* (New York: Knopf, 1986) contains a good section on this, 499–544.

28. Thomas M. Devine, *The Tobacco Lords: A Study of the Tobacco Merchants of Glasgow and Their Trading Activities, 1740–90* (Edinburgh: Edinburgh University Press, 1975); Jacob M. Price, *Capital and Credit in British Overseas Trade: The View from the Chesapeake, 1700–1776* (Cambridge: Harvard University Press, 1980); Wilbur Shepperson, *British Emigration to North America* (Minneapolis: University of Minneapolis Press, 1957); Charlotte Erickson, *Invisible Immigrants: The Adaptation of English and Scottish Immigrants in Nineteenth-Century America* (Ithaca and London: Cornell University Press, 1972); David Dobson has compiled a multivolume *Directory of Scottish Settlers in North America, 1625–1825* (Baltimore: Genealogical Publishing Co., 1984–86), and *A Directory of Scots Banished to the American Plantations, 1650–1725* (Baltimore: Genealogical Publishing Co., 1984). See also J. P. Maclean, *An Historical Account of the Settlements of the Scottish Highlanders in America Prior to 1783* (Cleveland: Helman-Taylor Co., 1978).

29. William C. Lehmann, *Scottish and Scotch-Irish Contributions to Early American Life and Culture* (Port Washington, N.Y.: National University Publications, 1978); Charles H. Haws, *Scots in the Old Dominion, 1685–1808* (Edinburgh: J. Dunlap, 1980); Ned Landsman, *Scotland and Its First American Colony, 1683–1760* (Princeton: Princeton University Press, 1985); Alan L. Karras, *Sojourners in the Sun: Scottish Migrants*

in *Jamaica and the Chesapeake, 1740–1800* (Ithaca, N.Y.: Cornell University Press, 1992).

30. Marilyn J. Westerkamp, *Triumph of the Laity: Scots-Irish Piety and the Great Awakening, 1625–1700* (New York: Oxford, 1988); Leigh Eric Schmidt, *Holy Fairs: Scottish Communions and American Revivals in the Early Modern Period* (Princeton: Princeton University Press, 1989).

31. Archie Turnbull, "Scotland and America, 1730–70," in *A Hotbed of Genius: The Scottish Enlightenment, 1730–1790*, David Daiches, Peter Jones, and Jean Jones, eds. (Edinburgh: Edinburgh University Press, 1986), 137–53.

32. Shepperson, "The American Revolution and Scotland," 8–9.

33. Garry Wills, *Inventing America* (Garden City, N.Y.: Doubleday, 1978).

34. William H. Brock, ed., *Scotus Americanus: A Survey of the Sources for Links between Scotland and America in the Eighteenth Century* (Edinburgh: Edinburgh University Press, 1982); Richard B. Sher and Jeffrey R. Smitten, eds., *Scotland and America in the Age of the Enlightenment* (Princeton: Princeton University Press; Edinburgh: Edinburgh University Press, 1990).

35. *List of American Documents* (Edinburgh: Her Majesty's Stationery Office, 1976); *The Scots in America: Historical Background, List of Documents, Extracts and Facsimilies* (Edinburgh: Scottish Record Office [hereafter SRO], 1994).

36. Duncan Rice, *The Scots Abolitionists, 1833–1861* (Baton Rouge and London: Louisiana State University Press, 1981).

37. Forrest McDonald and Grady McWhiney, "The Antebellum Southern Herdsman: A Reinterpretation," *Journal of Southern History* 41 (May 1975):147–66; Forrest McDonald and Grady McWhiney, "The Celtic South," *History Today* 30 (July 1980):11–15; Grady McWhiney and Forrest McDonald, "Celtic Origins of Southern Herding Practice," *Journal of Southern History* 51 (May 1985):165–82; Forrest McDonald and Ellen Shapiro McDonald, "The Ethnic Origins of the American People, 1790," *William and Mary Quarterly* 37 (1980):179–99; Grady McWhiney, *Cracker Culture: Celtic Ways in the Old South* (Tuscaloosa: University of Alabama Press, 1988); Roland Tappan Berthoff, "Celtic Mist over the South," *Journal of Southern History* 52 (November 1986):521–46.

38. E. Estyn Evans, "The Scotch-Irish: Their Cultural Adaptions and Heritage in the American Old West," in E. R. R. Green, ed., *Essays in Scotch-Irish History* (London: Routledge and Kegan Paul, 1969),

69–86; E. Estyn Evans, "Cultural Relics of the Ulster-Scots in the Old West of North America," *Ulster Folklife* 11 (1965):33–38; Rory Fitzpatrick, *God's Frontiersmen: The Scots-Irish Epic* (London: Weidenfeld and Nicolson, in association with Channel Four Television Company Limited and Ulster Television, 1989).

39. David Hackett Fischer, *Albion's Seed: Four British Folkways in America* (New York: Oxford University Press, 1989). Cf. also William C. Lehmann, *Scottish and Scotch-Irish Contributions to Early American Life and Culture* (Port Washington, N.Y.: Kennikat Press, 1978); and Ross, *The Scot in America.*

40. Erickson, *Invisible Immigrants.* James G. Leyburn, *The Scotch Irish: A Social History* (Chapel Hill: University of North Carolina Press, 1962) also believes the Scotch-Irish have similarly "disappeared."

41. William Kittredge, "The Best That Can Be: The Politics of Storytelling," *Halcyon* 14 (1992):1–5.

42. Wallace Stegner, "A Geography of Hope," in *A Society to Match the Scenery,* Gary Holthaus et al., eds. (Niwot, Colo.: University Press of Colorado, 1991), 224.

43. Richard L. Rapson, *Britons View America: Travel Commentary, 1860–1935* (Seattle and London: University of Washington Press, 1971); Allan Nevins, ed., *America Through British Eyes* (New York: Oxford University Press, 1948); Rowland Tappan Berthoff, *British Immigrants in Industrial America, 1790–1950* (Cambridge: Harvard University Press, 1953); Robert G. Athearn, *Westward the Briton: The Far West, 1865–1900 as Seen by British Sportsmen and Capitalists, Ranchers and Homesteaders, Lords and Ladies* (Lincoln: University of Nebraska Press, 1953); Lawrence M. Woods, *British Gentlemen in the Wild West: The Era of the Intensely English Cowboy* (New York: Free Press, 1989); John Merritt, *Baronets and Buffalo: The British Sportsman in the American West, 1833–1881* (Missoula: Mountain Press Publishing Co., 1985); Lee Olson, *Marmalade and Whiskey: British Remittance Men in the West* (Golden, Colo.: Fulcrum Publishing, 1993). See also Clark Spence, *British Investment in the American Mining Frontier, 1860–1901* (Ithaca: Cornell University Press, 1958); and Dorothy R. Adler, *British Investment in American Railways, 1834–1898* (Charlottesville: University Press of Virginia, 1970).

44. Jim Hewitson, *Tam Blake and Company: The Story of the Scots in America* (Edinburgh: Canongate Press, Ltd., 1993); James Hunter, *A Dance Called America: The Scottish Highlands, the United States and Canada* (Edinburgh and London: Mainstream Publishing, 1994).

45. Alexander Campbell McGregor, *Counting Sheep: From Open Range to Agribusiness on the Columbia Plateau* (Seattle and London: University of Washington Press, 1982); W. Turrentine Jackson, *The Enterprising Scot* (Edinburgh: Edinburgh University Press, 1968); W. G. Kerr, *Scottish Capital on the American Credit Frontier* (Austin: Texas State Historical Association, 1976); Bruce LeRoy, *Lairds, Bards and Mariners: The Scot in Northwest America* (Tacoma: Washington State American Revolution Bicentennial Commission, 1978); James Hunter, *Scottish Highlanders, Indian Peoples: Thirty Generations of a Montana Family* (Helena: Montana Historical Society Press, 1996).

46. Mae Reed Porter and Odessa Davenport, *Scotsmen in Buckskin: Sir William Drummond Stewart and the Rocky Mountain Fur Trade* (New York: Hastings House, 1963); Susan Bryant Dakin, *A Scotch Paisano in Old Los Angeles: Hugo Reid's Life in California, 1832–1852, Derived from His Correspondence* (Berkeley: University of California Press, 1978); William Norwood, *Traveler in a Vanished Landscape: The Life and Times of David Douglas* (New York: N. Potter, 1973). Douglas's journals have been collected in *Douglas of the Forests: The North American Journals of David Douglas,* John Davies, ed. (Edinburgh: P. Harris, 1979). See also Louise Shadduck, *Andy Little: Idaho Sheep King* (Caldwell, Idaho: Caxton Publishers, 1990); Steven Fox, *The American Conservation Movement: John Muir and His Legacy* (Madison: University of Wisconsin Press, 1985). Muir will be discussed later. There are two autobiographies, *An American Odyssey: The Autobiography of a Nineteenth-Century Scotsman, Robert Brownlee, at the Request of His Children* (1892); reprint, edited by Patricia A. Etter, published by the University of Arkansas Press, 1986; and four volumes of *Memoirs* (San Francisco: privately published, 1917–28) by shipping magnate Robert Dollar.

CHAPTER 2. SCOTTISH EXPLORERS AND FUR TRAPPERS: THE 1790S TO THE 1850S

1. *The Climate of Scotland: Some Facts and Figures* (London: Her Majesty's Stationery Office, 1989), 21.
2. R. L. Stevenson, "Edinburgh," in *The Lantern Bearers and Other Essays,* Jeremy Treglown, ed. (New York: Farrar Straus Giroux, 1988), 88.
3. James McCarthy, *Scotland: The Land and Its Uses* (Edinburgh: Chambers, 1994), 7.

4. For Johnson at his best, see Richard Ingrams, ed., *Dr. Johnson by Mrs. Thrale: The Anecdotes of Mrs. Piozzi in Their Original Form* (London: The Hogarth Press, 1984).

5. Maurice Lindsay, "Speaking of Scotland," *Collected Poems* (1940-90), as cited in McCarthy, *Scotland*, 14.

6. John Clive, "The Social Background of the Scottish Renaissance," in Clive, *Not by Fact Alone: Essays on the Writing and Reading of History* (New York: Knopf, 1989).

7. See J. D. Mackie, *A History of Scotland* (London: Penguin Books, 1964, 1978); Ross, *The Scot in America;* George Shepperson, "The Scot Around the World," in Harold Orel et al., eds., *The Scottish World: History and Culture of Scotland* (New York: Harry N. Abrams, Inc., 1981), 230.

8. Cited in Linda Colley, *Britons: Forging the Nation, 1701-1837* (New Haven and London: Yale University Press, 1992), 123.

9. Colley, *Britons*, 127; Dorothy Downs, "British Influences on Creek and Seminole Men's Clothing, 1733-1858," *The Florida Anthropologist* 33 (June 1980):50.

10. Cited in "The Hudson Bay Company," *Scottish Review* 35 (January 1900):226-27.

11. *Orkney Herald*, February 16, 1887, cited in *Orkney Islander* (1994), 10; James A. Troup, "Dr. John Rae: The Education of an Adventurer," *The Beaver* 73 (October/November 1993):4-9.

12. Edward Burt, vol. 1 of *Letters from a Gentleman in the North of Scotland* (Dublin: Peter Wilson, 1755), 26.

13. *Scotsman*, October 2, 1841; Information from Strathnaver Museum, Bettyhill, and the Wick Heritage Center, Wick; *Inverness Courier*, June 25, 1842.

14. Sir John Sinclair, *Analysis of the Statistical Account of Scotland with a General View of the History of That Country* (Edinburgh: Tait, 1825), 1:106-107. Cited in A. R. B. Haldane, *The Drove Roads of Scotland* (Edinburgh: Edinburgh University Press, 1952, 1968), 21.

15. A. Innes Shand, "Romance of the Fur Trade: The Companies," *Blackwood's* 164 (October 1898):498-500; A. Innes Shand, "Romance of the Fur Trade: The Mountain Men," *Blackwood's* 165 (January 1899):37-38; Peter C. Newman, *Company of Adventurers: The Story of the Hudson's Bay Company*, Vol. 1 (New York: Penguin Books, 1985), 89.

16. D. B. Warden, *A Statistical, Political, and Historical Account of the United States of North America* (Edinburgh: Archibald Constable and

Co., 1819), 3:186; William S. Coker and Thomas D. Watson, *Indian Traders of the Southeastern Spanish Borderlands* (Pensacola: University Presses of Florida, 1986). Chapter 1 is subtitled "Scotsmen All."

17. Jennifer S. H. Brown, *Strangers in Blood: Fur Trade Company Families in Indian Country* (Vancouver and London: University of British Columbia Press, 1980), 41. Hunter, *A Dance Called America*, 164.

18. Alexander Ross, *The Fur Hunters of the Far West*, Kenneth A. Spaulding, ed. (Norman: University of Oklahoma Press, 1959), 17.

19. Hiram Martin Chittenden, *A History of the American Fur Trade of the Far West* (Stanford: Academics Reprints, 1954) 1:381–83, 386–87. See also David Lavender, *The Fist in the Wilderness* (Albuquerque: University of New Mexico Press, 1964), 71–76; and Jennifer S. H. Brown, "A Parcel of Upstart Scotchmen," *The Beaver* (February/March 1988):5–12.

20. Chittenden, *A History of the American Fur Trade of the Far West*, 2:698–716; Hon. Judge Hall, *Letters from the West* (London: Henry Colburn, 1828), 271–75; quotation from 271.

21. John Myers Myers, *The Saga of Hugh Glass: Pirate, Pawnee, and Mountain Man* (Lincoln: University of Nebraska Press, 1963, 1976), 3–7, 21.

22. William Cochran McGaw, *Savage Scene: The Life and Times of Mountain Man Jim Kirker* (San Lorenzo, N.M.: High-Lonesome Books, 1972).

23. Henry J. Coke, *A Ride over the Rocky Mountains to Oregon and California* (London: Richard Bentley, 1852), 271–75, 301; quoted, 271.

24. David Stevenson, *The Covenanters: The National Covenant and Scotland* (Edinburgh: Saltire Society, 1988), 4–5.

25. Colley, *Britons*, 123.

26. Clive, "The Social Background of the Scottish Renaissance," 151–65.

27. Derek Pethick, *First Approaches to the Northwest Coast* (Vancouver: Douglas and McIntyre, 1976), 54–76. See also the review by Clifford Geertz, "Culture War," in the *New York Review of Books* (November 30, 1995), 4–6.

28. James P. Ronda, "Dreams and Discoveries: Exploring the American West, 1760–1815," *William and Mary Quarterly*, 3rd Series, 46 (January 1989):152. See also Alexander Walker, *An Account of a Voyage to the North West Coast of America in 1785 and 1786*, Robin Fisher and J. M. Bumsted, eds. (Seattle: University of Washington Press, 1982), 177–89.

29. Alexander Mackenzie, *Voyages from Montreal, on the River St. Laurence, through the Continent of North America, to the Frozen and Pacific Oceans: In the Years 1789 and 1793. With a Preliminary Account of the Rise, Progress, and Present State of the Fur Trade of That Country* (London: T. Carell, Jr., and W. Davis, etc., 1801).

30. Mackenzie, *Voyages*, 410.

31. Mackenzie, *Voyages*, 259.

32. Mackenzie, *Voyages*, 15, 381, 253, 411.

33. Barry Gough, *First Across the Continent: Sir Alexander MacKenzie* (Norman and London: University of Oklahoma Press, 1997) is the latest biography. Gough correctly reminds us that MacKenzie always had one eye out for his economic advantage.

34. Susan Delano McKelvey, *Botanical Exploration of the Trans-Mississippi West, 1790–1850* (Jamaica Plain, Mass.: The Arnold Arboretum of Harvard University, 1955).

35. McKelvey, *Botanical Exploration*, 26–60; William M. Olson, ed., *The Alaska Travel Journal of Archibald Menzies, 1793–1794* (Fairbanks: University of Alaska Press, 1993), 6. *The Clan Menzies Magazine* 1 (January 1977):10–15.

36. John Bradbury, *Travels in the Interior of America in the Years 1809, 1810, and 1811*, foreword by Donald Jackson (Lincoln and London: University of Nebraska Press, 1986), 15–19.

37. McKelvey, *Botanical Exploration*, 464–79, 481–85, 389.

38. O. B. Sperlin, "Our First Official Horticulturist," *Washington Historical Quarterly* 21 (July 1930):218–305, and in later issues.

39. *Journal Kept by David Douglas During His Travels in North America, 1823–1827* (London: William Wesley and Son, 1914), 69; McKelvey, *Botanical Exploration*, 299–339, 393–427.

40. *Journal Kept by David Douglas*, 129.

41. Davies, *Douglas of the Forests*, quoted, 18.

42. William Morwood, *Traveller in a Vanished Landscape: The Life and Times of David Douglas* (New York: N. Potter, 1973), believes it to be suicide. Ann Lindsay Mitchell and Syd House, *David Douglas: Explorer and Botanist* (London: Aurum Press, 1999) conclude that no one will ever know the circumstances that surrounded his death (172–74).

43. Brinsley Burbidge, "Scottish Plantsmen," in *The Enterprising Scot: Scottish Adventure and Achievement*, Jenni Calder, ed. (Edinburgh: Royal Museum of Scotland, 1986), 56.

44. Alexander Forbes, *California: A History of Upper and Lower California* (London: Smith, Elder and Co., 1839).

45. Forbes, *California*, 185, 221.
46. George F. Ruxton, *Adventures in Mexico and the Rocky Mountains* (London: John Murray, 1847), iv.
47. Forbes, *California*, 153, 313; quoted, 153.
48. Lester G. Engelson, "Proposals for the Colonization of California by England," *California Historical Society Quarterly* 18 (1939).
49. Forbes, *California*, 151–52.
50. Martha Voght, "Scots in Hispanic California," *Scottish Historical Review* 52 (1973):144.
51. Voght, "Scots in Hispanic California," 141; Robert F. Heizer, ed., *The Indians of Los Angeles County: Hugo Reid's Letters of 1852* (Los Angeles: Southwest Museum, 1968).

CHAPTER 3. SCOTLAND AND THE AMERICAN INDIANS

1. Anecdote heard at the Braemar Highland Games, August 1991. See the photo in Hewitson, *Tam Blake and Company*, 189. Iain Moncreiff of that Ilk, *The Highland Clans* (London: Barrie and Jenkins, Ltd., 1982), 154–58.
2. Sylvia Van Kirk, "Women and the Fur Trade," *The Beaver* (Winter 1972):4–21.
3. Dorothy Downs, "British Influences on Creek and Seminole Men's Clothing, 1733–1858," *The Florida Anthropologist* 33 (June 1980):51; Van Kirk has elaborated on her insights in *Women and the Fur Trade* (Norman: University of Oklahoma Press, 1983). See also Jennifer S. H. Brown, *Strangers in Blood*.
4. Downs, "British Influences," 48–51.
5. George MacDonald Fraser, *The Steel Bonnets: The Story of the Anglo-Scottish Border Reivers* (London: Harvill, 1971), 75n.
6. Allan I. Macinnes, *Clanship, Commerce and the House of Stuart, 1603–1788* (East Linton, East Lothian: Tuckwell Press, Ltd., 1996), ix, 122–23.
7. Hugh Murray, *An Historical Account of British North America*, 2 vols. (Edinburgh: Oliver and Botayd, 1839).
8. Warden, *A Statistical, Political, and Historical Account of the United States of North America*, 585.
9. Ishbel Aberdeen, *"We Twa": Reminiscences of Lord and Lady Aberdeen* (London: W. Collins and Sons, Ltd., 1925), 80. Robert M.

Crunden, *A Brief History of American Culture* (New York: Paragon House, 1995), 105.

10. James Browne, *A History of the Highlands and of the Highland Clans* (Glasgow: A. Fullarton and Co., 1840), 3:501.

11. W. Boyd Dawkins, "Review of H. H. Bancroft," *Edinburgh Review* 196 (October 1876):285; Mick Gidley, "Three Cultural Brokers in the Context of Edward S. Curtis's *The North American Indian*," in *Between Indian and White Worlds: The Cultural Broker*, Margaret Connell Szasz, ed. (Norman: University of Oklahoma Press, 1994), 197–215.

12. William Donaldson, *The Jacobite Song: Political Myth and National Identity* (Aberdeen: Aberdeen University Press, 1988).

13. Gilbert Imlay, *A Topographical Description of the Western Territory of North America* (London: Piccadilly, 1792), 371.

14. Murray, *An Historical Account of British North America*, 1:69.

15. I. F. Grant, *Highland Folk Ways* (London: Routledge and Kegan Paul, 1961).

16. John McPhee, *The Crofter and the Laird* (New York: Farrar Straus, 1970).

17. Hon. Judge Hall, *Letters from the West* (London: Henry Colboudin, 1828), 335.

18. See Angie Debo, *And Still the Waters Run* (Princeton: Princeton Uniersity Press, 1940).

19. Michael Lynch, *Scotland: A New History* (London: Pimlico, 1992), 369–72; J. M. Bumsted, *The People's Clearance: Highland Emigration to British North America, 1770–1815* (Edinburgh: Edinburgh University Press/University of Manitoba Press, 1982).

20. Robert Somers, *Letters from the Highlands on the Famine of 1846* (Inverness: Melvens Book Shop, Ltd., [1845] 1977), 116. Jim A. Johnson, *Tonque and Farr* (Thurso: Northern Printers, 1987), 11–13. James Campbell, *Invisible Country: A Journey Through Scotland* (New York: New Amsterdam Books, 1984), 79.

21. *Stornoway Gazette*, April 26, 1923, in Shawbost Schoolroom Museum, Isle of Lewis. The story of the *Metagama*, perhaps the most celebrated of the twentieth-century emigrant sailings, can be found in Jim Wilkie, *Metagama: A Journey from Lewis to the New World* (Edinburgh: Mainstream Publishing Co., Ltd., 1987). See also Marjory Harper, "Crofter Colonists in Canada: An Experiment in Empire Settlement in the 1920s," *Northern Scotland* 14 (1994):69–111.

22. Alexander Mackenzie, *The History of the Highland Clearances* (Glasgow: Alex MacLaren and Sons [1881] 1946), 307; John Prebble,

The Highland Clearances (New York: Penguin Books, 1963). Eric Richards, *A History of the Highland Clearances* (London: Croom Helm, 1982), is far more balanced. See also David Craig, *On the Crofters' Trail: In Search of the Clearance Highlanders* (London: Jonathan Cape, 1990).

23. Percy S. Cohen, "Theories of Myth," *Man* 4 (1969):337-55. See also Roland Barthes, *Mythologies* (London: Jonathan Cape, 1974); Henry Glassie, *Irish Folk History: Texts from the North* (Philadelphia: University of Pennsylvania Press, 1982), 11; MacPherson in preface to the reprint of Mackenzie, *The History of the Highland Clearances.*

24. Geddes MacGregor, *Scotland: An Intimate Portrait* (Boston: Houghton Mifflin, 1980), 5.

25. Anecdote heard in Aberdeen, Spring 1992.

26. See the observations on Indian time in Frank Waters, *Pumpkin Seed Point* (Athens, Ohio: Swallow Press, 1969).

27. Jacqueline Peterson with Laura Peers, *Sacred Encounters: Father de Smet and the Indians of the Rocky Mountain West* (Norman and London: The De Smet Project, Washington State University in Association with the University of Oklahoma Press, 1993), 78; Downs, "British Influences," 46-64.

28. William Bartram, *The Travels of William Bartram*, Mark Van Doren, ed. (New York: Facsimile Library, 1940), 394. See also Thomas P. Slaughter, *The Natures of John and William Bartram* (New York: Vintage Books, 1977, 1996).

29. J. Leitch Wright, Jr., *Creeks and Seminoles: Destruction and Regeneration of the Muscogulge People* (Lincoln and London: University of Nebraska Press, 1986), 36.

30. Dobson, *Scottish Emigration to Colonial America, 1607-1785,* 107.

31. Arthur Preston Whitaker, "Alexander McGillivray, 1783-1789," *North Carolina Historical Review* 5 (April/July 1928):181-203, 289-309.

32. R. S. Cotterell, *The Southern Indians: The Story of the Civilized Tribes Before Removal* (Norman: University of Oklahoma Press, 1958), 85.

33. See the accounts in Grant Foreman, *The Five Civilized Tribes: Cherokee, Chickasaw, Choctaw, Creek, Seminole* (Norman: University of Oklahoma Press, 1934, 1970); Wright, *Creeks and Seminoles;* and David H. Cockran, *The Creek Frontier, 1540-1783* (Norman: University of Oklahoma Press, 1967).

34. R. David Edmunds, *Tecumseh and the Quest for Indian Leadership* (Boston: Little, Brown and Company, 1984).

35. Gary E. Moulton, *John Ross, Cherokee Chief* (Athens and London: University of Georgia Press, 1978), 6.

36. Gary E. Moulton, ed., *The Papers of Chief John Ross*, Vol. 2, 1840–1866 (Norman: University of Oklahoma Press, 1985), 321.

37. Voght, "Scots in Hispanic California," 140–41.

38. David Macrae, *The Americans at Home: Pen-and-Ink Sketches of American Men, Manners, and Institutions* (Glasgow: John S. Marr and Sons, 1879), 340–44.

39. William Ferguson, *America by River and Rail: Or, Notes by the Way on the New World and Its People* (London: James Nisbet and Co., 1851), 414.

40. List from Davies, *Douglas of the Forests*, 166–69. See also John C. Jackson, *Children of the Fur Trade: Forgotten Metis of the Pacific Northwest* (Missoula: Mountain Press Publishing Co., 1995), especially 15–41, 69–81.

41. Donald MacDonald, *Lewis: A History of the Island* (Edinburgh: Gordon Wright Publishing, 1978), 165.

42. *Islander* (1994), 8.

43. Information from Stromness Historical Center, Stromness, Orkney, 1994.

44. Peter C. Newman, *Caesars of the Wilderness: The Story of The Hudson's Bay Company*, Vol. 2 (New York: Penguin Books, 1987), 250–51.

45. Irene Spay, ed., *The Papers of the Palliser Expedition, 1857–1860* (Toronto: Champlain Society, 1968), 169.

46. John West, *The Substance of a Journal During a Residence at the Red River Colony, British North America* (London: L. B. Seeley and Son, 1824).

47. On this theme see Szasz, *Between Indian and White Worlds*.

48. George Bryce, *The Scotsman in Canada*, Vol. 2 (London: Sampson Low, Marston and Co., Ltd., 1911).

49. John Ewers, *The Blackfeet: Raiders on the Northwestern Plains* (Norman: University of Oklahoma Press, 1958), 263.

50. The Smithsonian has recently recognized Murie's contributions by featuring him in an exhibit. See Alice Fletcher Cunningham, *The Hako: A Pawnee Ceremony by Alice C. Fletcher . . . assisted by James R. Murie*, music transcribed by Edwin S. Tracy. In *U.S. Bureau of American Ethnology 22nd Annual Report*, 1900–1901, pt. 2 (Washington, D.C., 1904), 5–172; James R. Murie, *Pawnee Indian Societies* (New York:

American Museum of Natural History, 1914). Such brokerage also came from the Scottish immigrants themselves. The writings and sketches of Scots-born Alexander MacGregor Stephen, who lived at Keams Canyon, Arizona, from 1880 until his death in 1894, provide numerous insights into the life-styles of the Hopi. The writings were eventually edited by Elsie Clews Parsons as *The Hopi Journal of Alexander M. Stephen* (New York: Columbia University Press, 1936). See also Louis A. Hieb, "Introduction," *The Hopi Indians of Arizona*, typescript.

51. *Holbrook [Arizona] Argus*, April 9–23, 1896.

52. Martin F. Schmitt, ed., *General George Crook: His Autobiography* (Norman: University of Oklahoma Press, 1946), 146–53; *Holbrook Argus*, April 9–23, 1896.

53. *Holbrook Argus*, April 9–23, 1896.

54. Juana Fraser Lyon, "Archie McIntosh, the Scottish Indian Scout," *Journal of Arizona History* 7 (Autumn 1966):103–22. See also Oliver Knight, *Following the Indian Wars: The Story of the Newspaper Correspondents Among the Indian Campaigners* (Norman: University of Oklahoma Press, 1960, 1993).

55. John G. Bourke, "General Crook in Indian Country," *The Century Magazine* 41 (March 1891):643–60.

56. They appeared in the *New North-West* on January 10, 17, 24, 31, and February 17, 21, 1879. Copies lent by Raphael Cristy. See also Albert J. Partoll, "Angus McDonald, Frontier Fur Trader," *Pacific Northwest Quarterly* 42 (April 1951):138–46.

57. *The Park County News*, September 7, 1925; *Circle Banner*, undated clipping, Montana Historical Society; *Fergus County Argus*, August 22, 1938. Montana Newspaper Association, December 31, 1926, cited in Raphael Cristy, "Legend Maker: Charles M. Russell's Historical Perspective in His Published Stories and Essays" (master's thesis, University of Montana), 2–4.

58. *The Billings Times*, November 4, 1935.

59. See a modern compilation, *Coyote and . . . : Native American Folk Tales*, retold by Joe Hayes (Santa Fe: Mariposa Publishers, 1983).

60. Reprinted in *Circle Banner*, June 6, 1932.

61. Story told to author by a Pueblo Indian in 1995.

62. Cited in Cristy, "Legend Maker," 32.

63. Charley M. Russell, *Trails Plowed Under* (Garden City, N.Y.: Doubleday, 1941).

64. Anecdote from L. G. Moses of Oklahoma State University.

CHAPTER 4. SCOTLAND AND THE VICTORIAN WEST: THE REALITY

1. *Journal and Letters of Philip Vickers Fithian, 1773–1774: A Plantation Tutor of the Old Dominion*, Hunter Dickinson Farish, ed. (Williamsburg: Colonial Williamsburg, 1943), 239–41.
2. W. Mackintosh Mackay, "Scottish Religion and Education," *The Scots Magazine* 8 (October 1927):254, makes this claim.
3. John Howison, *Sketches of Upper Canada* (Edinburgh: Oliver and Boyd, 1822), 190.
4. *Information for Emigrants to British North America*, 2d ed. (London: Charles Knight and Co., 1862), 53. The best guidebook, *Emigrant's Guide to the Western States of America* (Edinburgh: Oliver and Boyd, 1852), was written by Ayrshire émigré John Regan.
5. Laurence J. Saunders, *Scottish Democracy, 1815–1849: The Social and Intellectual Background* (Edinburgh: Oliver and Boyd, 1950), 1–3; Aspinwall, *Portable Utopia*, 186.
6. Bumsted cited in Clara Thomas, "Margaret, Morag, and the Scottish Ancestors," *British Journal of Canadian Studies* 7 (1992):92. There is even a Scottish "prayer" that asks: "O Merciful Lord! In thy infinite goodness, grant us that we may be, in some small measure, worthy of the high esteem in which we hold ourselves."
7. Burt, *Letters from a Gentleman in the North of Scotland*, 1:320.
8. *Inverness Courier*, May 18, 1847.
9. Hugh MacPhee, "The Trail of the Emigrants," *Transactions of the Gaelic Society of Inverness* 46 (1969–70):201.
10. Cf. Des MacHale, *The World's Best Scottish Jokes* (London: Argus and Robertson, 1988). See also *Scottish American*, November 3, 1893.
11. Rev. David Macrae, *The Americans at Home: Pen-and-Ink Sketches of American Men, Manners, and Institutions* (Glasgow: John S. Marr and Sons, 1879), 316–24.
12. Thomas Simpson Carson, *Ranching, Sport, and Travel* (London: T. Fisher Unwin, 1917), 120; Ross, *The Scot in America*, 2.
13. James Stuart, *Three Years in North America* (Edinburgh: Robert Cadel, 1833), 2:388–89; J. Cameron Lees, "Round the World," *The Scottish Church* 1 (1888):185.
14. R. L. Stevenson, *Travels with a Donkey/An Inland Voyage/The Silverado Squatters* (London: J. M. Dent and Sons, Ltd., 1984), passim.
15. Stevenson, *Travels . . .*, 216–17.
16. *Scottish American*, May 4, 1867.

17. Blanche M. Taylor, "The English Colonies in Kansas, 1870–1895," *Historical Magazine of the Protestant Episcopal Church* 41 (March 1972):24.

18. William T. Chapman, "The Wakefield Colony," *Kansas State Historical Society Collections* 10 (1907–1908):501–502.

19. Brian P. Birch, "Victoria Vanquished: The Scottish Press and the Failure of George Grant's Colony," *Kansas History* 9 (Autumn 1986):118–21.

20. James L. Forsythe, "George Grant of Victoria: Man and Myth," *Kansas History* 9 (Autumn 1986):102–14.

21. Oscar O. Winther, "The English in Nebraska, 1857–1880," *Nebraska History* 48 (October 1967):209; Oscar O. Winther, "The English and Kansas, 1865–1890," in *The Frontier Challenge: Responses to the Trans-Mississippi West*, John G. Clark, ed. (Lawrence: University Press of Kansas, 1971).

22. James Alexander, "Letter from Nebraska," *Aberdeen Daily Free Press*, January 3, 1873; John Imrie, "The Scot—At Home and Abroad," *Scots Magazine* 24 (June/November 1899). Cf. John Woods, *Two Years' Residence in the Settlement on the Prairie in the Illinois Country, United States . . .* (London: Longman, Hurst, Rees, Orme, and Brown, 1822), 205–16.

23. R. H. Campbell, "Scotland," in *The Scots Abroad: Labour, Capital, Enterprise, 1750–1914*, R. A. Cage, ed. (London: Croon Helm, 1985), 15.

24. Berthoff, *British Emigrants in Industrial America, 1790–1950*, 86–87.

25. James Paul Allen and Eugene James Turner, *We the People: An Atlas of America's Ethnic Diversity* (New York: Macmillan, 1988), 39–47.

26. Information from F. S. Buchanan.

27. Robert M. Horne, "James Fergus in the Colorado Gold Fields," *Colorado Magazine* 50 (1973):41–56; *History of the Union Pacific Coal Mines, 1868 to 1940* (Omaha: Coronado Press, 1973), 164; Robert L. Spude, "Cyanide and the Flood of Gold," *Essays and Monographs in Colorado History* 12 (1991):1–35.

28. Shepperson, "The Scot Around the World," 242.

29. Interview with John L. Garretson, Spring 1992.

30. Marjory Harper, "Emigrant Strikebreakers: Scottish Granite Cutters and the Texas Capitol Boycott," *Southwestern Historical Quarterly* 95 (April 1992):465–86.

31. Tony Dickson, ed., *Scottish Capitalism: Class, State and Nation from before the Union to the Present* (London: Lawrence and Wishart, 1980), 185.

32. W. R. Lawson, "Scottish Capital Abroad," *Blackwood's* 136 (October 1884):468.

33. Paul M. Edwards, "Scottish Investments in the American West," in *Scottish Colloquium Proceedings* 4–5 (University of Guelph, 1973), 70.

34. Clark Spence, *British Investments in the American Mining Frontier, 1860–1901* (Ithaca: Cornell University Press, 1958); W. G. Kerr, "Scotland and the Texas Mortgage Business," *Economic History Review* 16 (1963–1964):92–103.

35. *The Scots in America*, 32–34.

36. R. E. Tyson, "Scottish Investment in American Railways: The Case of the City of Glasgow Bank, 1856–1881," in Peter L. Payne, ed., *Studies in Scottish Business History* (London: Frank Cass, Ltd., 1967), quoted, 287.

37. W. R. Lawson, "Scottish Capital Abroad," 480; Edwards, "Scottish Investments in the American West," 73; W. G. Kerr, "Scottish Investment and Enterprise in Texas," in Payne, *Studies in Scottish Business History*, 367.

38. James Macdonald, *Food from the Far West* (New York: Orange Judd Co., 1878), vii, xiv, 47; Edward Everett Dale, *Frontier Ways: Sketches of Life in the West* (Austin: University of Texas Press, 1959, 1989), 14–16.

39. Bruce Lenman, *An Economic History of Modern Scotland, 1660–1976* (London: B. T. Batsford, 1977), 14.

40. Robert Trow-Smith, *A History of British Livestock Husbandry, 1700–1900* (London: Routledge and Kegan Paul, 1959), 5.

41. K. J. Bonser, *The Drovers* (London: Macmillan, 1970), 65–75, 126.

42. Terry G. Jordan, *North American Cattle-Ranching Frontiers* (Albuquerque: University of New Mexico Press, 1993), 52.

43. Haldane, *The Drove Roads of Scotland*, 8, 186.

44. William Ferguson, *America by River and Rail: Or, Notes by the Way on the New World and Its People* (London: James Nisbet and Co., 1856), 412.

45. Trow-Smith, *A History of British Livestock Husbandry*, 112, 250.

46. W. H. Marwick, *Scotland in Modern Times: An Outline of Economic and Social Development since the Union of 1707* (London: Frank Cass and Co., 1964), 71.

47. Edith H. Whetham, *Beef Cattle and Sheep, 1910–1940* (Cambridge: University of Cambridge Report of Land Economy, Occasional Paper H.5, 1976), 4.

48. Macdonald, *Food from the Far West*, 279.

49. Carson, *Ranching, Sport and Travel;* Thomas Simpson Carson, *The World as Seen by Me* (London: Heath Cranston, Ltd., 1922). See also Lowell H. Harrison, "Thomas Simpson Carson, New Mexico Rancher," *New Mexico Historical Review* 42 (1967):127–43.

50. Larry A. McFarlane, "British Remittance Men as Ranchers: The Case of Coutts Marjoribanks and Edmund Thursby, 1884–95," *Great Plains Quarterly* 11 (Winter 1991):56–58.

51. John Clay, *My Life on the Range* (New York: Antiquarian Press, Ltd. [1924] 1961). The only sketch of Mackenzie is in the *DAB*. Cf. W. M. Pearce, *The Matador Land and Cattle Company* (Norman: University of Oklahoma Press, 1964). *Denver Post Empire Magazine*, May 23, 1971; Harmon Ross Mothershead, *The Swan Land and Cattle Company, Ltd.* (Norman: University of Oklahoma Press, 1971), viii.

52. Gene M. Gressley, *Bankers and Cattlemen* (Lincoln: University of Nebraska Press, 1966), 134.

53. Peter Fleming, "Notes of a Tour in Oregon," *The Blairgowrie Advertiser and Strathmore and Stormont News*. Blairgowie, March 13, 1875. Copy, SRO.

54. Mothershead, *The Swan Land and Cattle Company, Ltd.;* Pearce, *The Matador Land and Cattle Company*.

55. Clay, *My Life on the Range*, 181.

56. Anne T. Ostrye, *Foreign Investment in the American and Canadian West, 1870–1914: An Annotated Bibliography* (Metuchen, N.J., and London: The Scarecrow Press, Inc., 1987), 1–10.

57. Jackson, *The Enterprising Scot*, 312.

58. Edwards, "Scottish Investments in the American West," 75; Kerr, "Scottish Investment and American Enterprise in Texas," 381.

59. Elinore Pruitt Stewart, *Letters of a Woman Homesteader* (Boston: Houghton Mifflin Co., 1913, 1988), 5, 75–76.

60. Larry A. McFarlane, "Opposition to British Agricultural Investment in the Northern Plains, 1884–1900," *Nebraska History* 67 (Summer 1986):16–17.

61. Haldane, *The Drove Roads of Scotland*, 189.

62. Mark Cocker, "A Country Diary," *Guardian*, May 11, 1992.

63. Malcolm Gray, *The Highland Economy, 1750–1850* (Edinburgh: Oliver and Boyd, 1957), 87.

64. Larkin, *A Tour in the Highlands in 1818*, 221, as cited in Haldane, *The Drove Roads of Scotland*, 194.

65. Trow-Smith, *A History of British Livestock Husbandry, 1700–1900*, 275; I. F. Grant, *The Economic History of Scotland* (London: Longmans, Green and Co., 1934), 310–14.

66. Haldane, *The Drove Roads of Scotland*, 26–27.

67. Joan Thirsk, ed., *The Agrarian History of England and Wales*, Vol. 4, 1500–1640 (Cambridge: Cambridge University Press, 1967), 197.

68. Arthur Redford, *The Economic History of England 1760–1860* (London: Longmans, 1960), 79–80.

69. Lenman, *An Economic History of Modern Scotland*, 198–99.

70. Haldane, *The Drove Roads of Scotland*, 202–203; Whetham, *Beef Cattle and Sheep*, 1910–1940, 1–3.

71. Judith Keyes Kenny, "Early Sheep Ranching in Eastern Oregon," *Oregon Historical Quarterly* 64 (1963):105, 109–10.

72. Edward Norris Wentworth, *America's Sheep Trails* (Ames: Iowa State College Press, 1948), 613. Information on Burnett, later 11th Baronet and 23rd Laird of Crathes Castle, from an exhibit therein.

73. Wentworth, *America's Sheep Trails*, 322–50.

74. Wentworth, *America's Sheep Trails*, 366.

75. *A History of Torrance County* (n.p., 1979), 328, 36–37.

76. John Minto, "Sheep Husbandry in Oregon," *Oregon Historical Society Quarterly* 3 (September 1902):230–31.

77. Harold Briggs, "The Early Development of Sheep Ranching in the Northwest," *Agricultural History* 11 (April 1937):162–63, 167.

78. Minto, "Sheep Husbandry," 235–36. See also Virginia Paul, *This Was Sheep Ranching: Yesterday and Today* (Seattle: Superior Publishing Company, 1976).

79. McGregor, *Counting Sheep*.

80. Shadduck, *Andy Little*, is the only biography. Cf. Louis W. Attenberry, "Celts and Other Folk in the Regional Livestock Industry," *Idaho Yesterdays* 28 (Summer 1984), 22. See also Carole Simon-Smolinski, "Idaho's Scots Americans," in Carole Simon-Smolinski and Laurie Mercier, eds., *Idaho's Ethnic Heritage: Historical Overview* (Boise: Idaho State Historical Society, 1990), 50–76.

81. Wentworth, *America's Sheep Trails*, 407.

82. Kenny, "Early Sheep Ranching," 110; telephone interview with Mrs. Mary Dundy, Miles City, Montana (May 4, 1993).

83. McGregor, *Counting Sheep*, 121.

84. Kathleen Neils Conzen et al., "The Invention of Ethnicity: A Perspective from the USA," *Journal of American Ethnic History* 12 (Fall 1992):12–13. See also Eric Hobsbawm and Terrence Ranger, eds., *The Invention of Tradition* (Cambridge: Cambridge University Press, 1983), especially Hugh Trevor-Roper, "The Invention of Tradition: The Highland Tradition of Scotland," 15–41.

85. John M. Duncan, *Travels through Part of the United States and Canada in 1818 and 1819* (Glasgow: The University Press, 1823), 335–39.

86. Wisconsin Scot, Letter of December 14, 1864, *Aberdeen Free Press*, Copy, Special Collections, University of Aberdeen.

87. Philip B. Kinhardt, Jr., et al., *Lincoln* (New York: Alfred Knopf, 1992), quoted, 263.

88. Found in Myron W. Reed Clipping File, Western History Department, Denver Public Library.

89. Carolyn Wells, ed., *A Parody Anthology* (New York: Dover, 1964, 1967), 46.

90. Herbert N. Casson, "The Sons of Old Scotland in America," *Munsey's Magazine* 34 (1906):600.

91. Ross, *The Scot in America*, 411.

92. *Scottish American*, September 25, 1901.

93. Typescript interview with Betty Hitt, Idaho Historical Society, Boise, Idaho.

94. George De Vos and Lola Romanucci-Ross, eds., *Ethnic Identity: Cultural Continuities and Change* (Palo Alto, Calif.: Mayfield Publishing Co., 1975), 15.

95. *Aberdeen Free Press*, January 3, February 21, 1873.

96. Telephone interview with Don McRae, Miles City, Montana, Fall 1993; Page, "Country Squires," 23.

97. Gerald Redmond, *The Caledonian Games in Nineteenth-Century America* (Rutherford, N.J.: Fairleigh Dickinson University Press, 1971).

98. Caroline Bingham, *Beyond the Highland Line: Highland History and Culture* (London: Constable, 1991), 186.

99. *Scottish American*, July 17, 1889.

100. *Scottish American*, July 10, 1889.

101. Howard N. Rabinowitz, "Macdonald Smith," *Golfiana* 6 (1994):29–33; Howard N. Rabinowitz, "Alex Smith and the Early Days of American Golf," *Golf Journal* 47 (October 1994):17–19; Howard N. Rabinowitz, "Golf's Aspiring Autocrat [Charles Blair Macdonald] *Golf Journal* 49 (May 1996):37–41.

CHAPTER 5. SCOTLAND AND THE VICTORIAN WEST: THE ROMANCE

1. J. Frank Dobie, *Some Part of Myself* (Austin: University of Texas Press, 1980), 37.
2. Jane Porter, *The Scottish Chiefs* (London: Ward, Lock and Co., 1880), iii, 8, 9, 11.
3. A. D. Hook, "Jane Porter, Sir Walter Scott, and the Historical Novel," *Clio* 5 (1976):181–91.
4. Albert B. Friedman, ed., *The Viking Book of Folk Ballads of the English-Speaking World* (New York: Viking, 1956, 1963), xii.
5. John Marsden, *The Illustrated Border Ballads: The Anglo-Scottish Frontier* (Austin: University of Texas Press, 1990).
6. Child quoted in Marsden, *The Illustrated Border Ballads*, 119.
7. William Donaldson, *The Jacobite Song: Political Myth and National Identity* (Aberdeen: Aberdeen University Press, 1988); Charles Mackay, *The Jacobite Songs and Ballads, of Scotland, from 1688 to 1746* (London and Glasgow: Richard Griffin and Co., 1861), 14; James Reed, *The Border Ballads* (London: Athlone Press, 1973), 7–8. See also David Buchan, *The Ballad and the Folk* (London and Boston: Routledge and Kegan Paul, 1972).
8. See also Peter van der Merwe, *Origins of the Popular Style: The Antecedents of Twentieth-Century Popular Music* (Oxford: Clarendon Press, 1989), 196–97; and "Ballad" in Maria Leach, ed., *Funk and Wagnalls Standard Dictionary of Folklore, Mythology and Legends* (London: New English Library, 1972), 105–11.
9. William B. McCarthy, "The Americanization of Scottish Ballads: Counterevidence from the Southwest of Scotland," in Joseph Harris, ed., *The Ballad and Oral Literature* (Cambridge: Harvard University Press, 1991), 98.
10. Friedman, *The Viking Book of Folk Ballads of the English-Speaking World*, 424–25. Louise Pound, "Traditional Ballads in Nebraska," *Journal of American Folklore* 26 (1913):362.
11. Jan Harold Brunvand, *The Study of American Folklore* (New York: W. W. Norton, 1978), 192; Louise Pound, "The Southwestern Cowboy Songs and the English and Scottish Popular Ballads," *Modern Philology* 11 (October 1913):1–13.
12. Duncan Emrich, ed., *Folklore on the American Land* (Boston: Little, Brown and Company, 1972), 506; Francis B. Gummere, *The Popular Ballad* (New York: Dover, 1959), 272.

13. Sir Herbert Maxwell, *The Honorable Sir Charles Murray, K.C.B.* (Edinburgh and London: William Blackwood and Sons, 1898), 78–80, 99.

14. Sir Charles Augustus Murray, *Travels in North America During the Years 1834 and 1836* . . . , 2 vols. (London: R. Bartley, 1839), 1:253.

15. Murray, *Travels,* 1:288.

16. Murray, *Travels,* 1:407–409.

17. Murray, *Travels,* 1:452, 393.

18. Murray, *Travels,* 2:22.

19. Maxwell, *The Honorable Sir Charles Murray,* 196–97.

20. Charles Augustus Murray, *The Prairie-Bird,* 3 vols. (London: Richard Bentley, New Burlington Street, 1844).

21. The *Times* [London], February 29, 1944. Copy in Sir Charles A. Murray Papers, GD.261, SRO.

22. Letter of February 2, 1843, to brother, Murray Papers, SRO.

23. Porter and Davenport, *Scotsman in Buckskin,* is the only biography.

24. The observation is from a Presbyterian minister who met him. As cited in William James Anderson, "Sir William Drummond Stewart and the Chapel of St. Anthony the Eremite, Murthly," *The Innes Review: Scottish Catholic Historical Studies* 15 (Spring 1964):152.

25. Alvin M. Josephy, Jr., "First Dude Ranch Trip to the Untamed West," *American Heritage* 7 (February 1956):8–15.

26. Cited in Olson, *Marmalade and Whiskey,* 18.

27. Joan Carpenter Troccoli, *Alfred Jacob Miller: Watercolors of the American West* (Tulsa: Gilcrease Museum, 1990), 45–48; Ron Tyler, ed., *Alfred Jacob Miller: Artist on the Oregon Trail* (Fort Worth: Amon Carter Museum, 1982), plate 101.

28. A. J. Miller to W. D. Stewart, March 27, 1839, GD 121/Box 101/Bundle 21/99, SRO.

29. Jacqueline Williams, *Wagon Wheel Kitchens: Food on the Oregon Trail* (Lawrence: University Press of Kansas, 1993), 180.

30. *Braves and Buffalo: Plains Indian Life in 1832. Water Colors of Alfred J. Miller,* introduction by Michael Bell (Toronto: University of Toronto Press, 1975), 108–20.

31. A. J. Miller to WDS, March 16, 1844, 122/22/87, SRO.

32. William Sublette to WDS, November 22, 1843, 121/22/77, SRO.

33. Robert Campbell to WDS, August 29, 1839, 101/21/122, SRO.

34. Robert Campbell to WDS, February 3, 1843. Grandtully Correspondence, 1841–1845, GD, 121/Box 101/22, SRO.

35. Sublette to WDS, June 16, 1841, 122/22/4, SRO.
36. Sublette to WDS, April 20, 1844, 121/22/91, SRO.
37. John I. Merritt, *Baronets and Buffalo: The British Sportsman in the American West, 1833–1881* (Missoula: Mountain Press Publishing, 1985), quoted, 38.
38. Anderson, "Sir William Drummond Stewart," 165.
39. Interview with Robert Stewart-Frothingham, July 6, 1994, Murthly, Scotland. See also William Fraser, *The Red Book of Grandtully*, 2 vols. (Edinburgh: n.p., 1868).
40. *Altowan; Or Incidents of Life and Adventure in the Rocky Mountains* (New York: Harper and Brothers, 1846), 106, 251, 57, 80, 150, 240.
41. It is still in print. William Drummond Stewart, *Edward Warren*, Bart Barbour, ed., with an introduction by Winfred Blevins (Missoula: Mountain Press Publishing Co., 1986).
42. Bernard de Voto, *Across the Wide Missouri* (Boston: Houghton Mifflin, 1947).
43. Michael Moss and John Hume, *Old Photographs from Scottish Country Houses* (Lancaster: Hendon Publishing Co., 1984), n.p.; Lenman, *An Economic History of Modern Scotland*, 198–99.
44. Innes Shand, "The Scot at Home," *Blackwood's* 118 (December 1875):736; C. W. Hill, *Edwardian Scotland* (Edinburgh and London: Scottish Academic Press, 1976), 9–10.
45. Moss and Hume, *Old Photographs from Scottish Country Houses*, n.p.
46. George Wray, "Diary of a Tour in the Rocky Mountains," GD 21/482/2, SRO.
47. Andrew Haggard, "Yankee Homes and Buffalo Haunts," *Blackwood's* 149 (February 1891):183–85; J. P. Maud, "A Fall Hunt in the Rockies," *Blackwood's* 142 (August 1887):264–72.
48. R. Tait Murray, "The Central Prairie: A Hunting Expedition," manuscript, GD 302/83, SRO. This manuscript has been reprinted in Brian P. Birch, ed., "Beyond Victoria, A Scottish Visitor's First Buffalo Hunt," *Kansas History* 6 (Autumn 1983):173–80.
49. Cited in Richard W. Etulain, "A Cultural History of the Modern West," manuscript.
50. Roger Taylor, *George Washington Wilson, Artist and Photographer, 1823–91* (Aberdeen: Aberdeen University Press, 1991), quoted, 50.
51. Marcus Halliwell, *Highland Landscapes: Paintings of Scotland in the Nineteenth Century* (London: Garamond Publishers Ltd., 1990), 6.

52. David Irwin and Francina Irwin, *Scottish Painters at Home and Abroad, 1700–1900* (London: Faber and Faber, 1975), 36, 365. See also Marilyn Slokstad, "Romantic Images in Art," in Orel, *The Scottish World*, 259–69.

53. William H. Goetzmann and Joseph C. Porter, *The West as Romantic Horizon* (Omaha: Center for Western Studies, Joslyn Art Museum, 1981).

54. Nancy K. Anderson, "Curious Historical Artistic Data: Art History and Western American Art," in *Discovered Lands, Invented Pasts* (New Haven and London: Yale University Press, 1987), 13.

55. "William Keith, 1839–1911," *California Palace of the Legion of Honor* 3 (July 1945):34–39.

56. Linnie March Wolfe, *Son of the Wilderness: The Life of John Muir* (Madison: University of Wisconsin Press, 1945, 1973), 162.

57. Paul Mills, *An Introduction to the Art of William Keith* (Oakland: Oakland Municipal Art Museum, 1956), 4.

58. James William Pattison, "William Keith—Poetical Painter," *Fine Arts Journal* 29 (1913):369; Jeanne Van Nostrand, *The First Hundred Years of Painting in California, 1775–1875* (San Francisco: John Howell Books, 1980), 68–69.

59. Helmut Gernsheim, *The Rise of Photography, 1850–1880: The Age of Collodian*, 3rd ed., enlarged and revised (London: Thames and Hudson, 1988), 120–23.

60. John Smith, *George Washington Wilson in Caithness and Sutherland* (Clapham, Lancaster: Dalesman Books, 1988), 29; Donald Macaulay, *George Washington Wilson in the Hebrides* (Keighley, West Yorkshire: Kennedy Brothers, 1984); John Smith, *George Washington Wilson in Orkney and Shetland* (Keighley, West Yorkshire: Kennedy Brothers, 1986).

61. Taylor, *George Washington Wilson*, quoted, 96.

62. Jackson, *Time Exposure* (Albuquerque: University of New Mexico Press, [1942] 1986) is the best source of his life.

63. Josephene Cobb, "Alexander Gardner," *Image* 7 (June 1958): 124–36; William Welling, *Photography in America: The Formative Years, 1839–1900* (Albuquerque: University of New Mexico Press, 1978, 1987), 178.

64. Michael L. Carlebach, *The Origins of Photojournalism in America* (Washington and London: Smithsonian Institution Press, 1992), 120. See also A. D. Morrison-Low, "Scottish Photographers Abroad During the Nineteenth Century," in *The Enterprising Scot: Scottish Adventure and*

Achievement, Jenni Calder, ed. (Edinburgh: Royal Museum of Scotland, 1986), 154–58.

65. Moray McLaren, *Understanding the Scots* (New York: Bell Publishing, 1961, 1972), 29.

66. Sir Harry Lauder, *Roamin' in the Gloamin'* (London: Hutchinson and Co., Ltd., 1928), 158.

67. "A King of the Vaudeville Stage," *Current Literature* 46 (January 1909):84.

68. Sir Harry Lauder, *A Minstrel in France* (New York: Hearst's International Library Co., 1918), 29.

69. C. A. Oakley, *The Second City* (London and Glasgow: Blackie and Son, Ltd., 1946), quoted, 265.

70. "A King of the Vaudeville Stage," *Current Literature* 46 (January 1909).

71. *Literary Digest* 64 (January 10, 1920):67; conversation with Ivan and Carol Doig, February 3, 1996.

72. Sir Harry Lauder, *Between You and Me* (New York: James A. McCann Co., 1912), 139.

73. Henry L. Snyder, "Romantic Images of Scotland—Words and Music," in Orel, *The Scottish World,* 254–58.

74. Harold Orel, "Scottish Stereotypes," in Orel, *The Scottish World,* 19.

75. B. A. Botkin, ed., *A Treasure of American Folklore: Stories, Ballads, and Traditions of the People* (New York: Crown Publishers, 1944), 132–33, 150–53.

76. Ralph E. Friar and Natasha A. Friar, *The Only Good Indians: The Hollywood Gospel* (New York: Drama Book Specialists, 1972); Gretchen M. Bataille and Charles L. P. Silet, *The Pretend Indians: Images of Native Americans in the Movies* (Ames: Iowa State University Press, 1980).

77. L. G. Moses, "Interpreting the Wild West, 1883–1914," in Szasz, *Between Indian and White Worlds,* 158–78; L. G. Moses, *Wild West Shows and the Images of American Indians, 1883–1933* (Albuquerque: University of New Mexico Press, 1996). See also the posters and photos in *The West of Buffalo Bill* (New York: Henry N. Abrams, Inc., 1974), 46–66.

78. Moses, "Interpreting the Wild West," quoted, 164–65.

79. John Burke, *Buffalo Bill: The Noblest Whiteskin* (New York: Capricorn Books, 1973), 169–200.

80. Don Russell, *The Lives and Legends of Buffalo Bill* (Norman: University of Oklahoma Press, 1960), 440–42.

81. *Edinburgh Evening News,* August 4, 1984; Undated Clippings, Edinburgh History Room, Edinburgh Public Library.
82. Aberdeen *Bon-Accord,* September 1, 1904, 8.
83. Aberdeen *Evening Express,* c. December 15, 1904, undated clipping.
84. Aberdeen *Daily Journal,* August 26, 1904; August 23, 1904; *Bon-Accord,* September 1, 1904, v; *Daily Journal,* August 27, 1904.
85. *Daily Journal,* August 26, 1904; *Bon-Accord,* September 1, 1904, 8. See also Sarah J. Blackstone, *Buckskin, Bullets and Business: A History of Buffalo Bill's Wild West* (Westport, Conn.: Greenwood, 1986); Joseph G. Rosa and Robin May, *Buffalo Bill and His Wild West* (Lawrence: University Press of Kansas, 1989); Stanley Vestal, *Sitting Bull: Champion of the Sioux* (Oxford: Oxford University Press, 1959); and Rita G. Napier, "Across the Big Water; American Indians' Perceptions of Europe and Europeans, 1887–1906," in Christian F. Feest, ed., *Indians and Europe: An Interdisciplinary Collection of Essays* (Aachen, The Netherlands: Raper Verlay, 1987).
86. On this theme, see Glassie, *Irish Folk History;* M. I. Finley, *The Use and Abuse of History* (London: Penguin Books, 1975), 11–34; Henry Glassie, "The Practice and Purpose of History," *Journal of American History* 81 (December 1994), 961–68; Richard Slotkin, *Regeneration Through Violence: The Mythology of the American Frontier, 1600–1860* (Middletown, Conn.: Wesleyan University Press, 1973); Richard Slotkin, *The Fatal Environment: The Myth of the Frontier in the Age of Industrialism, 1800–1890* (New York: Atheneum, 1985); Lee Clark Mitchell, *Witness to a Vanishing America: The Nineteenth-Century Response* (Princeton: Princeton University Press, 1981); Henry Nash Smith, *Virgin Land: The American West as Symbol and Myth* (Cambridge: Harvard University Press, 1950); Ray Allen Billington, *Land of Savagery/Land of Promise: The European Image of the American Frontier in the Nineteenth Century* (New York: Norton, 1981); Robert Coles, *The Call of Stories: Teaching and the Moral Imagination* (Boston: Houghton Mifflin Co., 1989).

CHAPTER 6. VARIETIES OF THE SCOTTISH WESTERN EXPERIENCE

1. LeRoy, *Lairds, Bards and Mariners.*
2. Cited in John C. Paige, "Country Squires and Laborers: British Immigrants in Wyoming," in *Peopling the High Plains: Wyoming's European*

Heritage, Gordon Olaf Hendrickson, ed. (Cheyenne: Wyoming State Archives and Historical Department, 1977), 23.

3. Carlisle to Robert Mitchell, May 24, 1815. GD 714/6, SRO.

4. James Joseph Hope-Vere to John P. Wood, 1828 Hopetoun Mss. (0888), SRO.

5. Jerrell G. Johnson, *The Arizona Scotsman* (Pine, Ariz.: Beaumaris Books, 1970).

6. Geo Sim to My Dear Sister, April 29, 1906. GD 1/756/2/7, SRO; Charles Lummis, "Garden in the Sky," in Gregory McNamee, ed., *Names in Stone and Glen: An Arizona Anthology* (Tucson: University of Arizona Press, 1993), 137–38; Frederick Stewart Buchanan, ed., *A Good Time Coming: Mormon Letters to Scotland* (Salt Lake City: University of Utah Press, 1988).

7. Cited in Kate B. Carter, comp., "British Contributions to Utah" (1940), 95. Pamphlet 282, Utah Historical Society. See also Carter, comp., "The Mormons from Scotland and Wales," Pamphlet 11913.

8. Frederick S. Buchanan, "Scots Among the Mormons," *Utah Historical Quarterly* 36 (Fall 1968):328–29.

9. P. A. M. Taylor, *Expectations Westward: The Mormons and the Emigration of Their British Converts in the Nineteenth Century* (Edinburgh and London: Oliver and Boyd, 1963), 140.

10. *The Edinburgh Review* 202 (April 1854):320–83. Increase McGeevan Dusay (pseud.), *Plain Questions for Mormonites: By One Who Knows They Are Not Saints* (London: Westheim and MacIntosh, 1852), 10.

11. *The Celtic Magazine* 10 (1885):243–44.

12. A Country Clergyman, *Friendly Warnings on the Subject of Mormonism: Addressed to His Parishioners* (London: Franas and John Rivington, 1850); *Edinburgh Review* 202 (April 1954):382.

13. Henry Mayhew, *The Mormons, or Latter-Day Saints: A Contemporary History* (London: Office of the National Illustrated Library, 1851), v.

14. Philip A. M. Taylor, "Why Did British Mormons Emigrate?" *Utah Historical Quarterly* 22 (July 1954):249–70.

15. *Edinburgh Review* 202 (April 1854):382.

16. Dusay, "Plain Questions for Mormonites," 10, 18.

17. Taylor, *Expectations Westward,* 346.

18. Buchanan, "Scots Among the Mormons," 344.

19. Robert Baird, *Religion in America,* Henry Warner Bowden, ed. (New York: Harper and Brothers, 1856, 1970), 129.

20. See, for example, Edward Arthur Wicker, *The Presbyterian Church in California, 1849–1927* (New York: Frederick H. Hitchcock, 1927).

21. Sam Menaul to Mark T. Banker, January 1, 1981. Archives, Menaul Historical Library [hereafter Menaul Library], Albuquerque, N.Mex. The data come from these folders: John Menaul; James Menaul; Charity Menaul; Menaul Family.

22. John Hanson Beedle, *The Undeveloped West: Or, Five Years in the Territories* (New York: Arno Press [1873] 1973), 524–31; George Wharton James, *New Mexico: The Land of the Delight Makers* (Boston: Page, 1920), 369–70.

23. James H. Fraser, "Indian Mission Printing in New Mexico: A Bibliography," *New Mexico Historical Review* 43 (1968):311–17.

24. John Menaul, "Characteristics of Pueblo Indians," *Home Mission Monthly* 6 (1891–92):80; John Menaul, "Work Among the Indians," in *The Field Is* (May 1893):197. In Archival Box 88-5, Menaul Library. See also typed sheet, "Rev. James A. Menaul," Menaul Library.

25. *Home Mission Monthly* 25 (February 1892):73.

26. *Home Mission Monthly* 16 (May 1877):n.p. See Mark T. Banker, "Presbyterian Missionary Activity in the Southwest: The Careers of John and James Menaul," in Ferenc M. Szasz, ed., *Religion in the West* (Manhattan, Kans.: Sunflower University Press, 1984), 55–61; Mark T. Banker, "Presbyterians and Pueblos: A Protestant Response to the Indian Question, 1872–1892," *Journal of Presbyterian History* 60 (Spring 1982).

27. *Idaho Statesman*, November 16, 1981.

28. Typescript of interview with Nellie Allen, Idaho Historical Society, Boise, Idaho.

29. Interview with Nellie Allen.

30. Typescript of interview with Betty Hitt, Idaho Historical Society.

31. Interview with Betty Hitt.

32. Travel Journal of Mrs. M. A. Pringle, GD 246/47, SRO.

33. Muriel E. Chamberlain, *Lord Aberdeen: A Political Biography* (London and New York: Longman, 1983), 339–40; Lucille Iremonger, *Lord Aberdeen* (London: Collins, 1978), 175. See also Wilbur Devereux Jones, *Lord Aberdeen and the Americas* (Athens: University of Georgia Press, 1958).

34. Aberdeen, *"We Twa,"* 314.

35. The Marquis and Marchioness of Aberdeen and Temair, *More Cracks with "We Twa"* (London: Methuen and Company, Ltd., 1929), 69.

36. Aberdeen, *More Cracks with "We Twa,"* 69–71. Olson, *Marmalade and Whiskey*, 129.

37. *Manchester Guardian,* April 19, 1939; *Aberdeen Press and Journal,* March 14, 1957.

38. A. G. Bradley, *Canada in the Twentieth Century* (New York: E. P. Dutton and Co., 1903), 201.

39. *The Best of Robert Service* (Philadelphia, Pa.: 1880), 22, 247. Thanks to Sandra V. MacMahan for this citation.

40. McFarlane, "British Remittance Men as Ranchers," 56–58.

41. R. M. Middleton, ed. and annot., *The Journal of Lady Aberdeen: The Okanagan Valley in the Nineties* (Victoria, B.C.: Morris Publishing, Ltd., 1986), 13, 59.

42. Aberdeen, *More Cracks with "We Twa,"* 91. For further details on the Aberdeens in the West, see The Countess of Aberdeen, *Through Canada with a Kodak* (Toronto: University of Toronto Press, 1994).

43. Doris French, *Ishbel and the Empire: A Biography of Lady Aberdeen* (Toronto: Dundurn Press, 1988), 121–22. See also Marjory Harper, "A Gullible Pioneer? Lord Aberdeen and the Development of Fruit Farming in the Okanagan Valley, 1890–1921," *British Journal of Canadian Studies* 1 (December 1986):256–81; Mark Zuehlke, *Scoundrels, Dreamers and Second Sons: British Remittance Men in the Canadian West* (Vancouver/Toronto: Whitecap Books, 1994).

44. Aberdeen, *More Cracks with "We Twa,"* 94.

45. A good capsule summary of his life can be found in Orlin Scoville, *Remittance Men, Second Sons and Other Gentlemen of the West* (Washington, D.C.: Patomic Corral, The Westerners, 1990), 31–43. See also *Pueblo Chieftain,* July 11, 1954.

46. Denver *Post,* May 28, 1945.

47. Denver *Times,* July 15, 1900.

48. John Monnett and Michael McCarthy, "Talk About Your Goodtime Charlie!" *Senior Voice* (December 24, 1989).

49. Denver *Times,* April 18, 1900.

50. Denver *Republican,* August 28, 1902.

51. Denver *Times,* April 18, 1900.

52. Denver *Times,* July 15, 1900.

53. Denver *Republican,* May 13, 1898; Denver *Times,* September 2, 1940.

54. J. D. A. Ogilvy, "L. Ogilvy and His Friends," *Empire Magazine,* December 24, 1974; May 23, 1971.

55. Floyd Baskette, "Legendary Uncle Lyulph," *Empire Magazine,* May 23, 1971; J. D. A. Ogilvy, "Certain Adventures of L. Ogilvy," *Empire Magazine,* October 18, 1970.

56. Denver *Republican*, May 13, 1898. Scoville, *Remittance Men, Second Sons, and Other Gentlemen of the West*, 32–40.

57. Gene Fowler, *Timber Line: A Story of Bonfils and Tammen* (New York: Covici and Friede, 1933), 111.

58. Jefferson Davis to My Dear Daughter, in Hudson Strode, ed., *Jefferson Davis: Private Letters, 1823–1887* (New York: Harcourt, Brace and World, Inc., 1966), 304, 305.

59. Anne B. Fisher, *No More a Stranger* (Stanford: Stanford University Press, 1946), 207–208. In *RLS: A Life Study* (London: Hamish Hamilton, 1980), Jenni Calder observes, "the trip, indeed the whole American experience, was a landmark in Stevenson's writing as well as in his personal life," 128.

60. Peter Conrad, *Imaging America* (New York: Oxford University Press, 1980), 107–108.

61. Graham Balfour, *The Life of Robert Louis Stevenson* (New York: Charles Scribner's Sons, 1911, 1915), 155.

62. Jonathan Rabin, "Introduction," in Robert Louis Stevenson, *The Amateur Emigrant* (London: Hogarth Press, 1984), n.p.

63. Clayton Hamilton, *On the Trail of Stevenson* (Garden City, N.Y.: Doubleday, Page and Co., 1975), 128–31.

64. David Daiches, *Robert Louis Stevenson and His World* (London: Thames and Hudson, 1973), 48–49.

65. Balfour, *The Life of Robert Louis Stevenson*, 152–53.

66. Anne Roller Issler, "Robert Louis Stevenson in Monterey," *Pacific Historical Review* 34 (August 1965):321.

67. See Nellie Van de Grift Sanchez, "In California with Robert Louis Stevenson, *Scribner's* 60 (October 1916):467–81; Roy Nickerson, *Robert Louis Stevenson in California* (San Francisco: Chronicle Books, 1982); Ian Bell, *Dreams of Exile: Robert Louis Stevenson: A Biography* (New York: Henry Holt, 1992), quoted, 129.

68. Stevenson, *Travels . . .*, 211, 215, 217, 219.

69. Bell, *Dreams of Exile*, passim; *Scotsman*, December 1, 1991.

70. Robert Louis Stevenson, "The Old Pacific Capital," *Fraser's Magazine* 22 (November 1880):647–57; Robert Louis Stevenson, *The Wrecker* (New York: Charles Scribner's Sons, 1922), especially chapter 8.

71. J. R. Hammond, *A Robert Louis Stevenson Companion: A Guide to the Novels, Essays and Short Stories* (London: Macmillan, 1974), 108.

72. Nickerson, *Robert Louis Stevenson in California*, 107–15; quoted, 114. See also J. C. Furnas, *Voyage to Windward: The Life of Robert Louis Stevenson* (London: Faber and Faber, Ltd., 1952), 142–67.

73. John Muir, *The Story of My Boyhood and Youth* (Madison and Milwaukee: University of Wisconsin Press, 1965), 3.

74. Muir, *The Story of My Boyhood and Youth*, 129.

75. Linnie Marsh Wolfe, *Son of the Wilderness: The Life of John Muir* (Madison: University of Wisconsin Press, 1945), 162; Robert Engberg, ed., *John Muir's Summering in the Sierra* (Madison: University of Wisconsin Press, 1984), 13. See also John Muir, *Wilderness Essays* (Salt Lake City: Peregrine Smith, Inc., 1980).

76. John Leighly, "John Muir's Image of the West," *Annals of the Association of American Geographers* 48 (December 1958):309–18; Roderick Nash, *The American Conservation Movement* (St. Charles, Mo.: Forum Press, 1974), 9.

77. C. Michael Hall, "John Muir's Travels in Australia: 1903–1904," in Sally M. Miller, ed., *John Muir: Life and Work* (Albuquerque: University of New Mexico Press, 1993), 304.

78. Catherine L. Albanese, *Nature Religion in America: From the Algonkian Indians to the New Age* (Chicago and London: University of Chicago Press, 1990).

79. Michael P. Cohen, *The Pathless Way: John Muir and American Wilderness* (Madison: University of Wisconsin Press, 1984), 127.

80. See *John Muir: Life and Legacy*, special issue of *Pacific Historian* 29 (Summer/Fall 1985).

81. Cited in Ronald H. Limbaugh, "Stockeen and the Moral Education of John Muir," *Environmental History Review* 15 (Spring 1991): 36–37.

82. See, for example, William Cronon, "Landscape and Home: Environmental Traditions in Wisconsin," *Wisconsin Magazine of History* 74 (Winter 1990/1991):97. In *The American Conservation Movement: John Muir and His Legacy*, Stephen Fox argues that Muir rejected his inherited Christianity to adopt a variety of pantheism. In *John Muir: Summering in the Sierra*, Robert Engberg suggests that he accepted a version of Eastern mysticism that viewed the earth as a universe of opposites: life and death; light and dark; yin and yang. He evolved this position from the fact that his family remained unified in spite of the vast differences among them. See also Stephen Fox, *The American Conservation Movement: John Muir and His Legacy* (Madison: University of Wisconsin Press, 1985); Engberg, *John Muir: Summering in the Sierra*, 7; Thurman Wilkins, *John Muir: Apostle of Nature* (Norman: University of Oklahoma Press, 1995), 6, 8.

83. Mark Stoll, "God and John Muir," in Miller, *John Muir: Life and Work*, 64–81.

84. Robert T. Handy, *A History of the Churches in the United States and Canada* (New York: Oxford University Press, 1976), 169; William Warren Sweet, *The Story of Religion in America* (New York: Harper and Brothers, 1950), 236–37. The best book on Restorationism in general is Richard T. Hughes and C. Leonard Allen, *Illusions of Innocence: Protestant Primitivism in America, 1630–1875* (Chicago: University of Chicago Press, 1988).

85. W. F. B. in the *DAB*, 116.

86. Don Weiss, "John Muir and the Wilderness Ideal," in Miller, *John Muir: Life and Work*, 120.

87. William Frederic Bade, ed., *The Life and Letters of John Muir* (Boston: Houghton Mifflin, 1924), 1:179; cited in Weiss, "John Muir," 120.

88. Ronald W. Limbaugh, "Introduction: John Muir's Life and Legacy," in Miller, *John Muir: Life and Work*, 8–9; Cohen, *The Pathless Way*; Frederick Turner, *Rediscovering America: John Muir in His Time and Ours* (New York: Viking, 1985); Wilkins, *John Muir*, 150n.

89. John Leighly, "John Muir's Image of the West," 307–10.

CHAPTER 7. THE WESTERN CANADIAN ALTERNATIVE

1. *Highland Clearances: Sufferings of the Outcasts in Knoydart and in Skye* (Glasgow: n.p., 1853), 10.

2. Francess G. Halpenny, "Scots in the Dictionary of Canadian Biography," in Catherine Kerrigan, ed., *The Immigrant Experience*, (Guelph, Ontario: University of Guelph, 1992), 23.

3. J. M. Bumsted, *The Scots in Canada* (Ottawa: Canadian Historical Association, 1982), 10–11; *The Scots in Canada: A Resource Based on a Scottish Record Office Exhibition* (Edinburgh: SRO, 1994), 1; John Murray Gibbon, *Scots in Canada: A History of the Settlement of the Dominion from the Earliest Days to the Present Time* (London: Kegan Paul, Trench, Trubner and Co., Ltd., 1911), 161. See also J. M. Bumsted, "Scots," in *Encyclopedia of Canada's Peoples* (Toronto: University of Toronto Press, 1999), 1115–42.

4. Helen I. Cowan, *British Emigration to British North America: The First Hundred Years* (Toronto: University of Toronto Press, revised and enlarged edition, 1961), 26–27.

5. Bumsted, *The Scots in Canada*, 1–15; Donald Aspey, "Where the Gaelic Lives," *Scots Magazine* 13 (April/September 1930):425. See also Charles W. Dunn, *Highland Settler: A Portrait of the Scottish Gael in Cape*

Breton and Eastern Nova Scotia (Wreck Cove, Cape Breton Island: Breton Books, 1952, 1991); R. A. MacLean, *A State of Mind: The Scots in Nova Scotia* (Hantsport, Nova Scotia: Lancelot Press, 1992).

6. See Rae Fleming, ed., *The Lochaber Emigrants to Glengarry* (Toronto: Natural Heritage/Natural History, Inc., 1994); Marianne McLean, *The People of Glengarry* (Montreal and Kingston: McGill-Queen's University Press, 1991); John Kenneth Galbraith, *The Scotch* (Boston: Houghton Mifflin, 1964).

7. Craig, *On the Crofters' Trail.*

8. "St. Andrew's Society of Detroit, Michigan 100th Anniversary, 1849–1949," pamphlet, Scottish National Library.

9. Ged Martin and Jeffrey Simpson, *Canada's Heritage in Scotland* (Toronto: Dundurn, 1989), 9.

10. *The Scots in Canada: Historical Background List of Documents, Extracts and Facsimiles,* 9.

11. Bryce, *The Scotsman in Canada,* 2:116.

12. Alan Artibise, *Winnipeg: An Illustrated History* (Toronto: James Lorimer and Co., 1977), 11–15.

13. Alan R. Turner, "Scottish Tradition in Canada (Toronto: McClelland and Stewart, 1976), 77.

14. John Luke Poett, "A Pioneer Veterinarian in Western Canada," *Journal of the West* 27 (January 1988):16–25.

15. Turner, "Scottish Settlement in the West," 80; Gibbon, *Scots in Canada,* 139, 141.

16. Bumsted, *The Scots in Canada,* 5.

17. Susan Jackel, ed., *A Flannel Shirt and Liberty: British Emigrant Gentlewomen in the Canadian West, 1880–1914* (Vancouver and London: University of British Columbia Press, 1982), 66–74, 217–20, xxvi.

18. Marjory Harper, "Nineteenth Century Exodus," *Leopard: The Magazine for North East Scotland* (February 1989):15–17; Walter Nugent, *Crossings: The Great Transatlantic Migrations, 1870–1914* (Bloomington: Indiana University Press, 1992), 47–48.

19. Marjory Harper, "Exodus: Persuading the Emigrant," *Leopard* (March 1987):18–20; cf. Marjory Harper, "Exodus—A Fresh Start for the Children," *Leopard* (May 1989):23–25.

20. Harper, "Nineteenth Century Exodus," quoted, 16; cf. Marjory Harper, "Exodus: The Transatlantic Tradesmen," *Leopard* (April 1989): 15–18.

21. Norman Macdonald, *Canada: Immigration and Colonization, 1841–1901* (Aberdeen: Aberdeen University Press, 1966), chapter 11.

22. *The New West* (Winnipeg: Canadian Historical Publishing Co., 1888), 127, 137.

23. Gibbon, *Scots in Canada*, 149.

24. James B. Hedges, *Building the Canadian West: The Land and Colonization Policies of the Canadian Pacific Railway* (New York: The Macmillan Company, 1939), quoted, 123.

25. G. G. Ramsay, "The Settlement of Highland Crofters in the Northwest of Canada," *Macmillan's Magazine* 51 (January 1885): 161–75; Gibbon, *Scots in Canada*, 149–50.

26. Gibbon, *Scots in Canada*, quoted, 158; Ramsay, "The Settlement of Highland Crofters in the Northwest of Canada," 175.

27. Hugh MacPhee, "The Trail of the Emigrants," *Transactions of the Gaelic Society of Inverness* 46 (1969–70):215–16.

28. Margaret MacDonell, *The Emigrant Experience: Songs of Highlands Emigrants in North America* (Toronto, etc.: University of Toronto Press, 1982), 151–55. (Excerpted from the longer poem.)

29. Harper, "Crofter Colonists in Canada," 71.

30. Wayne Norton, *Help Us to a Better Land: Crofter Colonies in the Prairie West* (Regina: Canadian Plains Research Center, 1994), 84.

31. Norton, *Help Us to a Better Land*, 27.

32. Kent Stuart, "The Scottish Crofter Colony, Saltcoats, 1889–1904," *Saskatchewan History* 24 (1971):41–50.

33. Stuart MacDonald, "Crofter Colonisation in Canada, 1866–1892: The Scottish Political Background," *Northern Scotland* 7 (1986):55.

34. *The Emigrants* (Edinburgh: SRO, 1994), 18; *Western Canada* (n.p., c. 1912), 18.

35. Harper, "Crofter Colonists in Canada," 69–108.

36. *Aberdeen Press and Journal*, October 10, 1936.

37. *Aberdeen Press and Journal*, February 27, 1933.

38. Biographical information drawn largely from Peter P. Remaley's account in the *DAB*.

39. Robert Service, *The Spell of the Yukon* (New York: Dodd, Mead and Co., [1907] 1942), 55, 61.

40. John West, *The Substance of a Journal During a Residence at the Red River Colony, British North America* (London: L. B. Seeley and Son, 1824), 51.

41. Bryce, *The Scotsman in Canada*, 2:277–84.

42. See the account in Ferenc Morton Szasz, *The Protestant Clergy in the Great Plains and Mountain West, 1880–1915* (Albuquerque: University of New Mexico Press, 1988); Norman MacDonald, *Canada:*

Immigration and Colonization, 1841–1903 (Aberdeen: Aberdeen University Press, 1960), especially chapter 11.

43. John S. Moir, "Scottish Influences on Canadian Presbyterians," *Scotia* 1 (April 1978):34. Moir discusses this theme in more detail in *Enduring Witness: A History of the Presbyterian Church in Canada* (Toronto, 1973).

44. Bryce, *The Scotsman in Canada,* 2:263–76.

45. *Home and Foreign Missionary Record* 14 (January 1883–December 1884):316; *Home and Foreign Missionary Record* 21 (1895):264; *Home and Foreign Missionary Record* 21 (1895):263; *Home and Foreign Missionary Record* 24 (1899):42–43.

46. *Home and Foreign Missionary Record* 14 (January 1883–December 1884):316.

47. Facts from respective sketches in the *Dictionary of Canadian Biography.*

48. Constance Whyte, *More Than a Legend: The Story of the Loch Ness Monster* (London: Hamish Hamilton, 1957), xv.

49. F. W. Holiday, *The Great Orm of Loch Ness* (London: Faber and Faber, 1968), 155; R. T. Gould, *The Loch Ness Monster and Others* (London: Geoffrey Bles, 1934), 5.

50. Tim Dinsdale, *Loch Ness Monster* (London: Routledge and Kegan Paul, 1961); Tim Dinsdale, *The Leviathans: The Mysterious Sightings of Lake and Sea Monsters Throughout the World* (London: Routledge and Kegan Paul, 1966); cf. Nicholas Mitchell, *The Loch Ness Story* (London: Gorgi Books, 1974), 52.

51. Mary Moon, *Ogopogo: The Okanogan Mystery* (North Vancouver: T. J. Douglas, 1977).

52. Paul H. LeBlond, "Sea Serpents of the Pacific Northwest," in Ferenc M. Szasz, ed., *Great Mysteries of the West* (Golden, Colo.: Fulcrum, 1993), 3–15.

53. Moon, *Ogopogo,* 15.

54. Gibbon, *The Scots in Canada,* 160–61.

EPILOGUE

1. Christopher Harvie, *No Gods and Precious Few Heroes: Scotland, 1914–1980* (London: Edward Arnold, 1981), 45–47.

2. William Wilson to Dear Mother, September 7, 1843, GD 121/Box 101/Bundle 22/No. 73, SRO.

3. Wilson to Dear Mother.

4. Typescript interview of Mrs. Nellie Allen, Idaho Historical Society, Boise. Although modern critics have correctly noted that the Scots educational system often ignored the "lass-o-parts," the opportunities for formal schooling for women still surpassed most contemporary offerings.

5. Hunter, *Scottish Highlanders, Indian Peoples,* 191.

6. Helen Corr, "An Exploration into Scottish Education," in W. Hamish Fraser and R. J. Morris, eds., *People and Society in Scotland, 1830–1914* (Edinburgh: John Donald, 1990), 290; Rosalind Mitchison, *Life in Scotland* (London: B. T. Batsford, 1978), 46.

7. *Scottish Contributions to the Making of America* (USIA, 1950), 3.

8. James Paul Allen and Eugene James Turner, *We the People: An Atlas of America's Ethnic Diversity* (New York: Macmillan, 1988); Rodger Doyle, *Atlas of Contemporary America* (New York: Facts on File, 1994), especially 31–32.

9. James Drawbell, "The Kilted California," *Scottish Field* 12 (June 1974):44–46.

10. Robert McCrum et al., *The Story of English* (New York: Viking, 1986), 127.

11. *The Scottish Banner* 17 (May 1994), 12.

12. Andrew F. Rolle, *The Immigrant Upraised: Italian Adventurers and Colonists in an Expanding America* (Norman: University of Oklahoma Press, 1968) has noted the same absence of Italian memoirs.

13. Patricia A. Etter, ed., *An American Odyssey: The Autobiography of a Nineteenth-Century Scotsman, Robert Brownlee. At the Request of His Children. Napa County, California, October 1992* (Fayetteville: University of Arkansas Press, 1986). Sandra Varney MacMahon is working on an article on Macmillan's life.

14. John L. Sinclair, *In Time of Harvest* (Albuquerque: University of New Mexico Press, 1943); Albuquerque *Tribune,* December 18, 1993; Albuquerque *Journal,* December 18, 1993.

15. Elspeth Cameron, *Hugh MacLennan: A Writer's Life* (Toronto: University of Toronto Press, 1981), x, 343.

16. Cameron, *The Other Side of Hugh MacLennan,* quoted, ix.

17. "Scotland's Fate: Canada's Lesson" (1973) in Cameron, *The Other Side of Hugh MacLennan,* 262.

18. "Scotchman's Return" (1958) in Cameron, *The Other Side of Hugh MacLennan,* 151.

19. Colin Nicholson, "'There and Not There': Aspects of Scotland in Laurence's Writing," in Colin Nicholson, ed., *Critical Approaches to*

the Fiction of Margaret Laurence (Vancouver: University of British Columbia Press, 1990), 162–63.

20. On Margaret Laurence, see Clara Thomas, *The Manawaka World of Margaret Laurence* (Toronto: McClelland and Stewart, Ltd., 1975); Patricia Morley, *Margaret Laurence* (Boston: Twayne, 1981).

21. Hunter, *A Dance Called America*, 146–48.

22. Ivan Doig, *English Creek* (New York: Harper and Row, 1984); Ivan Doig, *Dancing at the Rascal Fair* (New York: Harper and Row, 1987); Ivan Doig, *This House of Sky: Landscapes of a Western Mind* (San Diego: Harcourt Brace Jovanovich, 1978).

23. Norman Maclean, *A River Runs Through It and Other Stories* (Chicago: University of Chicago Press, 1976), 104.

Select Bibliography

Aberdeen, Ishbel (The Countess of Aberdeen). *Through Canada with a Kodak*. Toronto: University of Toronto Press, 1994.

———. *"We Twa": Reminiscences of Lord and Lady Aberdeen*. London: W. Collins and Sons, Ltd., 1925.

Adams, Ian, and Meredyth Somerville. *Cargoes of Despair and Hope: Scottish Emigration to North America, 1603–1803*. Edinburgh: John Donald Publishing, Ltd., 1993.

Arrington, Leonard J. *David Eccles: Pioneer Western Industrialist*. Logan: Utah State University Press, 1975.

Aspinwall, Bernard. *Portable Utopia: Glasgow and the United States, 1820–1920*. Aberdeen: Aberdeen University Press, 1984.

Baines, Dudley. *Migration in a Mature Economy: Emigration and Internal Migration in England and Wales, 1861–1900*. Cambridge, etc.: Cambridge University Press, 1985.

Bell, Ian. *Dreams of Exile: Robert Louis Stevenson: A Biography*. New York: Henry Holt, 1992.

Berthoff, Rowland Tappan. *British Immigrants in Industrial America, 1790–1950*. Cambridge, Mass.: Harvard University Press, 1953.

Bingham, Caroline. *Beyond the Highland Line: Highland History and Culture*. London: Constable, 1991.

Bradley, A. G. *Canada in the Twentieth Century*. New York: E. P. Dutton and Co., 1903.

Brown, Jennifer S. H. "A Parcel of Upstart Scotchmen." *The Beaver* (February/March 1988):5–12.

———. *Strangers in Blood: Fur Trade Company Families in Indian Country.* Vancouver and London: University of British Columbia Press, 1980.

Bruce, Duncan A. *The Mark of the Scots: Their Astonishing Contributions to History, Science, Democracy, Literature, and the Arts.* Secaucus, N.J.: Birch Lane Press, 1996.

Bryce, George. *The Scotsman in Canada.* Vol. 2. London: Sampson Low, Marston and Co., Ltd., 1911.

Buchan, David. *The Ballad and the Folk.* London and Boston: Routledge and Kegan Paul, 1972.

Buchanan, Frederick Stewart, ed. *A Good Time Coming: Mormon Letters to Scotland.* Salt Lake City: University of Utah Press, 1988.

———. "Scots Among the Mormons." *Utah Historical Quarterly* 36 (Fall 1968):328–52.

Bumsted, J. M. *The People's Clearance: Highland Emigration to British North America, 1770–1815.* Edinburgh: Edinburgh University Press/ University of Manitoba Press, 1982.

———. "Scots" in *Encyclopedia of Canada's Peoples.* Toronto: University of Toronto Press, 1999.

———. *The Scots in Canada.* Ottawa: Canadian Historical Association, 1982.

Burke, John. *Buffalo Bill: The Noblest Whiteskin.* New York: Capricorn Books, 1973.

Burt, Edward. *Letters from a Gentleman in the North of Scotland.* 2 vols. Dublin: Peter Wilson, 1755.

Cage, R. A., ed. *The Scots Abroad: Labor, Capital, Enterprise, 1750–1914.* London, etc.: Groom Helm, 1985.

Calder, Jenni. *RLS: A Life Study.* London: Hamish Hamilton, 1980.

———, ed. *The Enterprising Scot: Scottish Adventure and Achievement.* Edinburgh: Royal Museum of Scotland, 1986.

———, ed. *Stevenson and Victorian Scotland.* Edinburgh: Edinburgh University Press, 1981.

Cameron, Elspeth. *Hugh MacLennan: A Writer's Life.* Toronto: University of Toronto Press, 1981.

———, ed. *The Other Side of Hugh MacLennan: Selected Essays, Old and New.* Toronto: Macmillan of Canada, 1978.

Campbell, James. *Invisible Country: A Journey Through Scotland.* New York: New Amsterdam Books, 1984.

SELECT BIBLIOGRAPHY

Carrothers, W. A. *Emigration from the British Isles.* London: Frank Cass and Co., Ltd., 1965.

Carson, Thomas Simpson. *Ranching, Sport, and Travel.* London: T. Fisher Unwin, 1917.

Cohen, Michael P. *The Pathless Way: John Muir and American Wilderness.* Madison: University of Wisconsin Press, 1984.

Coker, William S., and Thomas D. Watson. *Indian Traders of the Southeastern Spanish Borderlands.* Pensacola: University Presses of Florida, 1986.

Cowan, Helen I. *British Emigration to British North America: The First Hundred Years.* Revised and enlarged edition. Toronto: University of Toronto Press, 1961.

Craig, David. *On the Crofters' Trail: In Search of the Clearance Highlanders.* London: Jonathan Cape, 1990.

Daiches, David. *Robert Louis Stevenson and His World.* London: Thames and Hudson, 1973.

———, Peter Jones, and Jean Jones, eds. *A Hotbed of Genius: The Scottish Enlightenment, 1730–1790.* Edinburgh: Edinburgh University Press, 1986.

Devine, Thomas M. *The Great Highland Famine: Hunger, Emigration and the Scottish Highlands in the Nineteenth Century.* Edinburgh: John Donald, 1988.

———. *Scottish Emigration and Scottish Society.* Edinburgh: John Donald, 1992.

———. *The Scottish Nation, 1700–2000.* London: Allen Lane/The Penguin Press, 1999.

———. *The Tobacco Lords: A Study of the Tobacco Merchants of Glasgow and Their Trading Activities, 1740–90.* Edinburgh: Edinburgh University Press, 1975.

Davie, George Elder. *The Democratic Intellect.* Edinburgh: Edinburgh University Press, 1961, 1999.

DeVoto, Bernard. *Across the Wide Missouri.* Boston: Houghton Mifflin Co., 1964.

Dobson, David. *Scottish Emigration to Colonial America, 1607–1785.* Athens: University of Georgia Press, 1994.

Doig, Ivan. *This House of Sky: Landscapes of a Western Mind.* San Diego: Harcourt Brace Jovanovich, 1978.

Douglas, David. *Journal Kept by David Douglas During His Travels in North America, 1823–1827.* London: William Wesley and Son, 1914.

Dunn, Charles W. *Highland Settler: A Portrait of the Scottish Gael in Cape Breton and Eastern Nova Scotia.* Wreck Cove, Cape Breton Island: Breton Books, 1952, 1991.

Engelbourg, Saul, and Leonard Bushkoff. *The Man Who Found the Money: John Stewart Kennedy and the Financing of the Western Railroads.* East Lansing: Michigan State University Press, 1996.

Erickson, Charlotte. *Invisible Immigrants: The Adaptation of English and Scottish Immigrants in Nineteenth-Century America.* Ithaca and London: Cornell University Press, 1972.

Friedman, Albert B., ed. *The Viking Book of Folk Ballads of the English-Speaking World.* New York: Viking, 1956, 1963.

Friesen, Gerald. *The Canadian Prairies: A History.* Lincoln: University of Nebraska Press, 1984.

Furnas, J. C. *Voyage to Windward: The Life of Robert Louis Stevenson.* London: Faber and Faber, Ltd., 1952.

Glassie, Henry. *Irish Folk History: Texts from the North.* Philadelphia: University of Pennsylvania Press, 1982.

Gough, Barry. *First Across the Continent: Sir Alexander Mackenzie.* Norman and London: University of Oklahoma Press, 1997.

Graham, Ian Charles Cargill. *Colonists from Scotland: Emigration to North America, 1707–1783.* Ithaca, N.Y.: Cornell University Press, 1956.

Gressley, Gene M. *Bankers and Cattlemen.* Lincoln: University of Nebraska Press, 1966.

Gummere, Francis B. *The Popular Ballad.* New York: Dover, 1959.

Haldane, A. R. B. *The Drove Roads of Scotland.* Edinburgh: Edinburgh University Press, 1952, 1968.

Harper, Marjory. "Crofter Colonists in Canada: An Experiment in Empire Settlement in the 1920s." *Northern Scotland* 14 (1944): 69–111.

———. *Emigration from North-East Scotland.* Vol. 2, *Beyond the Broad Atlantic.* Aberdeen: Aberdeen University Press, 1988.

Hennessy, James Pope. *Robert Louis Stevenson.* London: Jonathan Cape, 1974.

Hewitson, Jim. *Tam Blake and Company: The Story of the Scots in America.* Edinburgh: Canongate Press, Ltd., 1993.

Hook, Andrew. *Scotland and America: A Story of Cultural Relations, 1750–1835.* Glasgow and London: Blackie, 1975.

Hunter, James. *A Dance Called America: The Scottish Highlands, the United States and Canada.* Edinburgh and London: Mainstream Publishing, 1994.

———. *Scottish Highlanders, Indian Peoples: Thirty Generations of a Montana Family.* Helena: Montana Historical Society Press, 1996.

Issler, Anne Roller. "Robert Louis Stevenson in Monterey." *Pacific Historical Review* 34 (August 1965):305–21.

Jackel, Susan, ed. *A Flannel Shirt and Liberty: British Emigrant Gentlewomen in the Canadian West, 1880–1914.* Vancouver and London: University of British Columbia Press, 1982.

Jackson, John C. *Children of the Fur Trade: Forgotten Metis of the Pacific Northwest.* Missoula: Mountain Press Publishing Company, 1995.

Jackson, W. Turrentine. *The Enterprising Scot: Investors in the American West after 1873.* Edinburgh: Edinburgh University Press, 1968.

Johnson, Jerrell G. *The Arizona Scotsman.* Pine, Ariz.: Beaumaris Books, 1970.

Johnson, Jim A. *Tonque and Farr.* Thurso: Northern Printers, 1987.

Jones, Maldwyn A. *Destination America.* London: Weidenfeld and Nicolson, 1976.

Jordan, Terry G. *North American Cattle-Ranching Frontiers.* Albuquerque: University of New Mexico Press, 1993.

Kennedy, Ludovic. *In Bed with an Elephant: A Journey Through Scotland's Past and Present.* London, etc.: Bantam Press, 1995.

Kerr, W. G. *Scottish Capital on the American Credit Frontier.* Austin: Texas State Historical Association, 1976.

Kerrigan, Catherine, ed. *The Immigrant Experience.* Guelph, Ontario: University of Guelph, 1992.

Landsman, Ned. *Scotland and Its First American Colony, 1683–1760.* Princeton: Princeton University Press, 1985.

Lauder, Sir Harry. *Between You and Me.* New York: James A. McCann Co., 1912.

———. *Roamin' in the Gloamin'.* London: Hutchinson and Co., Ltd., 1928.

Lavender, David. *The Fist in the Wilderness.* Albuquerque: University of New Mexico Press, 1964.

LeRoy, Bruce. *Lairds, Bards and Mariners: The Scot in Northwest America.* Tacoma: Washington State American Revolution Bicentennial Commission, 1978.

Limbaugh, Ronald H. "Stickeen and the Moral Education of John Muir." *Environmental History Review* 15 (Spring 1991):25–43.

Lynch, Michael. *Scotland: A History.* London: Pimlico, 1992.

Lyon, Juana Fraser. "Archie McIntosh, the Scottish Indian Scout." *Journal of Arizona History* 7 (Autumn 1966):103–22.

McCrum, Robert et al. *The Story of English*. New York: Viking, 1986.
Macdonald, James. *Food from the Far West*. New York: Orange Judd Co., 1878.
MacDonell, Margaret. *The Emigrant Experience: Songs of Highland Emigrants in North America*. Toronto, etc.: University of Toronto Press, 1982.
McFarlane, Larry A. "British Remittance Men as Ranchers: The Case of Coutts Marjoribanks and Edmund Thursby, 1884–95," *Great Plains Quarterly* 11 (Winter 1991):51–69.
McGaw, William Cochran. *Savage Scene: The Life and Times of Mountain Man Jim Kirker.* San Lorenzo, N.M.: High-Lonesome Books, 1972.
McGregor, Alexander Campbell. *Counting Sheep: From Open Range to Agribusiness on the Columbia Plateau*. Seattle and London: University of Washington Press, 1982.
MacGregor, Geddes. *Scotland: An Intimate Portrait*. Boston: Houghton Mifflin, 1980.
McKelvey, Susan Delano. *Botanical Exploration of the Trans-Mississippi West, 1790–1850*. Jamaica Plain, Mass.: The Arnold Arboretum of Harvard University, 1955.
McLean, Marianne. *The People of Glengarry*. Montreal and Kingston: McGill-Queen's University Press, 1991.
Maclean, Norman. *A River Runs Through It and Other Stories*. Chicago: University of Chicago Press, 1976.
MacLean, R. A. *A State of Mind: The Scots in Nova Scotia*. Hantsport, Nova Scotia: Lancelot Press, 1992.
Maxwell, Sir Herbert. *The Honorable Sir Charles Murray, K.C.B.* Edinburgh and London: William Blackwood and Sons, 1898.
Miller, Kerby A. *Emigrants and Exiles: Ireland and the Irish Exodus to North America*. New York: Oxford University Press, 1985.
Miller, Sally M., ed. *John Muir: Life and Work*. Albuquerque: University of New Mexico Press, 1993.
Mitchell, Ann Lindsay, and Syd House. *David Douglas: Explorer and Botanist*. London: Aurum Press, 1999.
Moon, Mary. *Ogopogo: The Okanagan Mystery*. North Vancouver: T. J. Douglas, 1977.
Moses, L. G. *Wild West Shows and the Images of American Indians, 1883–1933*. Albuquerque: University of New Mexico Press, 1996.
Mothershead, Harmon Ross. *The Swan Land and Cattle Company, Ltd*. Norman: University of Oklahoma Press, 1971.
Murray, Sir Charles Augustus. *Travels in North America During the Years 1834 and 1836* . . . 2 vols. London: R. Bartley, 1839.

Naef, Weston J., and James N. Wood. *Era of Exploration: The Rise of Landscape Photography in the American West, 1860–1885.* Boston: New York Graphic Society, 1975.

Newman, Peter C. *Caesars of the Wilderness: The Story of The Hudson's Bay Company.* Vol. 2. New York: Penguin Books, 1987.

———. *Company of Adventurers: The Story of the Hudson's Bay Company.* Vol. 1. New York: Penguin Books, 1985.

Nickerson, Roy. *Robert Louis Stevenson in California.* San Francisco: Chronicle Books, 1982.

Norton, Wayne. *Help Us to a Better Land: Crofter Colonies in the Prairie West.* Regina: Canadian Plains Research Center, 1994.

Oakley, C. A. *The Second City.* London and Glasgow: Blackie and Son, Ltd., 1946.

Olson, Lee. *Marmalade and Whiskey: British Remittance Men in the West.* Golden, Colo.: Fulcrum Publishing, 1993.

Orel, Harold et al., eds. *The Scottish World: History and Culture of Scotland.* New York: Harry N. Abrams, Inc., 1981.

Payne, Peter L., ed. *Studies in Scottish Business History.* London: Frank Cass, Ltd., 1967.

Pearce, W. M. *The Matador Land and Cattle Company.* Norman: University of Oklahoma Press, 1964.

Porter, Mae Reed, and Odessa Davenport. *Scotsman in Buckskin: Sir William Drummond Stewart and the Rocky Mountain Fur Trade.* New York: Hastings House, 1963.

Rabinowitz, Howard N. "Macdonald Smith." *Golfiana* 6 (1994):29–33.

Redmond, Gerald. *The Caledonian Games in Nineteenth-Century America.* Rutherford, N.J.: Fairleigh Dickinson University Press, 1971.

Rice, Duncan. *The Scots Abolitionists, 1833–1861.* Baton Rouge and London: Louisiana State University Press, 1981.

Ross, Alexander. *The Fur Traders of the Far West.* Edited by Kenneth A. Spaulding. Norman: University of Oklahoma Press, 1959.

Ross, Peter. *The Scot in America.* New York: Raeburn Book Co., 1896.

Russell, Don. *The Lives and Legends of Buffalo Bill.* Norman: University of Oklahoma Press, 1960.

Sanchez, Nellie Van de Grift. "In California with Robert Louis Stevenson." *Scribner's* 60 (October 1916):467–81.

The Scots in Canada: A Resource Based on a Scottish Record Office Exhibition. Edinburgh: Scottish Record Office, 1994.

Shadduck, Louise. *Andy Little: Idaho Sheep King.* Caldwell: Caxton Printers, 1990.

Simon-Smolinski, Carole, and Laurie Mercier, eds. *Idaho's Ethnic Heritage: Historical Overview.* Boise: Idaho State Historical Society, 1990.

Sprague, Marshall. *A Gallery of Dudes.* Lincoln: University of Nebraska Press, 1967.

Stewart, Elinore Pruitt. *Letters of a Woman Homesteader.* Boston: Houghton Mifflin Co., 1913, 1988.

Stewart, William Drummond. *Altowan; Or, Incidents of Life and Adventure in the Rocky Mountains.* New York: Harper and Brothers, 1846.

———. *Edward Warren.* Edited by Bart Barbour, with an introduction by Winfred Blevins. Missoula: Mountain Press Publishing Co., 1986.

Szasz, Margaret Connell, ed. *Between Indian and White Worlds: The Cultural Broker.* Norman: University of Oklahoma Press, 1994.

Taylor, P. A. M. *Expectations Westward: The Mormons and the Emigration of Their British Converts in the Nineteenth Century.* Edinburgh and London: Oliver and Boyd, 1963.

Troccoli, Jean Carpenter. *Alfred Jacob Miller: Watercolors of the American West.* Tulsa: Gilcrease Museum, 1990.

Tyler, Ron, ed. *Alfred Jacob Miller: Artist on the Oregon Trail.* Fort Worth: Amon Carter Museum, 1982.

Van Nostrand, Jeanne. *The First Hundred Years of Painting in California, 1775–1875.* San Francisco: John Howell Books, 1980.

Welling, William. *Photography in America: The Formative Years, 1839–1900.* Albuquerque: University of New Mexico Press, 1978, 1987.

Wentworth, Edward Norris. *America's Sheep Trails.* Ames: Iowa State College Press, 1948.

The West of Buffalo Bill. New York: Harry N. Abrams, Inc., 1974.

Wicher, Edward Arthur. *The Presbyterian Church in California, 1849–1927.* New York: Frederick H. Hitchcock, 1927.

Wilkie, Jim. *Metagama: A Journey from Lewis to the New World.* Edinburgh: Mainstream Publishing Co., Ltd., 1987.

Wilkins, Thurman. *John Muir: Apostle of Nature.* Norman: University of Oklahoma Press, 1995.

Woods, Lawrence M. *British Gentlemen in the Wild West: The Era of the Intensely English Cowboy.* New York: Free Press, 1989.

Wright, J. Leitch, Jr. *Creeks and Seminoles: Destruction and Regeneration of the Muscogulge People.* Lincoln and London: University of Nebraska Press, 1986.

Zuehlke, Mark. *Scoundrels, Dreamers and Second Sons: British Remittance Men in the Canadian West.* Vancouver/Toronto: Whitecap Books, 1994.

Index

Abbotsford, Scot.: those at, 119
Aberdeen, Lord and Lady, 54, 162–67, 205
Aberdeen, Scot., 26, 89, 138, 145, 155; Buffalo Bill at, 148; those from, 5, 7, 68, 81, 86, 112, 162, 192, 197
Aberdeenshire, Scot., 121; those from, 31, 84, 100, 137
Adam, James N., 8
Adam, Robert, 37
Addams, Jane, 163
Agate, James, 141
Agriculture, 96, 170–71; American, 83–85; Canadian, 166, 191, 194, 205; Scottish, 22, 132–34; Spanish, 46
Aikman, Robert "Scotch Bob," 103
Alberta, Can., 191, 196
Alexander, James, 84
Alexander, John, 112
Allen, Nellie (from Keith), 160, 210
Anderson, Mary, 47
Angus, Scot.: those from, 168
Arizona, 72, 88, 92, 94, 152, 156–58, 165
Arrington, Leonard, 20
Artists, 47, 128, 136–38, 173

Aspinwall, Bernard, 13
Ayrshire, Scot.: those from, 43

Bailyn, Bernard, 12
Baird, Robert, 156
Balley, H. T., 74
Banchory, Scot.: those from, 194
Bannockburn, Scot.: those from, 86
Barbour, John, 55
Bartram, William, 62
Beadle, John Hanson, 157
Beattie, William, 43
Bell, Ian, 176
Benbecula, Scot.: those from, 194
Bennett, James Gorman, 144
Berthoff, Roland H., 10, 16
Bierstadt, Albert, 136
Black, George Fraser, 10
Black Isle, Scot.: those from, 192
Blair, James, 12
Blind Harry, 55
Blythe, John and Margaret, 156
Bodmer, Karl, 136
Botsford, Robert, 13
Bradbury, John, 42
Bradley, A. G., 165
Brady, Mathew, 140

Brahan, Scot.: those from, 98
Brigham, Sara M., 96
British Columbia, Can., 31, 71, 166, 186, 190, 197
Brooks, Phillips, 163
Brothroyd, Edith Gertrude, 171
Brown, George, 189
Brown, Jennifer S. H., 69
Browne, James, 54
Brownlee, Robert, 215
Bryant, William Cullen, 128
Bryce, Ebenezer, 156
Bryce, George (historian), 200, 201, 204
Bryce, James, 135
Bumsted, James M., 59, 80, 185, 187
Burke, John ("Arizona John"), 145
Burnett, Robert, 100
Burns, Robert, 5, 9, 55, 86, 107, 108, 110–15, 138, 140, 142, 152, 172, 218
Burt, Edward, 28, 80

Calderwood, John, 85
California, 8, 45–48, 66, 71, 81, 85, 86, 116, 137, 139, 172–84, 211–13, 215
Calley, Linda, 26
Cameron, Colin, 92
Cameron, John, 90
Campbell, R. H., 85
Campbell, Robert, 31, 127, 130
Campbell, Thomas and Alexander, 182
Canada, 6, 9, 17, 27–30, 41, 45, 47, 50, 53, 59, 68–70, 76, 78–81, 103, 156, 163, 185–208, 215–17; movement for confederation of, 189; U.S. border with, 162
Cape Breton Island, Can., 186, 215
Cardross, Scot.: those from, 48, 66
Carlisle, Thomas, 152
Carnegie, Andrew, 7, 8, 177, 211
Carson, Thomas Simpson, 81, 92
Carter, Robert, III, 78
Casson, Herbert N., 8
Cathcart, Lady Gordon, 193–95
Character: the Scottish, 8–10, 26, 28, 44, 79, 90, 107–13, 120–23, 150, 159, 165, 186, 194, 203, 205, 210; and names, 52, 205, 212; western, 145
Child, Francis James, 121, 122
Clans, 30, 53, 62–64, 103, 113, 216
Clark, William, 128
Clay, Henry, 124
Clay, John, 92, 94
Clement, Antoine, 127
Clerics, 8, 12, 37, 63, 67, 69, 80, 157, 163, 196, 200, 201–204; missionaries, 128, 157, 201
Clive, John, 12
Clydeside, Scot.: those from, 7
Cody, William F. ("Buffalo Bill"), 143–49
Coke, Henry J., 35
Colbert family, 66
Colorado, 85–86, 92, 110, 111, 134, 153, 163, 164, 168–72, 212, 213
Colvin, Sidney, 177
Connor, Ralph, 163, 202
Conolly, William, 50
Conzen, Kathleen Neils, 108
Cook, James, 38
Cook, Thomas, 136
Cooper, James Fenimore, 120, 125
Cope, John, 121
Corriechoille, Scot.: those from, 90
Craig, David, 186
Craigie Hall, Scot.: those from, 152
Crawford, Dugald, 7
Crook, George, 71, 72
Crooks, Ramsay, 31
Culloden, Scot., 25, 53, 63–64, 121
Culture, 12–16, 156, 161; borrowing, 62; Canadian, 186, 199, 204–206; conflicts, 188; costume, 7, 62, 108, 142, 204, 212; the double lens of, 14; entertainments, 84, 109–11, 113–16, 133, 141–44, 204, 212–14; food, 108, 111, 129; hero, 45; heroines, 6, 16; household, 160, 193–94; humor, 79–80; identity for, 107–12; museum of western, 130; music, 32, 47, 108, 111, 113, 120–23, 142, 143, 152, 156, 168, 186, 199, 204, 206; Scoto-Indian, 50–77. *See also* Literature

INDEX   267

Culture brokers, 69–76, 145
Cunningham, Alice Fletcher, 70
Curtis, Edward, 55

Dakin, Susan Bryant, 20
Davenport, Odessa, 19
Davie, George, 37
Davis, Jefferson, 119, 172
Dawkins, W. Bond, 55
Dawson, Y. T., 197
Debo, Angie, 59
Declaration of Independence, 5, 15
Devine, Thomas M., 14
DeVoto, Bernard, 132
Dinsdale, Tim, 206
Dinwiddie, Robert, 12
Disserte, Miss M. E., 159
Doane, Charlie, 103
Dobson, David, 14
Doig, Ivan, 210, 217
Doig family, 143
Dollar, Robert, 7, 211
Donahoe, Michael, 7
Donaldson, William, 121
Dorsey, George A., 70
Douglas, David, 20, 43
Douglas, Thomas, 187–89
Dowie, John Alexander, 153
Drummond, Henry, 163
Drummond, Thomas, 43
Dunbar, Scot.: those from, 178, 181, 183
Dunbar, William, 101
Duncan, Hugh, 153
Duncan, John, 112
Duncan, John M., 109
Duncan, William, 15
Dunfermline, Scot.: those from, 7

Eccles, David, 156, 211
Economics, 37, 195, 211; banking, 87, 197; depression, 94; failure, 152, 171, 196, 211; famine, 25, 60, 66; Panic, 88; poverty, 26, 66. *See also* Ranching
Edinburgh, Scot., 7, 14, 22, 26, 36, 44, 71, 87, 126, 146, 154, 155, 161, 182, 187, 190; those from, 89, 135, 197
Education, 12, 14, 36, 178, 210; Canadian, 204; Scoto-Indian, 63, 66, 68–70, 73, 74; Scottish Studies, 15, 213
Edwards, Paul M., 88, 94
Emerson, Frank, 151
Employment, 10, 12, 78, 82–87, 152, 156, 166, 172, 209–11; architects, 37; bankers, 7, 88; Canadian, 186, 189, 194, 196, 197, 200; chemist, 85; craftsmen, 85; drovers, 90–94; editors, 70; educators, 4, 8, 37; engraver, 137; explorers, 26, 128; gardeners, 43, 86; in government, 7, 10, 189; industrialists, 8, 189; informants, 7; inventors, 8; labor leaders, 85, 209; medicine, 37, 42, 43, 102; merchants, 7; philanthropist, 62; philosphers, 15, 37; photographers, 55, 138–41; remittance men, 164–67; scouts, 70; sociologist, 14; television, 16; women's, 160, 194. *See also* Artists; Literature; Naturalists
Erickson, Charlotte, 14, 17
Evans, E. Estyn, 16
Evans, John, 38

Falkirk, Scot., 80, 90; those from, 7
Farquharson, Joseph, 136
Ferguson, William, 68
Findlay, Jacco, 68
Findlay, James, 68
Finnie, Helen, 13
Fischer, David Hackett, 16
Fithian, Philip, 78
Fitzpatrick, Rory, 16
Florida, 26, 169, 178
Folklore, 16, 55–58, 61–64, 106, 112, 120–23, 170
Forbes, Alexander, 45–48
Ford, Henry Jones, 9
Fraser, George MacDonald, 52
Fraser, William, 154
Friedman, Albert, 120
Frith, Francis, 138

Gardiner, Meredith, 43
Gardner, Alexander C., 139–41, 153, 211
Garretson, John L., 86
Gaston, Charity Ann, 157
Gibbon, John Murray, 208
Gilchrist, Mary, 113
Glasgow, Scot., 12, 13, 22, 36, 43, 87, 88, 146, 154, 155, 209; those from, 7, 85, 109, 139, 156, 182, 197, 210
Glass, Hugh, 32–34
Glen Forest, Scot.: those from, 124
Golf, 116–17
Gordon, George, 8
Gowan, David Douglas, 152
Graham, Ian C., 13, 14
Graham, Peter, 136
Grant, Cuthbert, 188, 189
Grant, George, 83–84
Great Plains, 58, 84, 89, 125, 132–36
Greenock, Scot.: those from, 31

Hall, James, 58
Hammond, J. R., 176
Hammond, M. O., 74
Harper, Marjory, 191, 192
Harrower, John, 5
Hartwick, Scot.: those from, 101
Harvey, William "Coin," 96
Haws, Charles H., 14
Healy, Patrick, 100
Henderson, David, 8
Henry, Andrew, 32
Hewison, Graham, 102
Hewitson, Jim, 19
Highlands, Scot., 53, 56, 61, 62, 66, 82, 89–91, 97, 112–14, 121, 135, 187, 207, 215, 216; Clearances, 17, 29, 52, 59, 61, 185, 186, 190, 217; those from the Highlands, 13, 157
Hillers, C. Jack, 139
Hitt, Betty, 161
Hook, Andrew, 14
Hooker, William J., 43, 44, 45
Hope-Vese, James Joseph, 152
Howison, John, 78
Huckleberry Finn (Twain), 119
Huffman, L. A., 139

Hunter, James, 19, 31
Hutton, James D., 136

Idaho, 16, 103, 106, 111, 134, 152, 156, 160, 211
Illinois, 68, 81, 82, 153
Imlay, Gilbert, 56
Indians, American, 17, 30, 33, 34, 41, 44, 49–77, 124, 129, 135, 140, 145–48, 150, 157–59, 189, 205, 207, 210
Inverness, Scot., 22, 99; those from, 43, 62, 66, 101, 207
Iowa, 7, 32, 82, 88, 140, 143
Irving, Edward, 153, 154
Isbister, Alexander Kennedy, 68
Issler, Anne Roller, 175

Jackson, W. Turrentine, 19, 94
Jackson, William Henry, 139
James, George Wharton, 157
Johnson, Robert V., 179
Johnson, Samuel, 23
Judson, E. Z. C., 144

Kaller, William, 8
Kames, Lord, 37
Kansas, 82, 83, 124, 135, 144, 163
Karras, Alan L., 14
Keith, George, 211
Keith, Scot.: those from, 160
Keith, William, 137, 151, 153
Kennedy, John, 8
Kennedy, John Stewart, 7
Kennedy, William, 189
Kenny, Judith Keys, 100
Kentucky, 65, 124, 178, 182
Kerr, James, 81
Kerr, W. G., 19, 94
Kirker, James, 32, 34
Knox, John, 36, 154

Lancashire, Scot.: those from, 197
Landseer, Edwin, 136
Landsman, Ned, 14
Lauder, Harry, 141–44, 211
Laurence, Margaret, 204, 216
Lawson, W. R., 87

INDEX

Lees, J. Cameron, 81
Legends, 29, 32–35, 89, 103, 149, 168, 170, 177, 206
Lehmann, William C., 14
Lerner, Alan Jay, 206
LeRoy, Bruce, 19, 151, 160
Lerwick, Scot.: those from, 5
Lindsay, Maurice, 24
Literature, 108, 112, 172, 213; advertisements, 190; autobiography, 118, 178, 215; biography, 19, 124, 151, 176, 185, 207; Coyote, 58, 74–76; diaries, 44, 94, 111, 134, 161, 215; drama, 6, 141–44, 206, 215; essays, 14, 15, 48, 73, 85, 153, 174–76, 181, 187, 215; ethnic, 9; fiction, 24, 26, 54, 81, 96, 172–76; firsthand accounts, 48; history, 8–19, 29, 70, 73, 211, 215; illustrations, 119, 138, 140; journals, 16, 30, 42, 44, 46, 48; letters, 152; magazines, 8, 12, 56, 87, 111, 116, 131, 137, 163, 179, 193; memoirs, 125; natural history, 6, 206; novels, 14, 16, 118–20, 125, 131, 163, 202, 204, 215–18; poetry, 27, 55, 86, 107, 110, 121, 128, 165, 175, 194, 197, 199; political, 69; publishers, 48; reading society, 164; religious, 13, 15, 158, 159, 163, 203; short stories, 76; travelogues, 28, 35, 39, 46, 48, 54, 59, 62, 78, 80, 81, 92, 109, 161, 185, 194
Little, Andrew, 20, 103–107, 151, 211; wife of, 161
Loewe, Frederick, 206
Logan, James, 3
Logierait, Scot.: those from, 202
Lynch, Michael, 59

MacArthur, John Stewart, 85
McCombie, William, 91
McCulloch, Horatio, 136
MacDonald, Angus, 31, 50, 72, 210
McDonald, Duncan, 72–76
McDonald, Ellen Shapiro, 16
MacDonald, Finian, 68
MacDonald, Flora, 6
McDonald, Forrest, 16
McDonald, James, 89
McDonald, John, 31
Macdonald, John A., 189
MacDonell, Andrew, 196
MacDonnell, Miles, 188
MacDougall, Robert, 185
McFarlane, Larry A., 165
McGillivray, Alexander, 63–65
McGillivray, Farquahar, 63
McGillivray, John and Lachlan, 63–64
McGillivray of Dunnaglas, 63
McGillvary brothers, 101
McGregor, Alexander Campbell, 19
McGregor, Archie, Peter, and John, 102–103, 107
MacGregor, Geddes, 61
Macinnes, Allan I., 53
McIntosh, Archie, 70–72
McIntosh, Donald, John, and William, 101
McIver, Donald, 196
McKay, Donald, 71
Mackay, George Grant, 166
Mackay, James, 31
Mackay, John, 38
McKay, Robert, 203, 204
Mackay, Thomas, 81
McKelvey, Susan Delano, 42
Mackenzie, Alexander, 39–41, 187
McKenzie, Kenneth, 32
Mackenzie, Murdo, 92
Mackenzie, Miss Stewart, 98
Mackinnon, Donald, 194–95
McLachlan, James, 8
McLane, John, 8
McLaren, John, 86
Maclean, John, 203, 204
Maclean, Norman, 217, 218
MacLennan, Hugh, 215–16
MacLennan, John, 191–92
McLeod, James, 16
MacLeod, John, 43
McLoughlin, John, 32, 50
McLoughlin, William, 102
McMechan, Harriet, 157
Macmillan, Jessie, 215
MacNeil, David, 152

MacPhee, Hugh, 194
McPhee, John, 56
MacPherson, Ian, 61
MacPherson, James, 55
Macrae, David, 67, 80–81
McTaggart, William, 136
Mactavish, J. G., 50, 68
McWhiney, Grady, 16
Manitoba, Can., 48, 188–89, 193, 194, 196, 204, 216–17
Marjoribanks, Archie, 92, 164, 166
Marjoribanks, Coutts, 92, 164–67
Marjoribanks, Ishbel (Lady Aberdeen), 54, 162–67, 205
Martin, Ged, 186
Maud, J. P., 134
Mayhew, Henry, 155
Menaul, James, 158–59
Menaul, John, 157–59
Menaul, Matthew, 157
Menzies, Archibald, 42, 44
Meyer, Duane, 14
Miller, Alfred Jacob, 128–29, 136
Mining, 47, 85–86, 88, 94, 153, 197
Minto, John, 102
Missouri, 7, 31–38, 42, 86, 113, 124, 127, 129, 130
Mitchell, Alexander, 7
Mitchell, Elizabeth, 190
Mitchell, Margaret, 16
Mitchison, Rosalind, 210
Moffat, Scot.: those from, 103
Moir, John S., 201
Momaday, N. Scott, 150
Money, William, 48
Montana, 19, 31, 72–76, 84, 106, 107, 113, 139, 143, 153, 205, 210–12, 217
Moody, Dwight L., 163
Moon, Mary, 208
Moray Firth, Scot., 121; those from, 31, 190
Mormons, 17, 20, 85, 100, 152–56, 161
Morris, Will, 141
Moses, L. G., 77, 145
Muir, John, 8, 20, 137, 155, 177–84, 211

Mulliner, Samuel, 153
Mumford, Robert, 6
Murie, James R., 70
Murray, Charles Augustus, 123–26, 167–68
Murray, Hugh, 54, 56
Murray, John, 194
Murray, R. Tait, 135
Muybridge, Eadweard, 139

Nasmyth, Alexander, 136
Naturalists, 6, 8, 20, 42–45, 137, 179–84
Nebraska, 70, 84, 96, 101, 112, 171, 212
Newman, Peter C., 30
New Mexico, 32, 34, 92, 101, 111, 139, 157–59, 212, 213
Newport, Puss, 152
New York, 8, 56, 64, 109, 119, 129, 140, 144, 155
Nichols, Frank, 129
Nicholson, Colin, 216–17
Nicholson, Davis, 7
North Dakota, 84, 92, 96, 165
North Uist, Scot.: those from, 196
Norton, Wayne, 195
Norwood, William, 20
Nye, Ellen, 74

Ogilvy, Jack, 170, 171
Ogilvy, Lyulph, 167–72
Oglethorpe, James, 62
Okanagan Valley, Can., 70, 166, 205, 207
Oklahoma, 49, 61, 66, 70, 77, 145, 157, 212, 213
Oregon, 32, 35, 71, 72, 92, 102, 106, 168, 211
Orel, Harold, 143
Orkney, Scot., 22, 26–28; those from, 19, 30, 68, 97
Orrum, Eilley, 85
Osbourne, Frances (Fanny), 173
O'Sullivan, Timothy, 139, 140
Outer Hebrides, Scot., 25, 60, 80; those from, 193
Owen, Robert, 140

INDEX

Pacific Northwest, 58, 68, 70, 74, 88, 102, 107, 151
Paisley, Scot., 22; those from, 5, 6, 140
Palliser, John, 69
Palou, Francisco, 46
Patterson, Alan, 100
Patterson, William, 106
Peel, Robert, 162
Pennsylvania, 13, 32, 66, 72, 157, 158
Perthshire, Scot.: those from, 43, 126, 203
Peyri, Antonio, 46
Porter, Jane, 14, 118
Porter, May Reed, 19
Portobello, Scot.: those from, 141
Potts, Jerry, 70
Presbyterians, 3, 5, 62, 63, 79, 84, 110, 153, 156–59, 163, 173, 181, 182, 201–203, 215, 218
Preston, Robert, 43
Price, Jacob M., 14
Pringle, Mrs. M. A., 81, 161

Raban, Jonathan, 174
Rabinowitz, Howard N., 117
Rae, John, 26, 28
Railroads, 7, 24, 83, 88, 133, 139, 140–41, 144, 149, 190–93, 196, 204
Ramsay, G. G., 193–94, 195
Ranching, 19, 84, 88–107, 132–34, 164–67, 170–71
Rankin, Charles, 205
Red River, Can., 41, 48, 68, 69, 188–89, 193, 197, 200
Reed, Myron W., 110
Reid, Hugo, 20, 48, 66
Reid, Thomas, 15
Reigate, Scot., 138
Religion, 12, 13, 36, 44, 46, 52, 69, 70, 79, 83, 108–10, 129, 153–55, 158, 163, 180–84, 195, 196, 200–204, 214–15
Remittance men, 164–67, 169
Rice, C. Duncan, 16
Richmond, T. N., 201
Riley, John James, 139
Robertson, John, 203, 204
Robert the Bruce, 9, 112, 119

Robinson, Alfred, 47
Robinson, William, 37
Rocky Mountains, 39, 44, 62, 128, 132, 134, 136–38
Ross, Alexander, 31, 48, 50, 70, 189
Ross, James, 70
Ross, John, 66
Ross, Peter, 111
Ross Shire, Scot.: those from, 72
Russell, Andrew J., 139
Russell, Charles M., 76, 136
Ruxton, George, 46

St. Andrew, 63, 108–10, 186, 213
Sanders, Huskie, 68
Saskatchewan, Can., 68, 192, 203
Saxby, Jessie M., 190
Schacter, William David, 153
Schmidt, Leigh Eric, 15
Scotland, 49, 146, 148; Borders, 120; Highlands and Lowlands, 10, 24, 36, 119; Lowlands, 111–12, 155; those from Lowlands, 216. *See also* Highlands
Scott, Sir Walter, 9, 14, 26, 54, 55, 118–20, 125, 136, 138, 172, 218
Scott, Walter (evangelist), 182
Selkirk, Earl of (Thomas Douglas), 41, 187–89
Sellar, Patrick, 60
Service, Robert W., 86, 165, 197, 199–200
Seward, William Henry, 168
Shadduck, Louise, 20
Shand, A. Inness, 30
Shepperson, George, 13, 15, 25
Shepperson, Wilbur, 14
Sim, George, 152
Simpson, George, 32, 50
Simpson, Jeffrey, 186
Sinclair, John, 29, 97
Sinclair, John L., 215
Skirving, Adam, 121
Sloan, Douglas, 13
Small, Frank, 148
Small, William, 5, 37
Smith, Adam, 37
Smith, Alexander, 116

Smith, Donald A., 50, 190
Smith, George, 7, 211
Smith, John, 116
Smith, Joseph, Jr., 154
Smith, Macdonald, 116–17
Society, 107–16; and colonies, 80–84, 140, 163, 168, 186–89, 193, 195–96, 201; ethnicity, 8–10, 17, 24, 108–17, 213–15; eviction and exile, 6, 175–76, 189, 217; Scotland-America comparison, 78–79; Scoto-Indian, 52–53, 59; times of trouble, 59; travel network, 81
South Dakota, 77, 96, 212
South Uist, Scot.: those from, 6, 196
Spotswood, Alexander, 12
Stephen, George, 190
Stevens, Isaac I., 72
Stevenson, Robert Louis, 22, 81, 172–77, 218
Stewart, Christina, 126
Stewart, Clyde, 96
Stewart, Elinore Pruitt, (Mrs. Clyde Stewart), 94
Stewart, William Drummond, 20, 123–32, 168
Stirling, Elizabeth, 81
Stoll, Mark, 181
Stone, A., 74
Stone, Barton W., 182
Strentzel, Louise Wanda, 178
Stromness, Scot., 27; Scoto-Indian at, 68
Stuart, James, 81
Stuart, Robert, 30
Sublette, William, 130
Sutherland, Alexander Sinclair, 152

Tammen, Harry, 171
Taylor, P. A. M., 154
Taylor, Robert, 101
Texas, 43, 47, 81, 82, 86–87, 89, 92, 118, 130, 164–66, 212
Thompson, David, 74
Thomson, John, 152
Tillyfourie, Scot.: those from, 91
Tolmie, William Frazer, 43, 102

Turnbull, Archie, 15
Turner, Frederick Jackson, 194

Ulster, Scot., 16; those from, 157
Utah, 86, 154, 155–56, 161, 211

Valentine, James, 138
Vancouver, George, 42
Virginia, 5, 6, 12, 15, 16, 70
Vroman, A. C., 139

Wallace, William, 9, 118–19
Warden, D. B., 54
Washington, 19, 31, 43, 68, 86, 103, 111, 211, 212
Washington, George, 64, 113
Watkins, Carleton E., 139
Watt, George D., 154
Weem, Scot.: those from, 42
Wemyss, Jean Margaret. *See* Laurence, Margaret
Wertenbaker, Thomas Jefferson, 12
West, John, 69, 200
Westerkamp, Marilyn, 15
Western Isles, Scot., 21, 22, 26, 27, 55, 59, 60, 68, 89, 90; those from, 19, 31, 39, 102, 193, 196
Whytbank, Scot.: those from, 81, 161
Wills, Garry, 15
Wilson, Alexander, 6
Wilson, Edmund, 215
Wilson, George Washington, 138–39
Wilson, James, 8
Wilson, William, 210
Winnipeg, Can., 27, 164, 189, 201, 203, 204
Wisconsin, 110, 125, 152, 178, 181
Witherspoon, John, 5
Women, 28, 47, 81, 85, 94, 114, 128, 160–64, 190, 194, 202, 215
Wray, George, 134
Wright, Alexander, 153
Wright, J. Leitch, Jr., 62
Wyeth, N. C., 119
Wyoming, 85, 92, 96, 100, 111, 113, 151, 165, 169, 212

Printed in the USA
CPSIA information can be obtained
at www.ICGtesting.com
LVHW041744160923
758411LV00001B/54

9 780806 191256